T0305190

Governing Social Risks in Post-Crisis Europe

For Joan

Governing Social Risks in Post-Crisis Europe

Colin Crouch

Professor Emeritus, University of Warwick, UK
External Scientific Member of the Max Planck Institute for
the Study of Societies, Cologne, Germany

Edward Elgar
Cheltenham, UK • Northampton, MA, USA

Published by
Edward Elgar Publishing Limited
The Lypiatts
15 Lansdown Road
Cheltenham
Glos GL50 2JA
UK

Edward Elgar Publishing, Inc.
William Pratt House
9 Dewey Court
Northampton
Massachusetts 01060
USA

A catalogue record for this book
is available from the British Library

Library of Congress Control Number: 2014947026

This book is available electronically in the ElgarOnline.com Social and Political Science Subject Collection, E-ISBN 978 1 78100 401 2

ISBN 978 1 78100 400 5

Typeset by Servis Filmsetting Ltd, Stockport, Cheshire
Printed and bound in Great Britain by T.J. International Ltd, Padstow

Contents

Acknowledgements

In developing the ideas for this book I benefited very considerably from my collaboration in a research project funded by the European Commission's Framework Programme Seven (FP7), on 'The governance of uncertainty and sustainability: tensions and opportunities (GUSTO)' [1] (Grant no. 225301). Among the many colleagues involved in the project, I should mention my fellow coordinators: Jean-Claude Barbier, Dorothee Bohle, Paul Marginson, Antonio Martins, Ruud Muffels, Ralf Rogowski, Els Sol, Noel Whiteside; and those others whose contributions were particularly relevant to various themes of this book: Reinhard Bispinck, Barbora Brngalova, Luigi Burroni, Bernard Casey, Heiner Dribbusch, Manuela Galetto, Vera Glassner, Marta Kahancová, Maarten Keune, Ute Klammer, Ruud Luijkz, Guglielmo Meardi, Tibor Meszman, Oscar Molina Romo, Tomáš Sirovátka, Catherine Spieser, Imre Szabo and Axel van den Berg. Kam Johal served as an exceptionally able administrator to the project. Our two main project officers at the European Commission, Ronan O'Brien and Marie Ramot, were also extremely helpful and supportive. The book itself is my personal project, and neither any of the above nor of course the European Commission are responsible for nor necessarily share any of the conclusions and views expressed therein.

Chapter 1 makes considerable use of my joint chapter with Maarten Keune, 'The governance of economic uncertainty: beyond the "new social risks" analysis', in Bonoli, G. and Natali, D. (eds) (2012), *The Politics of the New Welfare State*, Oxford: Oxford University Press, pp. 45–67.

Chapter 2 is based heavily on my article, 'Beyond the flexibility/security trade-off: reconciling confident consumers with insecure workers' (2011), *British Journal of Industrial Relations*, 50, 1: 1–22.

NOTE

1. The key findings of the GUSTO project were summarized in a special issue of *Transfer*, 'Labour markets and social policy after the crisis', February 2014, 20, 1.

Abbreviations

AIAS	Amsterdams Instituut voor Arbeidstudies
ALMP	Active labour market policy
AT	Austria
BE	Belgium
BG	Bulgaria
CEE	Central and Eastern Europe
CH	Switzerland
CZ	Czech Republic
DE	Germany
DJØF	Danmarks Jurist-og Økonomforbund
DK	Denmark
EE	Estonia
EEA	European Economic Area
EIRO	European Industrial Relations Observatory
EL	Greece
EPL	Employment protection laws
ES	Spain
ETUI	European Trade Union Institute
EU	European Union
FDI	Foreign direct investment
FI	Finland
FR	France
GDP	Gross Domestic Product
HR	Croatia
HU	Hungary
ICTWSS	Database on Institutional Characteristics of Trade Unions, Wage Setting, State Intervention and Social Pacts
IE	Ireland
IMF	International Monetary Fund
ILO	International Labour Organization
IT	Italy
IZA	Forschungsinstitut zur Zukunft der Arbeit
JA	Japan
LV	Latvia

LT	Lithuania
MNC	Multinational corporation
MPIfG	Max-Planck-Institut für Gesellschaftsforschung
NBER	National Bureau of Economic Research
NEET	Not in education, employment or training
NL	Netherlands
NO	Norway
NSR	New social risks
NWE	North-west Europe
OECD	Organisation for Economic Cooperation and Development
PL	Poland
PT	Portugal
RO	Romania
RU	Russian Federation
SD	Standard deviation
SE	Sweden
SI	Slovenia
SK	Slovakia
SME	small and medium-sized enterprises
SWE	South-west Europe
UK	United Kingdom
UNCTAD	United Nations Conference on Trade and Development
UNDP	United Nations Development Programme
UNEP	United Nations Environment Programme
URR	Unemployment replacement rate of pay
US(A)	United States (of America)
WTO	World Trade Organization

1. Risk, uncertainty and class in European societies

The financial crisis of 2007–08 and its continuing aftermath have exposed the lives of many working people in the advanced societies to higher levels of economic uncertainty than they had been accustomed to experiencing in recent decades. For some observers this immediately suggests a need for policies that will reduce insecurity, perhaps by protecting workers from losing their jobs. But others contend that economic insecurity is just the other side of the coin of flexibility, and that it is only through some people losing their jobs and having to find others, or accepting lower wages, that the economy can move back to a level of successful innovation; and that without that vital step, everyone's job is insecure, including those ostensibly protected by employment protection law. But others again claim that exposing large numbers of working people to a high level of insecurity will undermine their capacity to consume, which will in turn undermine attempts to revive the economy. Against this it can then be contended that economic recovery does not have to depend on domestic consumers, but can be fuelled predominantly by exports of goods and services. The outcome of the conflict will vary from country to country. This does not mean that governments and others have ample scope for choosing what paths they will take. At any one point in history an individual country brings with it a set of inherited balances of social and political forces, institutional endowments and a location in international networks. These factors are likely to condition the pattern of responses that it makes.

The purpose of this book is to explore the relevant institutional capacities for confronting these questions of the countries of the European Union (EU) and European Economic Area (EEA), with some reference to certain leading extra-European economies: Japan, the Russian Federation and the USA. Contemporary Europe combines some highly developed, high-income countries in its north west; some slightly less wealthy ones in its south west; and some middle-income countries in the former state socialist bloc to the east. Together they provide a diversity of income levels and institutional types in which the issue can be explored.

The question at stake is not a functionalist one about which technical means best provide working people with security, but instead is deeply conflictual. In principle, the employers of labour seek the most flexible possible workforce, one whose anxieties about uncertainty are of no more relevance than that of a piece of machinery. That was often the reality of the relationship in the early years of industrialization; and it has returned to twenty-first-century capitalism in such forms, increasingly popular among employers, as the zero-hours contract. Here, workers are paid only for those hours when the employer calls on their labour; but they have to be in a state of readiness whenever that call comes and therefore cannot easily take on additional jobs to cover them for periods when the employer does not want them and their income sinks to zero. This is by no means the only type of labour contract that employers want. For many kinds of work they value experience, accumulated skill and loyalty; there is then a coincidence of interest between employers and employees in continuity and security. However, in a competitive market individual employers will always be seeking ways in which they can maximize flexibility by reducing their commitment to particular kinds of workers. This incentive has to be traded off against the value of stability in certain contexts. If all firms competing in the same product market face the same patterns of labour needs, there will be no market disadvantages to those who decide to grant security of employment to certain kinds of workers. But it must be assumed that all firms are constantly seeking ways of achieving their production goals with more flexible workforces.

At the level of a national economy the clash between employers' search for flexibility and workers' search for security takes a different form. Particularly where there is formal democracy, governments have two relevant requirements. First, they have to be sensitive to popular discontent at extreme insecurity. Second, they are concerned that the population has a capacity to consume, that is, make purchases, with confidence; the less secure that a working population feels, the less confidently it can spend money. The nation state is the political level at which the tension between flexible labour and confident consumers bites, because it is here that the most intense elections are fought and where economic accounts have to be balanced. The EU is a part-way supra-national stage in this process; in other regions of the world there is little beyond the nation state. This political engagement in the issue means that an analysis of the positions of labour and capital is not enough to exhaust its study. We have to add social policy.

Finally, the tension appears at a different level when capital confronts its own simultaneous needs for flexible workers but confident consumers to whom it can sell its products. In this study we shall primarily present the issue of labour security from the perspective of this tension, both in general between capital and labour and nationally in labour market and social policy.

This is not a general study of varieties of capitalism, nor of the causes of economic success and failure, nor a detailed study of security policies. Our task is very specifically to examine the tension between consumption and labour flexibility, and the ways in which different balances of power between capital and labour affect the ways in which it is resolved, and the forms of governance that provide these different outcomes.

The present chapter examines the broad concepts within which the study will be conducted. Chapters 2 and 3 then provide the more immediate operational framework for the research. Chapters 4 to 6 present the evidence. Chapter 4 considers the extent to which the conundrum can be resolved by consumers and workers being different sets of persons. Chapter 5 examines ways in which a population's consumption possibilities can be separated from its labour income. In Chapter 6 we explore the functioning of welfare state institutions that might ease the tension between flexibility in the labour force and confident consumption within the labour market itself. From this account will emerge certain provisional conclusions about the characteristics of the majority of the countries being considered. These are brought together in Chapter 7 within the overarching theme of the different forms of governance available. Chapter 8 then looks at overall trends in these characteristics and their wider implications.

FROM *SOZIALPOLITIK* TO INDUSTRIAL RELATIONS – AND BACK

We must first examine the range of policy areas that need to be taken into account in such a project. For several decades now the study of labour issues has been a specialized field, rather cut off from the rest of sociology and economics. It used to be known as 'industrial relations', an essentially Anglo-American construction, and concentrated on relations between employers and organized labour in manufacturing, mining, construction, and a few other sectors where trade unions and collective bargaining were strongly established. University departments and journals used the phrase 'industrial relations' in their titles. The importance of trade unions began to decline in some countries after the 1970s, partly because economic change led to a decline in industrial employment in the core countries, partly because governments in the UK, the USA and elsewhere began expelling unions from the organizations that they would consult over policy in relevant areas. The term 'industrial relations' became embarrassing to some university managers, and by the 1980s departments started to be renamed as 'human resource management'. This narrowed the field even further to a management perspective on how to get the most effective work out of employees.

Meanwhile, however, the subject of labour organization was requiring exactly the opposite: a broadening of focus. 'Industrial relations' itself had long seemed too narrow for many continental European scholars, accustomed, until forced to come to terms with Anglo-American domination of the social sciences, to speak of *politique sociale, Sozialpolitik* and similar terms (Barbier 2008a). While these can be translated easily enough as 'social policy', the English term has always had a narrower meaning, referring to certain institutions of the welfare state or even more narrowly to social benefit payments. The equivalents in other European languages described both that area and the whole field implied by 'industrial relations'. The unifying principle was that both had been seen as addressing the great *question sociale* (or *soziale Frage*) of the late nineteenth and early twentieth centuries: how to incorporate the industrial working class within civil society. The social settlements around the place of labour in society that had been established around the end of World War II in most of western Europe – somewhat earlier in Scandinavia and (though then more temporarily) in the USA – included the establishment or consolidation of both welfare states and industrial relations regimes that recognized certain social rights of workers' representatives to participate in settling terms and conditions of work. The two policy fields then went their separate ways, as it seemed that the task of class incorporation had been achieved, leaving some important technical policy issues, addressing which required increased specialization among academics, policy makers and practitioners.

For much of the second half of the twentieth century the main public policy concern in the industrial relations field was containment of the inflationary tendencies of Keynesian demand management. This presented a number of classic collective action problems, which provided the main analytical frame for academic study (Crouch 1993: chapter 2; Olson 1982). Social policy in its own new specialized sense sometimes played a subsidiary role; elements of welfare policy provided material for agreements between governments and unions over how to manage inflation, but it was mainly seen as a different subject, to be studied with different if related analytical tools. While there was always a diversity of employment statuses, in general that of the male, full-time, dependent employee with an indefinite work contract was dominant, as self-employment and various forms of job tenure associated with agriculture declined. Policymaking in all these fields was largely contained at the level of the nation state. Economic growth was seen as entirely beneficial, and questions were not asked about the environmental impacts of the kinds of activity that produced such growth.

The major inflationary crises of the 1970s brought industrial relations and social policy together again, but in a very specific way. Both wage bargaining in a context of politically guaranteed full employment and governments' alleged tendencies to finance improving social welfare provision through money creation rather than taxation were regarded as major factors in inflation. During the 1980s and 1990s – the timing varies in different countries – public policy changed. Governments turned to monetary as opposed to demand management policies, creating new environments in both policy areas. For labour issues this approach implied improving flexibility by intensifying insecurity without compensation, drawing much from the so-called 'supply-side revolution' in the analysis of the labour market in economic theory. Beginning as the revolt against taxation from the US centre-right known popularly as 'Reaganomics', in economic writing this was a more general concern for looking at the conditions of labour supply, replacing the earlier concern of Keynesian policies with levels of demand in the economy (Canto et al. 1983; Roberts 1984). This became part of the more general economic policy orthodoxy known as neoliberalism, demanding a market economy free from constraints by governments, regulation and such organizations as trade unions. The initial impact of all this was to reduce the importance of both industrial relations and social policy, but the longer-term consequences have been rather different, and have brought about a need to bring the two bodies of knowledge fully together once more.

The business of industrial relations shifted away from inflation management to being a series of deals and conflicts over how the burdens of economic uncertainty should be distributed, and through what forms of social policy and employment contracts. In this process several institutions have engaged in new practices; and there has been a new diversity of employment forms and tenures. Social policy has become reintegrated with employment and industrial relations practices, being central to the distribution and redistribution of uncertainty. A certain wheel has turned full circle, returning us to an ensemble of policies reminiscent of that of the late nineteenth century's, though with very different content. As we shall see in subsequent chapters, this has happened partly through the rise of the social investment welfare state, including active labour market policy and childcare support for working families (Hemerijck 2012a), and also through the reappearance of social policy issues in industrial conflict; in some countries, particularly France, major strikes have tended to be about pensions rather than pay. In most of Europe, these changes have taken place during, and under pressure from, a period when economic growth could no longer be taken for granted. This then raises the priority of growth as a policy objective, but at precisely the moment when environmental concerns have also made it a priority to consider qualitative as well as quantitative characteristics of growth.

Countries in central and eastern Europe had a different experience during the western Keynesian period, but the state socialist regimes also, in their way, protected working populations from economic uncertainty. Today these countries share a similar policy agenda to their western counterparts, but usually with far higher levels of uncertainty and within very different institutional contexts.

By 2008, when the Anglo-American banking crisis triggered a global financial recession and a specific crisis in some countries of the Eurozone, the terms of policy conflict changed again. The primary cause of the linked crises was the behaviour of banks in a deregulated global financial market, and therefore it was a crisis of the dominant neoliberal economic model. However, because the solution adopted was for states to use public money to rescue the banks, pressure was placed on public finances that could be eased only by cutting back on other state expenditure, especially social policy. Further, in several countries governments had financed welfare state spending through bank borrowing rather than through adequate taxation. These loans now had to be repaid, at the expense of very extensive reductions in social spending. Further still, business interests were able to argue that they could recover from the deep recession only if they were freed from regulation, particularly labour regulation, but also other areas of social and environmental policy. Without such changes there would be deepening unemployment and reduced *de facto* labour security. In this way, a crisis caused by neoliberal deregulation (of financial markets) produced a pressing demand for more neoliberal deregulation, and a renewed challenge to social policy and labour market institutions (Mirowski 2013).

RISK, UNCERTAINTY AND DEBT

Policies for protecting workers from uncertainty have therefore become matters of intense disagreement and conflict. Measures that provide people with security in their working lives are often seen as *ipso facto* reducing their flexibility: as limiting employers' ability to fire employees, reduce their incomes or change their working conditions in order to adapt to competitive pressures. If employers cannot do these things, it is argued, they will lose business and therefore the capacity to employ. During the Keynesian period governments accepted an obligation to maintain the level of employment – or, rather, of male employment. While democratic governments have never really been able to escape from being held responsible by voters for problems of unemployment, the decline of the Keynesian priority has had a dramatic impact on the perspectives of trade unions and employers in their negotiations. The potential impact of their actions on employment levels has become the central issue in much of what they do. Employment has become what Évelyne Léonard has called 'the new general equivalent', or the currency against which all developments in collective bargaining and labour market policy are measured (Léonard 2001). Streeck (2008) makes a similar but broader point when he argues that citizenship and social policy expectations are being reformulated until labour is required to accept all manner of risks just to get employment. This does not mean that bargainers and policy makers are then called upon to try directly to safeguard employment by such measures as strict employment protection laws; far from it. Such direct measures are often seen as reducing flexibility and, in anything more than the short term, as harming employment rather than safeguarding it.

Many discussions of labour market and social policy, especially in the EU, have started from an assumption of this tension between flexibility and security (European Commission 1993, 2005, 2006, 2007; OECD 1994). However, the appearance of policy combinations that optimize both demonstrates that constructive and positive compromises can be envisaged between these two forces. Interest in Europe has concentrated on 'flexicurity', based initially on important policy initiatives in Denmark and the Netherlands (Bredgaard et al. 2007, 2008; European Commission 2007; Jørgensen and Madsen 2007; Klammer and Tillmann 2002; Muffels and Luijkx 2008a, b; Wilthagen and Tros 2004). During the crisis itself there was a growth of temporary agreements that maintained workers' jobs in exchange for reduced working hours and pay – reflecting a joint interest between employers wanting to hold on to valuable skilled workers and the workers' own need for job stability (Glassner et al. 2011; Marginson et al. 2014). In fact, the overall range of policies and practices involved in the reformulation of the balance between flexibility and security is considerably more extensive than this (Burroni and Keune 2009; Crouch and Keune 2012; and see Madsen 2009 for the Danish case in particular). These various policies are however usually seen as compromises. At least among policy makers there is a strong assumption that markets would be more efficient if they were not troubled by these demands for security. This became evident in 2012, when, as noted above, faced with a need to tackle urgent economic problems in Ireland and southern European member states of the European single currency, the EU demanded simple neoliberal market flexibility. This could be seen particularly in the detailed conditions imposed on Greece in exchange for its bailout (Government of Greece 2012). All 'flexicurity' talk of combining labour flexibility with new kinds of security that would help upgrade the economy was thrown out of the window.

Flexibility and security relate asymmetrically to the problem of market externalities. Flexibility is by definition a market variable, as it implies requiring labour to adjust to market demands. Self-employed workers adjust directly to market forces; employed workers' adjustment is filtered through managerial hierarchies and is possibly negotiated by trade unions. Security, defined here in terms of workers' desires or needs for protection from uncertainty, is only incidentally reflected in market forces. It will be such, for example, when employers want to ensure that they retain skilled workers in order to save recruitment and training costs, or to keep work-forces together during temporary downturns. But in general, workers' concerns for their security are seen as external to the market; this is why they appear in most economic literature as a constraint on it, and why responses to them are seen as a problem. However, if one accepts that the concern for protection from uncertainty is a legitimate human aspiration, the problem can be redefined as a market failure to deal with an important externality. That is of course precisely what had happened in the past, as over the years a range of public policies were developed to provide protec-tion against uncertainty: public pensions and social insurance, protection of employment legislation, minimum wages, rights of trade unions to represent employees against the power of employers to dispose of their labour (Freedland 2006; Knegt 2008). For much of the twentieth century the gradual accretion of these protections was seen as social progress, recognition that labour markets potentially embodied some undesirable externalities. This changed during the last quarter of that century, protec-tion coming increasingly to be seen, like all other attempts to withstand market forces, as self-defeating.

However, we can take discussion beyond this simple opposition between the market and restraints on it. The externality we have identified can be subdivided into a private and public component. To the extent that the consequences of insecurity are contained within the private lives of the individuals affected, and dealt with in some way or another within indi-viduals' domestic circles, they can be regarded as of no public importance. But there are several ways in which they acquire such importance and therefore become a matter of public policy. First, if labour insecurity translates into low consumer confidence, or even civil discontent, govern-ments may become concerned at inadequate demand. This is a problem defined partly in economic rather than social terms, but it is still a market externality, as the market cannot provide the means of its own existence. Second, workers, if the numbers concerned are large enough, are able to turn their private anxieties into public questions. Only in democracies can they do this by placing issues on the electoral agenda; but in democracies and authoritarian regimes alike they might respond by threatening social order. Under these circumstances governments, and other agencies responsive to public problems, try to balance the externality perceived as a market failure with a need also to strengthen the market in the interests of pursuing flexibility. Only rarely therefore has there been a solution to the antagonism between flexibility and security through the total triumph of the former.

This formulation may seem to imply that the employers' 'side' in the conflict is represented by a demand for flexibility in a context governed by the market, while the employees' 'side' constitutes a demand for security protected by public policy and perhaps trade unions. The former is an oversimplification. First, the 'employer' is often a public authority and not a property owner. More importantly, employers of all kinds depend on public protection as much as do employees. The right to own property requires definition in law and an ability to call the forces of order to enforce it. Also, capital may call on state aid and protection at least as much as labour when it gets into difficulties. Such aid will not necessarily be offered, and the principles for offering it are usually not as strictly defined as those for labour protection, but from time to time firms are rescued or their conditions eased by government. It had been widely considered that such interventions had been ended by the same wave of neoliberal thinking that defined employees' rights as a problem rather than a social advance. But the financial crisis of 2008 demonstrated exactly the opposite. So important had the financial risk-trading sector of the economy become, that the failure of major players in it was seen as a massive market externality against which governments had to act. Banks had very successfully defined their private need for reduced uncertainty as a collective one.

Uncertainty and Risk

For the great majority of humankind economic uncertainty is a source of deep anxiety and awareness of helplessness. For a fortunate and sizeable minority in wealthy countries it is a problem against which there are various though limited possibilities for protection, but also a potential source of opportunities. For a tiny minority in all parts of the world uncertainty constitutes a chance to make enormous gains through skilful investments in markets at risk. It is not surprising that in a world of rapid and massive change and therefore uncertainty, inequality within and between nations has risen steadily. That rise has been intensified as the post-2008 bank rescues protected that tiny minority from catastrophic errors in its risk calculations.

These inequalities in the ways in which uncertainty presents itself to people in different circumstances come about through differential capacity to translate uncertainty into risk. As Knight (1921) established long ago, risk is calculable uncertainty in terms of probability theory. Being calculable, risks can be traded. There are therefore markets in risk, and the estimation, trading and management of risk in this sense have become major activities of the financial sector of many economies. People in different economic circumstances stand in very different relationships to these markets. To access them one needs both wealth (to deploy in risk trading) and knowledge (to know how to go about doing so). In general, the more wealth a person owns, the stronger his or her incentive either directly to acquire that knowledge or to pay for the professional advice of those who have it. Therefore, the more wealth one has, the more one is likely to gain from engaging in risk trading (though there will always be a small number who are either very unlucky or very ill advised, and who make major losses).

Most people do not have such wealth. Some individuals are rich enough to engage in a little investment activity and gain minor rewards from risk trading, but they, like the vast numbers of those who have no tradable wealth at all, will primarily depend for their standard of living on earnings from work, either their own or that of family members or persons otherwise close to them. Limiting our attention to people living in relatively advanced economies, economic uncertainty is likely to affect them through potential loss of a job or deterioration in the rewards it brings, or potential loss of capacity to work through health problems or old age. These are forms of uncertainty that threaten to knock people down from the levels of living they have achieved. There will also be uncertainties around attempts to raise one's level of living: applications for new jobs, or promotions, or attempts to expand a business. These are positive uncertainties and of less interest to us than the negative ones, provided failure in the attempt to improve leaves the person no worse off than before.

If negative uncertainty is a 'bad', we should expect to see many attempts at reducing its implications; only its implications, not uncertainty itself. The problem can never be resolved by creating certainty, as it is not possible to provide this quality in economic life without killing off all innovation and change. This was more or less the social policy deal offered by governments in the Soviet bloc, and it ended in disaster. Instead, steps are taken to manage or govern uncertainty. This might be done through the market, as in the risk trading described above, or through state action, corporate practice, the actions of trade unions or the work of families.

Actors remain free to choose to take risks; an environment of economic security protects them only from the negative consequences of risks that are not of their own choosing.

The Knightian concept of risk as tradable uncertainty still leaves a degree of uncertainty that cannot be calculated (or which is left over when the laws of probability have been applied), or which results when risk calculations fail – as they did spectacularly in the global financial markets in 2008. This residual uncertainty, that part of uncertainty that either cannot be marketed or which is vulnerable to market failure, is therefore equivalent to what we have termed here the market externality of risk.

It was noted above that for the best part of the twentieth century the protection of labour from uncertainty was seen as a justified response to this externality, but that this perception changed among increasing numbers of observers and politically influential interests. This change has been paralleled in the predominant account given in the recently developed sociology of risk (Beck 1986; Luhmann 1991). This maintains that a change took place at a certain point in the development of modern societies, when large numbers of people started to change their approach to uncertainty. Instead of seeing it as something menacing, to be either avoided or accepted, people came to regard it as something they could use and turn into calculable opportunities. In other words they could turn it into risk: hence Beck's concept of *die Risikogesellschaft*, or the 'risk society' as a way of characterizing modern societies. Potential social policy implications of this were perceived by a number of scholars (Bonoli 2007; Giddens 1994, 1998; Häusermann 2012; Taylor-Gooby 2004), who distinguished between 'old' and 'new' social risks. Old social risks were those that had been designed to compensate the working-class population of industrializing societies against basic uncertainties of the kind we have considered above: insurance against unemployment, ill health and old age; trade union rights and employment protection. These were essentially passive forms of protection that assumed populations who could do little to improve their situation, suited to the rigid hierarchies of class society. New social risks (NSR) were those that could comfortably be accepted by workers in affluent post-industrial societies, with more flexible, less hierarchical work organizations, declining class structures and increased social mobility, who did not need protection from the old risks. These people aspired to opportunities; for them, uncertainties were becoming risks that they could *use*. This does not mean that risks had become pleasant experiences. Post-industrial societies still presented their citizens with difficulties and challenges, but they were those typical of wealthy, classless populations: the new social risks were therefore population ageing and associated care problems; the balance of family life and female employment; risks that one's educational qualifications will not facilitate employability.

The NSR approach enables us to take account of major changes that have affected advanced societies since the major reformulation of welfare state arrangements around World War II. Important examples are deindustrialization, female labour-force participation, increased mass longevity (and hence population ageing), flexibilization and an increased variety of employment relationships. It shows how these changes have created new vulnerable groups; and it also shows that welfare policies have changed, bringing increasing diversity rather than convergence across Europe. Perhaps its most important contribution has been to identify the intricate set of relationships that link care policies (for children, the elderly and other vulnerable groups) to women's labour-force participation, and to family structures, breaking down the divisions that led to these being viewed as separate areas during the heyday of male-breadwinner, industrial economies (Esping-Andersen 1999).

However, the insistence of much analysis of this kind that the 'old' problems of class society have been transcended leads its proponents to overlook or discount some major issues. As argued by Crouch and Keune (2012), NSR analysis sees welfare states as having to be reoriented to *reflect* changed socio-economic circumstances, these circumstances themselves being taken for granted as fixed. People must adapt to the market rather than reduce their exposure to it; the individual is seen as responsible for ensuring his or her own employment and can choose from the jobs offered, become self-employed or seek forms of education that will improve his or her employability. Unemployment is thus an individual problem to be addressed through education, though with some collective help through active labour market policies (ALMP). The most obviously weak point in this reasoning is that it assumes that, apart from ALMP, ordinary individuals have a capacity to predict and identify the kinds of job for which they should prepare themselves in future, although in reality even specialist job-research institutions have difficulty making such predictions. The NSR approach also fails to take into account that it is often employers, managers and financial capital that drive and define the uncertainties that emerge in the new circumstances; these are not 'natural' phenomena transmitting technical information about an inevitable reality. There is some capacity for choice of strategies, including their effects on welfare and uncertainty.

A conflict of interests between classes is therefore obscured by the NSR school. This is curious because risk, the core concept of the approach, is, as noted above, subject to extremes of inequality related to the most fundamental of class concepts: property ownership. The risks related to the work and welfare of the mass of the population are seen as a kind of sealed box bounded by social and labour market policy. Their connections to the trading in risk in which the wealthy can engage are simply not perceived. There is a continuum of risk extending across whole societies, and the sociology of risk needs to take account of it all. For example, the ability of moderate-income families to cope with insecure labour markets may be considerably improved if they can take out a 120 per cent mortgage on their home and use it to fund their daily consumption. But their ability to do that will depend on traders in financial markets being able to make money from selling such unsecured loans. These traders might be more willing to take on such risks if they have secure expectations of high earnings in other markets. They might be able to do this – and this is precisely what they have done – by investing in pension funds that do not offer pensioners guaranteed rates of benefit, but benefits that depend on stock-market valuations at the moment of their retirement. These latter, 'defined contributions' pensions throw the risk of pension inadequacy on to the pensioner, reducing it for investors (Ebbinghaus 2012; Whiteside 2014). These arrangements will have implications for old-age poverty in future years. As those so wealthy that they can make high earnings by extracting the tradable risk from uncertainty carry out their operations, they pass the untradeable bundle of uncertainty down until it rests with those unable to do the same.

Risk and Class

Relationship to the risk/uncertainty mix is a classic class relationship because it is very closely related to relationship to property ownership. Far from class in this sense declining in post-industrial societies, it has become increasingly important. This results from the central role of the financial sector, the area of the economy where pure wealth counts more than anywhere else. The fact that, compared with the first half of the twentieth century, far more people own some property does not reduce this. There is a fundamental difference between liquid and illiquid assets. The inequalities between a family whose property consists almost entirely of the home in which it lives and one with millions invested in stocks and shares is greater than is expressed by the quantitative difference. There are severe limits to the risks one can take with one's sole residential property, and therefore to the interest rates that one can expect to earn, compared with liquid assets that one is using just for investment. Attempts to transcend this problem in the USA and elsewhere by encouraging remortgaging of such property, the resulting debt then being traded as a liquid asset, was a proximate cause of the 2008 crisis.

When observers talk of a decline in class in post-industrial societies they mean the decline in clearly marked social groups that have accompanied the decline of the factory as the paradigm of hierarchical social relations. In fact there has never been a society in which a majority (even of male persons) had lives related to factories, but the social hierarchy of the factory projected a powerful image to societies accustomed to the even more rigid hierarchies of post-feudal rural economies. The paradigmatic factory had:

- some owners who possessed the property, and whose income was derived from profits from the risk of their investment;
- some managers and professionals, who did not own extensive property, but who were highly rewarded because of their relationship of trust with the owners, and who therefore could accumulate wealth over time;
- various grades of clerical and other support staff to the managers working alongside them in offices and sharing some of the basis of trust, but on relatively lower earnings and unlikely to accumulate much wealth;
- various grades of manual workers, whose incomes depended on their skill level, enabling those with the highest skills gradually to accumulate some wealth.

The social segregation between office (where workers typically wore suits and had white collars) and factory (where workers wore overalls with blue collars to protect themselves from a typically dirty environment) produced the sociocultural reality of a distinction between middle and working classes (factory owners being perhaps a dimly perceived small upper class, if they were wealthy enough). It also represented a broad political hierarchy of power and authority, proceeding from owners through successive levels of management on to the factory floor. There was a rough link between this politico-sociocultural reality and different levels of property ownership, giving a similar very broad pattern of three classes. The matching was imperfect, particularly because the lower levels of office workers earned less and exercised less power at work than skilled manual workers, despite being on the other side of the office/factory divide. In time however these lower level office workers became primarily female, and women were simply disregarded in images of class society, whether in popular imagination or professional sociology (Crompton 1989; Goldthorpe 1983). Women 'took their class' from their husband, so in turn women's occupations – even those of unmarried women – dropped out of class analysis. While this was unacceptable for the study of the class position of occupations, it had some logic for class as related to property. To the extent that people lived in families, occupational earnings would contribute to a common pool of wealth. If, as was usually the case, husbands earned more than their wives, their earnings would contribute more to that stock.

Class in this sense could be simultaneously clear and vivid, with profound political implications, and very vague or rough. As already noted, only a minority ever worked in factories in any capitalist economy, other occupations finding their place in class society through analogy. For example, schoolteachers resembled in their educational (and usually family) background the professionals (engineers, accountants) in the factory office, and had broadly similar if lower earnings. They were assimilated to the same class.

Also, wealth and earnings form a continuum, while classes form clearly separated categories. Mapping the former on to the latter always produces distortions and ambiguous cut-off points. It has long been argued (Giddens 1973; Weber 1919) that this was a distinctive feature of capitalist society, feudal and post-feudal forms of society coming, as it were, with ready-made, really existing hierarchies of rank. This is a profound misconception of those societies. Pre-industrial societies had highly complicated continua of land ownership, trading wealth and earnings from labour. What appear to be the clearly demarcated classes or estates of those societies represent attempts by kings and aristocrats to impose an order on the continua, often in order to protect their own position as the formal apex of the system despite the accumulation of superior levels of wealth by some bourgeois. Sometimes they might exclude whole categories of persons from certain activities (e.g., Jews from land-holding), but often all that they could do was to define artificial categories that gave different levels of rights and often implied important cultural distinctions, but not the reality of wealth ownership. A person without an inherited aristocratic position could be excluded from using certain titles, from participating in certain kinds of decision-making or even from wearing certain garments. But there was a constant tension between the two realities of social differences that resulted from divisions defined by political authority and those that emerged from various forms of property ownership. The former made broad, fairly clear categories, the latter continua.

Industrial class society was very similar, except that the categories were defined not so much by political authority as by factory owners and managers designing the hierarchies through which they would carry on their businesses, the broad rankings of the factory hierarchy listed above. There was a kind of privatization of class definition. Even this was not entirely true. The modern state and army developed before the modern factory as large-scale work organizations, and to some extent furnished models for employers on how to order the hierarchy of a factory. The division between office and factory paralleled that between officers and other ranks in armies. German employers modelled the idea of the trusted manager on the distinctive Prussian state concept of the civil servant (*Beamter*) (Kocka 1981).

The industrial state took a more active and decisive role in a paradoxical way; not so much by defining manual workers in terms of an absence of rights, but by defining protective rights for them. This development was linked to the rise not so much of political democracy itself as pressure for it or the threat of it. Trade unions and radical, sometimes socialist, political parties were capable of disrupting social and economic order and demanding radical limitations to the power of property ownership. Again, Germany provides the *locus classicus*, with the Bismarckian welfare state designed to pacify working-class agitation by reducing the degree of economic uncertainty in workers' lives through limited social insurance schemes (Palier 2010c). These and other initiatives took it for granted that employers were in positions of power over their workers, especially manual workers, and that the lives of the latter were characterized by insecurity, and often by poverty. Governments did not wish to change that power relation; indeed, they guaranteed it through the laws of property that made it possible for some people to command the labour of others and to extract profit from the process. They also usually maintained rules for access to the suffrage that defined property and gender rights, marking arbitrary category lines across the continuum of property ownership. But they sought to take some of the sting out of that fundamental inequality through limited legislation for labour rights and social welfare (Knegt 2008; Sinzheimer 1921). The social problem was defined relatively unambiguously as that of urban, male industrial workers and their dependent wives and children. These workers were the ones who might threaten social order through their mass status. Rural workers might have worse living conditions but were rarely successful in organizing protests. Self-employed workers of various kinds might be even less secure but had virtually no capacity to combine. Some office workers had little chance to provide security against eventual calamities, but usually felt they had more to lose from setting themselves in opposition to the managers with whom they mixed directly and personally within the office. Some or all of these groups were usually excluded from the new policy measures. The *question sociale* was an essentially urban, industrial, male, manual worker question, and the *politique sociale* that responded to it also took that form. As a result, and paradoxically, urban industrial class differences were to some extent made legal, and thereby politicized, by measures to offset their implications. These measures constituted responses to what came to be seen as the 'old' social risks.

As the second half of the twentieth century progressed, these sharp contours of class society softened in western European societies. The property-less had gained admission to the electorate, reducing the most pointed political definition of class boundaries. In most societies, protective legislation originally limited to manual workers in industry was extended to rural workers, the self-employed and non-manual employees, eventually becoming citizenship rights rather than measures to compensate for subordination and chronic insecurity. With the rise of the various services sectors, employment in industry began to decline, reducing the power of the factory paradigm of class structure. Women joined the paid workforce in large numbers, going in particular to occupations that did not form part of that paradigm. In different but related developments, the growing sophistication and professionalization of the welfare state led to an increasing division between it and labour policies, once inextricably bound together as *politique sociale*.

As industrial passed into post-industrial society, the universalization of citizenship, the declining sociocultural presence of class following deindustrialization, but then the intensification of class as inequalities of property ownership increased again, all moved this ensemble in different directions. The former two, in their different ways, reduced the importance of class identity and its political salience; the last reinforced its importance but in an invisible, politically insignificant way. Meanwhile, new groups of highly insecure workers in precarious forms of employment were forming a potential new class as a 'precariat' (Standing 1999, 2011). Apart from its acute awareness of their gender aspects, NSR analysis emerges as an unreflective consequence of these developments. The first two processes are seen as having removed the class significance of the role of the welfare state in coping with risk, leaving it to technocratic concerns. The invisibility of the third prevented analysts from seeing the class connections that led from risk trading to the economic uncertainty of working people. And the precariat were relegated to a social problem, not a class.

TOWARDS A NEW APPROACH

If the NSR school is rooted in certain premises about the mainly benign character of the forces at work in post-industrial economies, then in trying to go beyond the achievements of this school we need to rebalance that assumption of benignity (Crouch and Keune 2012). Rapid change and globalization, as well as the move away from Keynesian demand management, have together brought new vulnerabilities to working people's lives, uncertainties that are in the first instance defined and managed by employers and the owners of finance capital. Through their decision-making in corporate hierarchies, as well as through trading in risk markets, they have considerable scope to decide how uncertainties, experienced initially as exogenous shocks, will impact on different parts of the population, both within and beyond the labour force. The crude 'old risks' associated with labour's helplessness in the face of major market forces have not disappeared (Rogowski 2008a; Schmid 2008) – only the clearly tangible class structure that enabled these to be voiced and to influence public policy. Social policy, in the once-again expanded sense of all interventions (positive and negative) that come between economic shocks and the lives of working people, now has to be studied in terms of this process, distinctions such as that between old and new risks being secondary to it. This then leads us to examine various phenomena that go beyond the scope of the NSR agenda.

The economic uncertainty of people with limited personal wealth and dependent on their place in the labour market for their security re-emerged as a central organizing theme for research through the dialectic over flexibility and security discussed above. But the stance of policy had changed radically since an imperative of protecting workers from insecurity informed earlier generations of social policy. Under the influence of neoliberal ideas, policy in all fields has become increasingly governed by the ideal of the frictionless labour market, in which uncertainty would be resolved and shocks countered through rational actors' adaptation of expectations. Such an approach has little time for contemplating market externalities. Instead, it identifies measures to protect workers from insecurity as impediments to the market, which it then sees as the only force that can in the long term provide a kind of security; attempts to provide it by interfering with the market in order to recognize externalities will be self-defeating. If public policy has a role in this perspective, it is in facilitating the inception of this ideal through remedying certain market failures in order to: maximize labour force participation in order to reduce dependency rates and increase the tax base; improve the capacity of individuals to prepare themselves for participation in the labour market; and increase work flexibility among those within the existing workforce and those outside it. This activating role for policy replaces the protective one (Pascual and Magnusson 2007; Van den Berg and De Gier 2008). Davies and Freedland, who in 1993 were able to remark that employment law was primarily about protecting workers from insecurity, have more recently declared that, at least in the UK, this has changed: employment law is now about fitting workers to the exigencies of the market and maximizing labour force participation (Davies and Freedland 1993, 2007; see also Knegt 2008; Rogowski 2008a: 13; Verhulp 2008). They point out, in particular, how legislation that seems to be giving workers new rights (such as laws for the promotion of employment among women or elderly people) is actually about increasing the supply of labour. Policy for skills is about improving potential employees' quality and therefore their employability. One might summarize by saying that, if earlier labour law was concerned with human rights, today's law is concerned with human resources.

The NSR approach is fully consistent with this, though 'pure' neoliberal policy makers are not at ease with it. These latter point instead to the importance of individuals making provision from their own resources to convert the uncertainties they face into financial risk products, through private pension and insurance provision, and other purchases of financial assets. This is the narrow space around which policy debate now revolves: pure neoliberalism versus mixtures of it with strong ingredients of proactive, technocratic social policy.

It was argued above that flexibility stands in a relationship of some tension, not only with the demand of working people for stability in their lives, but also with the dependence on consumer confidence of an economy based on mass consumption. The concentration on the supply side of neoliberal economics has drawn attention away from the fundamental fact that an economy needs both supply and demand. To the extent that labour incomes are an important constituent of demand, and to the extent that consumer confidence is dependent on workers' confidence in the continuity of their income, the tension between flexibility and security may not only be one between the market and the welfare state, but a condition of the operation of markets themselves. Some forms of labour flexibility are therefore unwelcome to employers, if it becomes difficult to sustain continuity of employment among skilled and well-trained staff, or where firms are trying to develop strong corporate cultures. Streeck (2008, 2009b) has argued further that capitalism needs the workforce to be reproduced. The conditions of working life seem to be throwing this in some doubt today, as birth rates decline in many parts of Europe. Business interests may therefore favour 'family-friendly' policies, from public childcare to regulation of working hours (see also Klammer 2013).

The perfect labour market is an impossible dream. It is not possible for economic models to incorporate all shocks. It cannot be assumed that actors in the labour market have adequate knowledge rationally to anticipate likely uncertainties and to be able to turn them into tradable risks. Not all the externalities produced by the labour market can be either incorporated within the market itself or ignored as unimportant. If that is the case, then measures to provide for various kinds of security against economic uncertainty may be necessary to sustain the confidence – economic, political and social – of labour-market participants in mass-consumption democracies. But, of course, measures of this kind then impede the progress towards the perfect labour market.

This dilemma has been recognized by policy makers in two different ways. First, they have found it politically impossible to remove social policy supports for economic security in the way recommended by the economic theory. Second, and more constructively, there is important evidence that some forms of security provision do not seem to impede labour market efficiency but are even positively associated with it. This has now been recognized in the OECD's 2006 follow-up to its 1994 *The Jobs Study* (OECD 2006), as well as in significant academic research (Amable 2003).

If this was already the case, the search for the perfect labour market was even more thoroughly thrown off course by the financial crisis of 2008. As noted above, this was a crisis at the heart of the neoliberal model of market governance. Financial markets of the Anglo-American type, the type responsible for the crisis, had been seen as the purest expression of what could be achieved by the pure market, with their capacity for perfect anticipation and future discounting through calculated risk-sharing (Fama 1971, 1991). As we shall discuss further in later chapters, these markets have also been directly relevant to the problem of the labour market: instead of depending on social security benefits and job protection, workers could offset their labour-market uncertainty by taking on unsecured loans, the risky character of which was 'lost' by being extensively traded in secondary markets. The consumer spending unleashed by these loans stimulated demand in the economy, further reducing uncertainty. It achieved similar goals to Keynesian demand management, but using market means alone and without recourse to government intervention – a kind of 'privatized Keynesianism' (Bellofiore and Halevi 2009; Crouch 2009).

We now know that this model was not sustainable. First, it is questionable whether the deregulated global financial system really meets the criteria of the pure market. It seems to depend on traders not knowing the dimensions of the risks concealed within the bundles of assets in which they trade, whereas models of the perfect market assume rational actors motivated to acquire perfect knowledge. Second, the rush by governments to sustain the banking system after its collapse made that system dependent on political intervention of a kind completely incompatible with the rules of the market. The model is however surviving; the interests vested in it are too powerful for it to be permitted to collapse (Crouch 2011a). But it can no longer be seen as a pure market solution to problems of economic uncertainty. It is yet another distorted market, itself dependent on government regulation and financial support. Whether or not the moral hazard introduced by governments intervening in this way will lead to worse outcomes than if governments had allowed the markets to engage in their own major correction is as yet unknown.

In this context, existing doubts surrounding the search for pure labour markets are doubly reinforced. First, if the financial system can exist only with external public support, should the labour market be expected to be any different? Second, if, in some countries, insecure or flexible labour markets were only feasible because workers had access to sources of credit not dependent on their labour incomes, what was to happen after the collapse of the sub-prime mortgage and other unsecured credit markets? If that system was the market's answer to labour-market insecurity, was it really more cost-effective and efficient than orthodox social policy?

It is therefore necessary to revisit the whole question of labour market uncertainty and the most appropriate measures for reconciling workers' demands for protection from it with the need for flexibility. The crisis in unsecured credit enables us to see that it is not only formal public labour market and social policy that are relevant to attempts to reduce economic security; and we should not assume that unsecured credit has been the only other relevant set of practices. Several other areas of life, such as the family, have also been important, in at least some societies; areas that have not been involved in the central ideological conflict between markets and public social policy.

Policy makers, including senior managers of large corporations, have not been presented with the simple possibility of tearing down protections that they had come to see as inhibiting economic performance, but they have been required simultaneously to provide alternative forms of assurance to at least some sections of the working population that, barring natural disasters and the unforeseen, they should be able to plan their lives with reasonable confidence. This includes consideration of different forms of labour flexibility, which can have very different implications for security; hence 'flexicurity' and other initiatives that will be discussed in the following chapters. New approaches are now needed for bringing together analysis of the full ensemble of issues affecting labour market policies, related social policies, class relations and industrial relations regimes, in terms of collective action games around the distribution of uncertainty. This can be tackled as a collective problem, in various ways, or it can be one of 'dumping' the uncertainty burden on different sections of the population. In the next chapter we shall develop an analytical scheme that tries to fulfil this aim.

2. Widening the perspective: an analytical scheme

In the previous chapter I asserted that, to the extent that labour incomes are an important constituent of demand, and to the extent that consumer confidence is dependent on workers' confidence in the continuity of their income, the tension between flexibility and security will not only be one between the market and the welfare state or economy and social order, but also a condition of the operation of markets themselves. This is a central puzzle for capitalist economies. It is of course possible for work income not to be the main source of demand. Indeed, for most of human history traded demand was concentrated on luxury products for elite minorities. The mass of the people existed at a subsistence level. This remains the case in large areas of the world today. The industrial revolution brought an expansion of mass goods, but initially of low value-added products. The mutual fuelling of growth in both mass demand and mass supply dates back only as far as the Fordist revolution in mass-production methods of the early twentieth century, limited initially to the USA and later parts of Europe. Even that, which seemed to constitute a pure market solution to the problem, was contingent on economic conjuncture and did not offer long-term security to mass workers; development of the Fordist system was followed by the economic collapse of the 1930s. In many European countries, mass democracy was also not well established until either the inter-war years or later. It was as a response to the 1930s collapse, to World War II, and to the full establishment of democracy that serious policy-making linking labour security, consumer confidence and economic strength really dates.

By starting from this perspective, analysis does not turn solely to the state or collective employment relations as the prime locus of protection against market uncertainty but is open to a wide range of institutional possibilities. Examination of different ways in which supply and demand are related to each other provides a distinctive route to the study of different forms of the *Volkswirtschaft* – those aspects of economic life that concern the earnings and expenditure of the mass of the population. Such a study includes that of labour and social policy regimes, but seeks to go further. The object of research becomes a range of policies of public and private actors, as well as practices which, while not consciously constructed as policies, have an impact on life that can be as strong as explicit policy. The agenda of risk is more extensive, and ways of coping with it extend further – including ways of 'dumping' risk on some people rather than others.

At the heart of this complexity is the question: when are workers 'secure' anyway? The obvious answer from labour law might be: when they have rights to their jobs and cannot be easily dismissed or made redundant without compensation. An answer from social policy might stress rights to generous unemployment pay and help in securing a new position. But an economist might contend that the only security comes from being in a flourishing market economy that provides chances and choices of a wide range of jobs, irrespective of formal rights and welfare provisions. It is not easy to determine when anyone has been objectively economically secure, except retrospectively. Subjective security can be more easily assessed by asking people if they feel secure. Feelings are very important here, because if someone feels insecure, even if objectively they are not, then their behaviour will exhibit the symptoms of insecurity – for example, wary spending and consumption, hostility to people (such as immigrants) whom they feel to compete with them for jobs. Also, vice versa, if people are made to feel secure by, for example, the availability of easy but highly risky credit, they might exude an unwarranted but economically useful confidence. However, as we learned in the financial crisis, subjective beliefs that stray far from a base in whatever eventually imposes itself as some kind of reality can be brought to the ground with a nasty bump.

These considerations hardly make it any easier to establish when labour-market security actually exists, but rather suggest taking a lateral approach, concentrating on the relationship between labour flexibility and consumer confidence. This enables us to concentrate on how labour-market risk is managed, recognizing class conflicts and compromises, rather than technical solutions in that management. Compromises are certainly possible, as studies of the shared interests of capital and labour in the development of social policy have shown (e.g., Swenson 2002), but they are not inevitable and are not always constructive.

Our first need is to establish a framework for the different forms that can be taken by the relationship. The puzzle is conceived heuristically: those engaged in tackling it do not necessarily conceive it in this way; and it is not necessarily an historical process. Such an approach does however provide a lens through which it is useful to observe structures and changes. While the aim is to be comprehensive and to be able to capture unexpected linkages, it is neither feasible nor methodologically acceptable to go in search of as many facts as possible and then try to make sense of them. Instead, we need a disciplined, theoretically based analytical framework that suggests why and how a particular area of policy or practice is relevant for investigation. The basic empirical elements of the approach will also be found in Crouch (2010); the theoretical framework itself in Crouch (2011b). The present discussion draws heavily on this latter article.

We can identify three fundamental approaches to resolving the dilemma of achieving a flexible workforce without problems being created by workers' insecurity, discontent or inability to consume. The first (I) does so by separating populations into those who bear the risk of labour-market flexibility and those who have the security to consume, without the former being able to pose a social challenge. The second (II) separates capacity to consume from the rewards of labour without separating the people who consume from those who provide labour, but by differentiating these functions within the same persons. The third (III) seeks a resolution within the labour market relationship itself.

These approaches will normally be observed within particular societies at particular periods of time, and it is common for research to isolate its cases in place and time in this way. This is however misleading, as different places and times relate to each other. The present scheme will therefore consider three different contexts, corresponding roughly to the three fundamental adverbial forms: place, time and manner. The third will then be further subdivided into 'internalizing' and 'internally externalizing' contexts, as will be shown below.

If we are to relativize the idea of society in this way, it is necessary that we clarify what we mean by 'societies' for our purposes. Human individuals are unable to provide unaided an environment for their own security, as the provision of an environment requires collective action of some kind. Very rich and powerful people can solve this problem by ordering the collective action of others to provide such environments for them, using either political or economic means, and perhaps hiring other people as staff. The great majority of people, however, depend on their membership of one or more collectivities for this provision. The term 'community of fate' was introduced into modern sociology by Arthur Stinchcombe (1965) to describe such collectivities. He defined this term to mean an organization in which the success of individual participants is closely linked with the success of the larger collectivity. Writing for a handbook on organizations, he was particularly concerned with that form of human institution we call organizations, but the term can also be applied more generally to include looser forms of association. Indeed, it is most often used today to refer to nations. The term 'community' is confusing here, as in the rest of this book the word will be used in its stricter, normal sociological meaning, referring to primary, tight, face-to-face and largely informal groupings. The term 'fate' might also seem to imply powerlessness in the face of a fixed destiny.

What Stinchcombe wanted to identify by his term were a whole range of collectivities within which life chances are determined. In this book I shall therefore use the term 'collectivities' instead of 'community of fate', but always using this word with Stinchcombe's meaning for the earlier term.

Stinchcombe's concept is further troublesome, as forms of it in various European languages (e.g., *Schiksalsgemeinschaft*) had earlier been used by fascist movements presenting the ethnic nation as a mystical union of solidarity, a connotation that has never left the term. Stinchcombe is innocent of this as he is concerned only to identify objective groupings of shared life chances. However, it remains important to be able to distinguish between collectivities where this is simply a fact of life and those where political and other actors seek actively to realize the potentiality of this fact in social policy. For example, take two societies, in both of which the population depends for its welfare on a high level of education being available. In one, policy makers use this fact as a reason to develop policies for maximizing the level of educational success within the population; in the other, they do nothing. Both societies remain 'communities of fate' in Stinchcombe's sense, but in only the former is there an attempt to make a reality of that community by calling on a felt solidarity to make collective action possible. In Chapter 8 we shall have reason to consider this difference. We shall call the former 'solidaristic collectivities' and the latter 'non-solidaristic collectivities'. It is important to bear in mind that a given collectivity may be uneven in this respect, and may be solidaristic about some issues or in some ways but not in others, and to distinguish among different degrees of collectivity membership among different types of person. It is also a concept that is placed under considerable pressure by globalization (Ferrera 2012).

The issue of place enables us to address these points most directly. It should not be assumed that the central puzzle has to be resolved within one geographically defined society or jurisdiction (treated here for simplicity as nation states). This is especially important in a global economy with much production organized by transnational corporations. We must therefore ask (a) *where*, literally and geographically, confidence and insecurity are distributed. Turning next to time, we encounter the scope that exists for risks being pushed into the future in order to reduce uncertainty today; and for today to gain security from the products of past insecurity: the question (b) *when*. Finally, considering the manner in which the central puzzle is confronted within specific places and times (the question *how*) brings us to the normal field of policy research. While there is an enormous diversity in potential answers to the 'how' question, we shall here simplify it into a choice between two extremes. First, (c) refers to 'internal externalizing' contexts – in which burdens are 'dumped' on specific groups within the society, just as use of the place and time dimensions allows dumping on people in other jurisdictions or living at other periods; we shall call this process 'exclusionary' for simplicity. It captures the point made above about different people having different degrees of belonging-ness to a society. Second, (d) refers to 'internalizing' contexts – in which burdens are, at least in principle, shared evenly among all members of a specific society. We shall call this 'inclusive'. Thus, two of the contexts (time and place) involve the society of reference externalizing uncertainty on to outsiders; two (both of manner) internalize within the society, but one of these externalizes within itself.

Combining the three approaches and the four contexts gives us the potential analytical frame shown in Table 2.1. Two of its cells remain logi-cally empty. Segregation by place separates different people, and is there-fore incompatible with universalism; cell I(d) is always empty. Integration of security and flexibility is not possible across different spaces, so cell III(a) is also empty. There are therefore potentially ten combinations of different approaches and contexts. The numbered items within the cells in the table refer to the examples of policies and practices in the following discussion. It must be stressed that these are only empirical examples; the list tries to be extensive, but it is not exhaustive, and the importance of the examples varies considerably. It is the analytical frame that claims to be exhaustive, in the sense that any approach to resolving the central puzzle will be able to be located in one or more of these cells.

I. THE SEPARATION OF CONSUMERS FROM WORKERS

I(a) Separation by Place

The most fundamental means for separating consumers and workers into two non-overlapping groups, such that the confidence of the former is in no way affected by the vulnerability of the latter, uses the international division of labour. It is assumed that the vulnerable workers in the latter group are unable to express any discontent caused by their insecurity. It can be argued that the aim of the banks operating the global financial system is to develop secondary and derivatives markets that become entirely self-referential in this way. The values being traded are gener-ated within the financial system alone and have no reference to what is sometimes called the 'real' economy. If this could be fully achieved, the financial sector and those who derive their earnings from it would be autonomous of any working population anywhere. Considerable progress

Table 2.1 Approaches and contexts for resolving the confident consumption – flexible labour puzzle

Approaches	Contexts			
	(a) Place	(b) Time	(c) Manner: exclusionary	(d) Manner: inclusive
I Separating workers from consumers	1 International trade 2 Supply chains	3 Enjoying the fruits of past labour 4 Squandering the resources of the future 5 Inherited property ownership	6 Labour market segmentation 7 Shadow economy 8 Sector-based separation	
II Separating consumption from labour income	9 Emigrant remittances and returns	10 Private insurance 11 Collective insurance	12 Intra-family transfers 13 Traded, unsecured debt	14 Public services and transfers as decommodifying
III Integrating consumption and labour income		15 Demand management	16 Collective bargaining 17 Public services as employment facilitators 18 Activation policies 19 Employment law	

was made towards the achievement of this when international account-
ancy rules were changed to require corporations to calculate their value in
terms of their tradable financial assets rather than trade in the substantive
goods and services they sell. However, the system still needed to be related
ultimately to something outside of itself, and in the end this something
became in part the unsecured debts of millions of households whose
consumption had outrun what they could earn in the labour market. The
2007–08 crisis showed that, at least for the time being, financial markets
still need to 'touch base' with reality from time to time. They are however
able to make use of their near-perfect geographical mobility to avoid
dependence on specific populations. There was, for example, only a small
cost to be borne by transnational banks in having extreme austerity policies imposed on the Greek population. The fate of Greek people was an
externality for the financial markets, once the banks had been compensated for the losses they had occurred in making loans to the Greek and
other debtor governments. Displacement by place is still relevant for these
fluid markets. This basic geography needs to be established before we treat
countries as equal 'cases', expected to respond in the same way to the same
policies. There are two different but interrelated means: international
trading patterns and supply chain organization.

Example 1: international trade. In a world of sovereign national jurisdictions, the central puzzle can be resolved if confident consumers live in
some locations and precarious, highly flexible workers in others. In an
oversimplified theoretical case, we can assume that there are two kinds of
locations: those that export production by insecure workers, who do not
themselves consume much; and those where confident consumers, whose
own employment is in sectors not vulnerable to the fluctuations of production, import the products of the former.

The former case covers countries having two characteristics: at least
temporary restraints on domestic mass consumption; and success in producing exportable goods. A regime of this type was dominant in the Bonn
Republic during the early years of post-war recovery in the 1940s and
1950s. German workers were very poor, but World War II victor countries
and various neutrals were on a different economic path and provided mass
markets for German goods. Today, some developing countries in the Far
East have made major use of this resolution of the puzzle.

The other side of this coin is the existence of countries that import
the products of the exporting countries, and who themselves depend on
domestic production and consumption (probably mainly of services), debt
or other devices to finance mass consumption. These are better able to
protect their workers' consumption, as their labour demand is less elastic:

a decline in demand for goods will mainly affect labour in exporting countries. Such countries would however be running long-term trade deficits. This is therefore a sustainable approach only for financially powerful countries, whose debts others find it advantageous to hold; collapse of confidence in their debts threatens the viability of the approach.

Example 2: supply chains. A second way in which the international division of labour comes into play is through the development of international internal markets, subcontracting and supply chains organized by the managers of transnational corporations. These usually offer explicit or implicit guarantees of employment and/or stable incomes to some sections of the workforce, located in certain parts of the world, but not to others. The protection offered to insiders is partly dependent on outsiders bearing the brunt of any instability produced by market fluctuations. This is very commonly the case with clothing and textiles, where most production is carried out in China and other parts of Asia, at very low wage levels and under low conditions of labour security, while corporate headquarters and final product markets are to be found in wealthy countries (Miller 2009). As with international trade, employment (and therefore mass consumption) remains relatively stable in the privileged locations, for whom there is a response to the central puzzle. There is not however a response for the countries at the unstable end of the supply chain.

I(b) Separation over Time

The time dimension is relevant to the division of populations into consumers and workers if one envisages divisions over a period sufficiently long that there is little or no overlap between the two. The location in time of human communities is considerably more complex than that concerning space. The collectivity that constituted the nation of France in the eighteenth century is not the same as that of the twenty-first-century society that occupies the same territory. But this happens only gradually, as humans not only live across several decades, but also identify strongly with their children and probably at least one further generation. At what point does postponement of the resolution of a problem – say, the funding of a pension scheme or putting an end to environmental damage – cease to constitute sharing within the same entity, and become one of externalizing on to a future one? If we take a narrower view and examine the issue from the perspective of particular groups of decision makers, externalization might be considered to start as soon as a new generation of office-holders arrives on the scene, a time lapse of only a few years. Unless time displacement is done over long periods of time, it may be difficult to distinguish from conflict between generations existing alongside each other: an issue that more properly belongs under the fourth possibility to be discussed below. Nevertheless, we can see the use of time as a separator between labour and consumption in such ways as the following:

Example 3: enjoying the fruits of past labour. Consumption standards at time t may be enhanced by the use of assets and resources accumulated at time $t - 1$, whose construction may have been possible only because workers at the earlier time were not compensated to a degree that enabled them to consume. This was a common feature of the past accumulation of capital and infrastructure, but also of institutions, enjoyed by today's wealthy societies, even though the process took various different forms (Rostow 1965). This makes it easier for their populations to consume at high levels now. Labour and social policy research usually takes such matters for granted, but in comparing countries with very different historical backgrounds it can be highly relevant. This is especially so when considering countries trying to develop very rapidly today, requiring populations to forego current consumption in ways that are not necessary for those in already-wealthy countries. Like the issues discussed under I(a), it produces cross-national differences that need to be considered in comparative studies.

Example 4: squandering the resources of the future. The other side of this coin is when a generation at time t consumes at high levels because it is able to ignore externalities produced by this consumption that will negatively affect a generation living at time $t + 1$. The latter will presumably have to work harder with poorer consumption opportunities. In this way environmental damage and man-made climate change – major examples of how this can operate – can be incorporated in the study of labour and social policy.

Example 5: inherited property ownership. A major means for using time to separate consumption opportunities from work obligations is the existence of large wealth holdings, extracted from labour incomes at time $t - 1$ and giving consumption opportunities without a need to work for an inheritor generation at time t. Consumption at time t is then heavily concentrated among non-working elites, while the rest of society provides flexible, poorly rewarded labour, hardly able to afford to consume beyond subsistence levels. This is the solution to the central puzzle that has predominated for most of human history and across most of the world, unless and until mass domestic consumer markets developed. As a regime it has two principal disadvantages. First, without mass markets there are severe limits to possibilities for economic growth; consumption growth is concentrated in luxury goods. Second, it depends on the economic, social and political exclusion of the mass of the population, which often requires an extensive apparatus of suppression. Property inheritance also takes place among contemporary generations, so this is not only a factor that operates across time. It is always exclusionary, as only wealthy groups can participate in it.

I(c) Separating Types of Person at the Same Place and Time

Inherited property has contemporary implications as well as those over time. In most societies small wealthy minorities distinguish themselves from their contemporaries by their capacity to consume without having to work. Therefore in Table 2.1 the cell containing point 5 extends into I(c). Many other factors also provide scope for a segregation of people into consumers and workers within one society, but by concentrating consumption among majorities who work but have strong expectations of security and income levels that give scope for spending. An excluded minority lacks security but, since its incomes are low, this does not have important implications for consumption. Its minority status also restricts its capacity for protest.

Example 6: labour market segmentation through demographic character-istics. As noted above in connection with international differences in levels of security experienced by workers in different parts of the world, managers of large corporations usually develop internal labour markets, subcontracting and supply chains offering different levels of exposure to risk. The same processes occur within societies, partly through supply chains, but also through other factors that result in different terms and conditions being offered to different kinds of people. Managers make use of contracts of different types and duration, including labour-only sub-contracting, to distinguish between secure, well-paid core workforces and precarious, usually low-paid ones. While among employees there tends to be a positive correlation between security and income, as employers can indicate the value of an individual or category of worker through both, among people on self-employment contracts the opposite can be the case. Some contractors (such as consultants) may be very highly paid but with no security, deriving their consumer confidence from the strength of their market position. Low-paid self-employed, on the other hand, have neither contractual nor financial security. These various forms of exclusion are achieving increasing prominence in many societies, producing an issue of increasing importance.

Various demographic characteristics become an important basis for allocating people among these categories. The main examples are:

- *Ethnicity, 'foreignness'.* Members of ethnic or cultural minorities may enjoy lower formal citizenship rights, excluding them from various forms of labour security. Illegal immigrants are an important example in many contemporary advanced societies. Alternatively, discrimination takes place informally, through general social exclusion or weaker access to markets.
- *Gender.* Their role in childbearing has presented many reasons for relegating women to less secure labour-market positions, ranging from formal discrimination against their access to employment rights to consideration of their employment as less important to that of the 'breadwinner' males with whom they are assumed to live. In most societies, women constitute a majority rather than a minority, but they are usually a minority of the remunerated workforce.
- *Age.* Both extremes of the age range can be exposed to low security and low wages. The young may have difficulties accessing strong positions or rights, which are often based on tenure in a job; or, like women, they may be considered to have access to family resources to support their consumption. The old may be regarded as providing less efficient labour, or again may be considered to have access to family support, or where there are pensions, may be regarded as not needing labour income to support their consumption.

Example 7: shadow economy. Most studies of labour protection regimes and flexibility usually consider formal rules and assume that these are effectively implemented. In doing so they miss both part of the reality of labour market regulation and important numbers of employed people, as the shadow economy does not appear in any official statistics (Burroni and Crouch 2008; Schneider 2005). It is important that research takes full account of the size and place of the shadow economy because it forms a major device for separating consumers from producers, and certain producers from others. In developing economies illegal work and firms without a legal existence are the norm. The shadow economy overlaps with, or can be an aspect of, discrimination against illegal immigrants, but it is not limited to their case.

Example 8: sector-based separation. Different kinds of economic activity may offer different degrees of protection from insecurity and different levels of income. These differences may result from government protectionist strategies towards favoured sectors or from market processes. Sometimes public employees enjoy particular protection from economic uncertainty. A different form of stability of employment chances in the face of market fluctuations can occur where large numbers of firms, particularly but not solely small and medium-sized enterprises (SMEs), in related areas of activity, cluster within geographical areas or industrial districts. Both the craft sector of the Italian economy (Beccattini 2000) and the Californian information technology industry (Kenney 2000) provide examples of this phenomenon. Workers in such situations perceive that they have a diversity of employment opportunities available to them within a geographical range and within social networks. The fragility of individual small firms does not therefore necessarily threaten employment and income levels. Of course, districts and other clustered activities move from being particularly resilient to being particularly brittle when there is a collapse of the whole sector in which the area is specializing, as this frequently leaves few employment opportunities, leading to a crisis of confidence and a decline in purchasing power. They are however a useful example of how individuals may find forms of security apart from social policy.

II. THE SEPARATION OF CONSUMPTION FROM LABOUR INCOME

II(a): People might practise their precarious labour activities in one jurisdiction but consume in another, the former economy not being disturbed by the interruptions to consumption that are involved.

Example 9: emigrant remittances and returns. Emigrant workers may provide this kind of place flexibility in two ways. First, they send a part of their labour earnings home to their families. For some economies (e.g., the Philippines) these payments can form a major component of national income. If the workers lose their jobs, the economy of the host country does not bear so much loss from the decline in their consumption, as this is concentrated in their country of origin. Second, when emigrant workers find their labour insecurity intolerable, they often return home, again sparing the host country the costs of unemployment support.

II(b), with II(c) and II(d) Separation over Time and within Time

Individuals can sometimes separate their consumption from their labour income by making use of time, though as the time horizons are short, in practice it is sometimes difficult to distinguish this from in-time separations; hence the extended cells across (b), (c) and occasionally (d) for some items here.

Example 10: private insurance. In a pure market the central puzzle posed in this book does not arise. Since participants in such a market have perfect knowledge, and prices adjust marginally and immediately to any change, there are no endogenous shocks. All adjustments are smooth; flexibility does not imply uncertainty of a kind that should damage confidence to consume. There are two problems with this. First, the market is not proof against exogenous shocks, and while the range of exogeneity can in principle be reduced by extending the scope of the market, such things as natural disasters and wars will remain capable of imposing shocks. Second, no one starts from the position of being in a pure market; there are market distortions throughout economies, some caused by public policy interventions, others by inability to achieve perfect knowledge, others again by imperfections in competition. It is possible to resolve this problem within the market through the private insurance principle and the consequent sharing of risk. Apart from major and unpredicted catastrophes, those whose risks are insured can continue to spend without making their own full provision against possible losses. Risk is shared, and the sharing operates primarily across time, as it is over time that the insurance funds are accumulated.

Important though this model is for many forms of risk, it is not common for the mass of a workforce to insure privately against labour market risk – though for an example of how workers in less generous unemployment protection regimes use such devices as mortgage protection plans to gain some more risk protection see Clasen's (2007, 2009) studies of the British case. Such behaviour is vulnerable to three forms of market failure. First, the costs of such insurance would take the poor to very low levels of subsistence; their risks are high, implying large premiums, but their means to pay them are low. This would lead them to fail to insure, as they have to rank a small improvement in comforts today over provision for the future. Second, more generally than this, individuals are myopic in relation to major but often unpredictable economic developments and find it hard to make rational calculations concerning their insurance needs. Third, the classic reasons for breakdown of insurance markets – adverse selection and moral hazard – are likely to be a severe problem, particularly for insurance against sickness and unemployment. The main exception to this general under-provision concerns private retirement pensions, though even these tend to be restricted to higher-income groups. In general, understanding the problems faced by people on moderate incomes when insurance of this kind is considered helps explain why for them so much risk remains as a bundle of uncertainty.

Example 11: collective insurance. Given that there is a collective interest in resolving the flexibility/security confrontation, and that individuals must be expected to take precautions below the level needed for this collective purpose, this is an area where governments and associations, sometimes individual corporations, have intervened, typically providing insurance-type policies to sustain purchasing power under conditions of the instability or disappearance of employment income such as unemployment, sickness and retirement. There is an important difference here between so-called 'Bismarckian' schemes, which enrol certain types of employee in category-based funds, which tend to be exclusionary (category (c)) and 'Scandinavian' or universal schemes that embrace all workers in a society (category (d)). Today there are strong trends to convergence between these two once very distinct types, as states underwrite the accounts of increasingly inclusive category schemes (Hinrichs 2010; Palier 2010b), while immigrants are often excluded from 'universal' schemes. Company-level and employer-managed occupational pension schemes, often ignored in studies (but see Shalev 1996), come under category (c).

II(c) (and II(d)) Separating Consumption and Work at the Same Place and Time (Usually Using Exclusion, but Occasionally Universal)

Example 12: intra-family transfers. Studies of social policy and redistribution usually concentrate on relations between markets and state provision, leaving out the activities of the family. While its welfare role was historically considerably reduced by the rise of the welfare state, it remains fundamental for the living standards and security of persons not participating in the labour market, whether because of age, disability, household responsibilities or unemployment. It is also an important channel for inter-generational transfers, for example for housing finance. However, whereas pension and other insurance schemes are in theory capable of balancing security and risk over lengthy periods of time, internal family transfers exercise their trade-offs contemporaneously.

While elements of the role of the family can be seen in most societies, there is considerable diversity. In the case of young people, there is major difference in mean ages for leaving the parental home – ranging from the early 20s in north-west Europe to over 30 years of age in the south-west (Jurado Guerrero 1999; Jurado Guerrero and Naldini 1996). Social norms play a part in determining such differences, but these are sometimes supported by social and fiscal policy. In several wealthy societies the pensions and home ownership being enjoyed (or confidently expected) by older generations is enabling them to sustain the living standards of their adult children who find themselves in the precarious labour market (Kohli 1999; Kohli et al. 2010). These inter-generational transfers offset the conflict between generations that is often predicted, but rarely occurs, between an older cohort that enjoyed the post-war welfare state and a younger one coping with the rigours of the neoliberal economy. To some extent that economy is being sustained by the past legacy of a stronger, no longer renewed, welfare regime. Since the resource endowments of different families are very unequally distributed, this is a form of contemporaneous separation of consumption from labour income that does not operate universally; it is therefore an instance of II(c).

Example 13: traded, unsecured debt. Practices developed in financial markets for completely different purposes have also had the effect of separating individuals' consumption behaviour from their labour market income, again to some extent operating over time, but over short intervals. This is the main example of what was referred to in the previous chapter as risk trading in financial markets being part of a continuum of policies and practices that also includes welfare and labour legislation. These practices have involved facilitating consumer debt, either backed by collateral that is independent of labour market position or completely unsecured. They evolved in a major way in a number of countries. They required three conditions. The first was a general rise in home ownership funded by mortgages, giving individuals on moderate and even low incomes forms of collateral partly independent of labour market position. The second was the growth of secondary financial markets that enabled the risks associated with housing and other forms of debt (such as credit cards, which were growing during the same period) to be shared among an increasing number of players in the financial markets. The third was a gradual deregulation of financial markets on a global scale, which enabled more and more players and holders of different kinds of funds to enter these markets. Eventually risks were being shared so widely that collateral requirements on mortgages, credit cards and other forms of debt became nugatory. The sums that people could borrow both rose strongly and – the point that is relevant to our present discussion – became detached from their labour market positions.

As discussed in the previous chapter, the system can be seen as a market-generated functional equivalent of government demand management – a form of 'house price Keynesianism' (Hay et al. 2008), or 'privatized Keynesianism' (Bellofiore and Halevi 2009; Crouch 2009). However, whereas under straight Keynesianism (to be considered below) government used its own borrowing to smooth fluctuations in labour income over time by sustaining the level of employment, under privatized Keynesianism consumption is sustained by separating purchasing power from labour income among individuals, and with no time horizon. Borrowing is undertaken by individuals themselves on the basis of property mortgages or credit card ratings largely divorced from labour market situation. The collective goods element in this practice – the maintenance of consumer confidence – has meant that public policy eventually became involved in sustaining it. The model depends on continued housing market buoyancy, and governments might intervene to ensure this situation. This regime is vulnerable to eventual questioning of the value of the risks being traded, as was demonstrated in the financial crisis.

These practices have some relation to the role of property ownership in Example 6, discussed above, except that they have been far less exclusionary. It had been a major project of post-World War II conservatives in many countries to promote a 'property-owning democracy', with the hopes of persuading many mass voters that their interests lay with property ownership rather than with their labour power. They therefore encouraged home ownership and investment by mid-income people. The approach may have had some success at the level of political identity, but by itself it could never produce a lower-middle or upper-working class for whom property income was more important than that from labour. As suggested in the previous chapter, the inequalities remained too wide. The small, illiquid kinds of property represented by mortgage-supported home ownership did not enable their owners to engage in profitable risk trading. However, once the unforeseen association between secondary markets in risk and housing and credit card debt was forged, the project became more realistic as a substantive separation of many people from dependence on an increasingly precarious labour income for their consumer confidence. It became a kind of privatized welfare state. The project never became strictly universal and hence can be listed under II(c), there always being large numbers of people too poor to gain a mortgage or even a credit card.

II(d) Separating Consumption and Work at the Same Place and Time

Example 14: public services and transfers as decommodifying. When public services are funded by taxation and provided free or at very low cost at the point of receipt, they become decommodified, or removed from the market. This relieves people of the need to make provision for them out of their labour incomes, reducing any anxiety imposed by labour market flexibility and any negative effect on private consumption. The same applies to social assistance and basic pensions programmes. The macroeconomic (as opposed to individual) stabilizing effect of these policies may not have been part of their design, but they are among their consequences. These schemes are normally potentially available to all members of the society concerned, with the exception of illegal immigrants.

III. INTEGRATING CONSUMPTION AND LABOUR INCOME

III(b), with III(c) and III(d) Integration across Time

Example 15: demand management. The integration of policies and practices so that flexibility and security (or labour insecurity and consumption confidence) operate together is not easy, and usually requires conscious collective policy-making rather than the incidental consequences that we have observed in many of the other examples considered above. The use of time as a separating dimension can be important in this, though again it is difficult to distinguish past from present or future. It is also not always easy to tell a priori whether policies are operating in an exclusionary or inclusive way, though research can do this.

Under so-called 'Keynesian' demand management, government uses its own spending to boost the economy to avert recession and to cool it during inflation. By damping the fluctuations of the trade cycle over time it seeks to reduce the degree of insecurity in the labour market. This was the main macroeconomic strategy pursued in the USA, the UK and the Nordic countries for the first three decades after World War II. It contained within itself the risk that democratic governments would find it easier to expand demand (increasing employment, creating more services and/or cutting taxes) to ease recessions than to reduce it (increasing unemployment, cutting services, raising taxes) to prevent an economy from overheating. It was therefore likely to be inflationary, and fell into relative disuse after it was considered to have worsened the inflationary crises of the 1970s, though it has remained in the policy repertoire of many governments. Its effects are felt at the level of the general economy rather than by individual groups, so it can be classed as a universal set of policies, and therefore operates in III(b) and III(d).

III(c) and III(d) Integration within Time

It is within these last categories that we find most of the institutions usually associated with industrial relations and labour policy. When groups of these are operated together, usually as explicit public policy, we observe what have become known as 'flexicurity' policies (Jørgensen and Madsen 2007; Muffels et al. 2002; Muffels and Tros 2004; Wilthagen 2002), and those for the 'social investment welfare state' (Bonoli and Natali 2012a; Esping-Andersen et al. 2003; Giddens 1998; Hemerijck 2012a; Morel et al. 2012; Vandenbroucke et al. 2011).

Example 16: collective bargaining. Collective bargaining between trade unions and either individual firms or groups of employers is normally associated with reinforcing labour-market stability of a kind that can support consumer confidence, but at the expense of flexibility. However, because collective bargaining involves negotiation and is capable of operating at a strategic level, it is possible for the participants in bargaining to trade flexibility and security (Burroni and Keune 2009). They typically achieve this through encompassing bargaining, where negotiators represent such a large proportion of the labour force that they cannot externalize, at least within their own society (Olson 1982); or when there is a significant role for unions and associations representing important exposed sectors of the economy (Traxler 2003; Traxler et al. 2001; Traxler et al. 2008a). Alternatively, when bargaining takes place at the level of the individual firm, workers' representatives may have to trade the short-term protection of their members' security against possible needs for flexibility if the firm is to survive. This is generally known as concession bargaining.

Whether collective bargaining operates in an exclusionary (III(c)) or inclusive (III(d)) way depends very much on these same differences in how associations are structured and whom they represent. Fully encompassing bargaining can be universal in its impact, but if unions represent certain skill levels, age groups, ethnicities or a gender, their impact may combine with that of Example 6 under I(c) and protect the security (and therefore the consumption) of insiders at the expense of a flexible labour force of workers with limited rights.

Collective bargaining remains primarily national, while managements in large corporations are operating globally, restricting considerably the scope of bargaining to develop an autonomous approach to the flexibility/security trade-off. There have been some examples of EU-level action and concerted cross-border responses, which, though small in proportion to the overall level of economic activity, may be important harbingers of future developments (Erne 2008; Traxler et al. 2008b).

There is occasionally an extension of the reach of collective bargaining into III(b) (i.e., use of a time dimension). Unions may seek to use collective bargaining counter-cyclically, accepting restraint and the priority of competitiveness during periods of rising costs, but seeking to boost consumption through high wages during recessions.

Example 17: public services as employment facilitators. The direct provision of public services – discussed above with reference to the separation of consumption from labour income – has had a secondary, originally accidental consequence, which is better considered under the current heading. While its decommodifying role in consumption was discussed under Example 14, here we address its commodifying role in the labour market. Public services offered in kind include a range of care services: childcare, sickness care, elderly care. Where these services are provided by the market, they tend to be too expensive for people on modest incomes to afford, so there is under-provision. They are often provided, as in much of southern Europe, within the family, primarily by women. In that case the provision exists, but not as part of the true labour market. Where government provides or subsidizes services, they are still primarily provided by women, but within the labour force, generating jobs and incomes, and therefore purchasing power (Bonoli 2007). Further, other women relieved of family caring roles by the availability of the public services, enter other parts of the labour force. This leads to a kind of 'femino-multiplier' of job creation. Within Europe, those economies that provide high levels of publicly funded direct services have higher levels of female *and aggregate* employment (Esping-Andersen 1999). This has had a number of implications for the flexibility/security trade-off. To the extent that populations live in male/female partnerships, the increase in female participation has brought the stability of two separate employment incomes to households. Given the differences in the sectors in which men and women are likely to work (with women less likely to work in the exposed sectors), the dependence of individual households on individual industries will often be reduced. There is a further element, only partly linked to the gender issue. Not only is publicly subsidized consumption *relatively* excluded from market fluctuations, but so is employment in the delivery of such services. The larger the population that works in sectors partly protected from market forces in this way, the larger the overall stabilizing impact of public policy.

Again, inspection of the full details of schemes is necessary before one can determine whether they are exclusionary or inclusive. For example, childcare support may be provided on a universal basis or may be available only for those able to afford it from private resources. The role of public employment in providing relatively secure work for many men and women might well operate as an exclusionary device on behalf of privileged public employees, or it might provide a general support to confident consumption throughout an economy.

Example 18: activation policies. Government programmes for the unemployed are in many countries increasingly being linked to ALMP measures (Bonoli 2007; Hemerijck 2012a; Morel et al. 2012). These are a form of publicly supported personal insurance that takes the form of investment in one's own education. However, its future orientation is relatively short term, as it is expected to have a pay-off after a few months, so it is rightly considered in the current category and not as insurance. Included here are some Danish and Dutch 'flexicurity' measures (Bredgaard et al. 2007; Muffels et al. 2008; Pedersen 2006; Rogowski 2008a). These can be distinguished from simple workfare policies, where workers are given strong negative incentives to take any job that is available; these do not provide support for personal education investment, only punishment for refusal to work. ALMP are potentially inclusive in coverage, but might also operate in exclusionary ways.

Example 19: employment law. Labour law is another major policy area, which can operate universally or in an exclusionary way dependent on its terms. As noted in the previous chapter, the main purpose of labour law in most advanced countries has been to protect the rights of employees against employers who are regarded as being prime facie more powerful than they are (Davies and Freedland 2007; Knegt 2008). It has therefore been a force on the security side of the flexibility/security equation. As such, and also discussed in the previous chapter, it has come under sustained criticism from economists and others during recent years when employment has been seen to depend on increasing flexibility. The aim of much of this criticism has been to encourage labour law to accept a role in achieving a balance between security and flexibility. Labour protection laws might be exclusionary rather than universal, partly because they can have the effect of discouraging employers from offering jobs that rapidly become secure, thereby reducing overall employment in an economy; and partly because they might encourage employers to create forms of temporary contract excluded from their protection.

METHODOLOGY

In the following chapters we shall explore how the positions of different countries stand on these diverse variables, though in some cases it is not possible to find data that adequately express the issues at stake. The primary emphasis is on numerical data provided on a more or less comparable basis by international organizations, as these give some (though by no means complete) assurance of comparability. Occasionally it has been necessary to use more limited or national databases. The temptation to use qualitative or solely national narratives has however been resisted, as these make it possible for researchers to find persuasive evidence to support their hypotheses. The result is a somewhat stilted account without interesting nuances. This is a necessary antidote to the tendency for developments in individual countries to be regarded as distinctively associated with particular national institutions, when a comparative quantitative perspective reveals them to be more general. For example, it would seem to follow from parts of the argument in the present and previous chapters that the use of high household debt to finance consumption would be found in countries with highly flexible labour markets. It is found there, but also in some other surprising cases. Where use has been made of narrative accounts to supplement the statistical material, I have tried to reduce national particularism by concentrating on books and articles that themselves subject a number of countries to a common analytical frame. Several recent books of this kind enable the reader to fill out my skeletal study with richer, detailed narratives as well as more nuanced statistical data (see, in particular Bohle and Greskovits 2012; Bonoli and Natali 2012b; Bosch et al. 2009b; De Beer and Schils 2009b; Emmenegger et al. 2012; Gallie 2013; Gumbrell-McCormick and Hyman 2013; Hemerijck 2012a; Kettunen and Petersen 2011; Lehndorff 2012b; Palier 2010c; Rogowski 2008b; Rogowski et al. 2011; Schömann et al. 2013; Vaughan-Whitehead 2011). This has the unfortunate effect of using mainly English-language sources, as this is the language of so much comparative work in contemporary social science.

I shall try to examine the situation in European labour markets at two points in time: the start of the present century, and the most recent years for which internationally comparable data are available. Before 2000, the institutional and economic situations in central and eastern Europe (CEE) were too unstable to make possible a useful comparison with western countries, and the inclusion of countries in that region in comparative datasets was too limited. The idea of comparing the two points of time selected was to consider how and to what extent the crisis has been associated with distinctive changes. However, the implications of the crisis are still unravelling, especially in south-west Europe (SWE). Further, there is a time lag of around three years for the publication of most international data. We are therefore unable to pronounce on any new stage of stability that has been reached; some of what is being written here will be out of date by the time it is published, and even more before it is read. But perhaps there will be no stable state, and only future historians will be able to discern what is really happening in labour markets at this time.

As stated in the previous chapter, our concern is with Europe, defined as the member states of the EU and the EEA, but leaving out those countries with populations of less than one million (Cyprus, Luxembourg, Malta). These very small countries usually have highly specialized economies and often occupy extreme positions on variables that makes it difficult to use them comparatively. There will also be an attempt to locate Europe within a wider perspective by comparing its nation states with three major extra-European comparators: Japan, the Russian Federation and the USA. Eurostat provides considerable data on EU member states, usually Norway and Switzerland as well, but often leaving out Croatia, which joined the EU only as recently as 2013. For the years around 2000 it sometimes also lacks data for several CEE countries. Occasionally it provides comparable data on Japan and the US too, but only rarely on Russia. The OECD provides data for its member states, which includes all countries considered here except Bulgaria, Croatia, Latvia, Lithuania, Romania, and for the years around 2000 also Estonia and Slovenia. It occasionally presents Russian data. The coverage of other data sources that are used will be discussed when they are encountered.

The research does not test hypotheses through the calculation of correlation coefficients, though these coefficients are frequently used to help describe the data. This is because of the small numbers of cases concerned. I have not followed the common practice of increasing the *n* by presenting annualized data in order to enable proper use of regression analysis, as the hypotheses being developed here are not appropriate for that technique. We are focusing on deeply rooted institutions that change slowly, and whose effects cannot be expected to be seen in year-to-year variations. The hypotheses themselves do not anticipate such variations. Rigour therefore has to be found in different ways.

A central question for research of this kind is to develop standards for assessing the relative importance of the different variables. For those that are measured in terms of proportions of national income, this is relatively straightforward. For others, means will have to be devised at relevant points. A second question is how to determine whether a country's performance ranks as high or low on a particular variable. A strict approach will be taken here and applied to each variable. It is assumed that the question can be addressed only relatively. A country ranks as having a 'high' ('low'), or 'strong' ('weak') value on a particular variable if it is high (low) or strong (weak) relative to other countries, using the formula: (X-M)/SD, where X = the value for the country concerned on the variable being examined, M = the unweighted mean of all European countries (less Croatia) for which data are available and SD = the standard deviation. (Croatia has been excluded from calculation of the European means, though data on the country are included in the tables and figures wherever possible, because there are often doubts about their comparability with those from other European countries. It was therefore thought better to exclude it from something as important to the whole study as the calculation of means and standard deviations.)

Where a country's performance on a variable is at or above 2.00 SD or at or below −2.00 SD, it will be consistently described as 'extremely' high (low) (or strong [weak]). Performances between (−)1.00 and (−)1.99 SD will be described as 'very' high (low), etc. Those between (−)0.50 and (−)0.99 SD will be 'high' (low), etc. Those between (−)0.10 and (−)0.49 will be 'moderately' high (low), etc. Those between −0.09 and +0.09 will be described as 'marginal'. The raw data will be found in tables in the statistical appendix at the end of the book. Within each chapter they will be presented for each variable in graphical form following their conversion into variations around the means, enabling a comparison across issues.

This methodology assumes that the range of values on particular variables constituted by the empirical results from individual countries constitutes a benchmark: no country could score higher than the highest score actually attained, and none lower than the lowest. This is empirically the case, and when (as often) there is a more or less normal distribution, this is a defensible means of determining whether a particular national score is 'high' or 'low'. Problems arise when one or two countries have outlier scores. For example, we shall learn in Chapter 7 that the level of collective bargaining coordination in Austria is over three times the standard deviation. This score then has an effect on the relative position of all other countries' scores, in particular truncating differences among those below the mean. Consideration was given to excluding outliers from calculations of means, but that would raise different problems of distortion. The aim of making these relative calculations is to express an individual country's position in relation to the totality of empirical possibilities revealed by the range of national experiences. Outliers have therefore been retained.

By taking countries as our units I am conniving at the practice of 'methodological nationalism': most data are produced at the level of nation states, and they provide useful units for examining bundles of variables. It is a dubious approach, for two opposite reasons. First, to concentrate on the national level is to ignore important internal heterogeneity. For example, in Italy, the USA or post-unification Germany there is enough geographically rooted diversity to make units like regions or internal 'states' objects of study in their own right. On the other hand, international institutions like multinational corporations or the EU make rules that operate across national jurisdictions, leading a nation-based study to exaggerate the extent to which nation states are autonomous units. Some recognition will be given to these factors in the following chapters, but we are concentrating on nation states, partly for methodological convenience, but partly because these do still exist as objective collectivities, and often as highly solidaristic ones. It is usually still at this level that the tensions between flexibility and security, between people as workers and as consumers, are most acutely felt. At the same time, in exploring the importance of the nation state we should also discover its limits and therefore the extent of the need to look elsewhere.

3. Modes of economic governance and class relations

The various components of the relationship between labour flexibility and consumption discussed in the previous chapter become part of social action as forms of governance. Governance is a useful concept for this purpose, as it refers to a wide variety of ways in which human behaviour is regulated, going far beyond government and law, and including some forms that are implicit, even unconscious. This has been developed in an important literature on 'new modes' of governance (to select a small number of key examples, see Héritier and Lehmkuhl 2008; Kooiman 1993; Ronit and Schneider 2000).

There are however some problems with the way in which governance theory has developed. Interestingly, these overlap considerably with the problems of the NSR school of analysis of labour market and social policy discussed in Chapter 1. Both schools emerged during the past 20 years, in a period where it seemed to some that various forms of hierarchy and inequality associated with industrial society had been transcended. Like NSR, new modes of governance theory tries to define the changed institutions of post-industrial society, claiming that a new diversity of governance has been replacing what it sees as the monolith of the state. The market (a horizontal, implicit form) plays a stronger role, as also do more flexible, almost informal arrangements called networks – ways in which informal, changing sets of relationships among varying numbers and configurations of groups can regulate and even control the conduct of their members, perhaps without anyone involved knowing that this is what they are doing. In their concern to describe a shift from vertical (state) to horizontal (market and network) governance, 'new modes' theorists tend not to notice the growing role of the vertical governance of individual large corporations, particularly as these increasingly become global and lack commitment to any one jurisdiction. For example, multinational corporations (MNCs) can set the terms of new forms of labour contracts in global and supply chains, and replace defined benefits pension schemes with less reliable defined contributions schemes. These authors also fail to notice the *reduction* in governance diversity that is taking place with the decline in associational or corporatist governance. Employers' associations are declining, as large corporations prefer to manage their own industrial relations and lobby governments by themselves (Bouwen 2002; Coen 1997, 2007); trade unions are declining in membership everywhere. As a result of both trends, corporatist collective bargaining is declining as a form of managing labour relations, being replaced by the unilateral managerial hierarchies of corporations. In turn, these hierarchies are tied heavily to a shareholder value maximization model of business that further favours the risk-trading financial sector and reduces the diversity of forms of capitalist governance. Such forms of capitalism as mutualism are disappearing. It is by no means clear that economic governance is becoming more varied and less hierarchical overall. A plausible case can even be made for the opposite hypothesis.

Modes of governance are relevant to the present study, as varying instances combine with different constellations of class interests to cut across the different means of tackling the consumption and labour security conundrum that was set out in the previous chapter. In using the governance concept here we are not tying ourselves to the thesis of a specific direction of historical change embedded in the dominant literature. We shall use the idea of governance modes as a purely analytical category; possible directional trends might be a finding, but not an initial assumption. The best account of different modes of governance, which goes beyond perception of the three forms of state, market and network, and which does not embody any presumed historical sequence, is that developed by Hollingsworth and Boyer (1997) (see also Crouch 2005). In its latest form it identifies the following modes, which are here associated with the different approaches summarized in Table 2.1 in the previous chapter:

- *The polity*, subdivided as:

    Government actions: here we find the whole field of employment and social policy, including the more extended aspects of the latter, and including regional and local government and transnational levels like the EU, as well as national level. In the framework established in Chapter 2 it plays the central part in Examples 11 (collective insurance), the public part of 13 (debt), 14 (public services and transfers), 15 (demand management), 17 (public employment) and 18 (activation policies). It also influences Examples 3 and 4 (the use of past and future resources), 6 (the rules governing labour market segmentation) and 19 (employment law).

    The law: in states under the rule of law the law has to be separated from government. Its influence on the framework is seen most directly in Example 19 (employment law), but it underpins many other examples in the list, such as 5 and 12 (the rules of property ownership, inheritance and intra-family transfers), (negatively) 7 (the shadow economy), 10 and 11 (the rules underpinning private and collective insurance) and 16 (many of the rules governing collective bargaining).

- *The economy*, subdivided as:

  The market: not only does the strength in the labour market of workers with different kinds of skill and capacity determine their ability to demand different levels of security guarantees from their employers, but the market (combined with corporate hierarchy and redistributed by government through fiscal means), determines income levels, capacity to save from income being a major form of uncertainty protection – and also a major source of uncertainty itself if individuals without extensive financial assets have to rely on it for their future security. It is therefore directly relevant to: Examples 1 and 2 (international trade and supply chains), 3 and 4 (the use of past and future resources), 9 (flows of immigrant remittances), 5 and 12 (the use of property inheritance and intra-family transfers), 6, 7 and 8 (forms of structuring the labour market), 10 (private insurance), 13 (the organization of private debt), as well as influencing 16 (the outcomes of corporatist collective bargaining), and virtually all other items in some way.

  Corporate hierarchies: the important role of individual firms in establishing forms of working and associated labour statuses and balances between flexibility and security is often unthinkingly included within 'market', but when firms establish their own organizational structures they are able, not by any means to ignore, but to shape and structure the market's outcomes. In particular, corporate hierarchies shape Example 2 (supply chains), affect 6, 7 and 8 (the structure of the labour market), 10 (corporate-level private insurance) and constitute important actors in 16 (collective bargaining). Unfortunately the research methods available to us in this study do not enable us to distinguish between market and corporate hierarchy as governance forms. They therefore have to be amalgamated, which reduces the power of our analysis. Authors who have done better include Marginson et al. (2013), and Kahancová (2011).

- *Society*, subdivided as:

  Associations: prominent in the bipartite negotiation of labour standards and tripartite social pacts, primarily operative only in Example 16 (corporatist collective bargaining), but also in the operation of some forms of 11 (collective insurance) and 19 (employment law).

Networks: despite the prominence placed on them in modern governance theory, networks do not feature strongly in labour market and social policy, except as informal alternatives to associations, possibly enabling some firms to undermine obligations to negotiate with unions if their relations adopted the formal shape of associations.

Communities: although governance by familial and community obligations seems to be primarily associated with traditional economies, it enters our framework at several points, in particular the organization of Examples 5 (inheritance), 7 (shadow economy), 9 (immigrant remittances) and 12 (intra-family transfers), on which governments may place increasing reliance to complement or substitute for the welfare state.

Different classes and forces relate in diverse ways to these modes. This is why the study of governance should not be seen as a functionalist, technical exercise; it is shot through with the exercise of power, conflict and compromise. In a capitalist society, dominance by powerful elites will be most clearly embodied in corporate hierarchies, as (occasionally subject to limited co-determination rules) the managers and owners of companies have considerable discretion over how they structure labour markets, subject to market forces. Power will be embodied in the market itself to the extent that income and wealth are unequally distributed. Challenge may come to this dominance of wealthy classes from the democratic state and the laws it produces, as the interests of poorer classes have some opportunities to express themselves here. However, this will be limited by the extent to which dominant interests also have influence over the state. It is by no means impossible, especially where democratic institutions are weak, that market forces might favour workers' interests to a greater extent than political interests. Associational bargaining, implying the representation of employees by trade unions, brings a more direct challenge to dominant interests, though the outcomes will depend on a bargaining power that is ultimately grounded in the market. Also, some worker interests might be excluded from the coverage of associational governance. Finally, informal networks and communities operate in an unpredictable way.

At a very general level, we can expect that those elements of the Chapter 2 framework that are primarily regulated by associational governance (mainly Example 16) will be associated with the most universal risk-sharing and therefore with the most egalitarian outcomes – with the proviso that some groups within a society might be excluded from its scope. Those elements that are dominated or strongly influenced by the market (Examples 1–9, 12, 13), and even more by corporate hierarchy (2, 6–8, 10) will be associated with restricted risk-sharing and the highest levels of inequality. The outcome of regulation in the polity will depend on political configurations, but is likely to be more egalitarian than pure economic regulation and to be more universal in its reach than associational governance (3–7, 10–19).

A central hypothesis is, therefore, that the more market governance is challenged by state (government and law) and associational governance, the more egalitarian a society will be, and the more widely distributed the chances of its members to enjoy some form or other of labour market security. But this must then be subjected to a number of conditions:

1.　The overall tendency may be limited by the existence of certain excluded groups.
2.　There is no straight trade-off between the interests dominant in economic and political governance, so the correspondence will be only approximate.
3.　The hypothesis contains no presumption concerning the likely economic efficiency of any particular combination of governance forms and level of inequality; this has to be separately investigated.
4.　One must be careful not to jump to conclusions about causal direction in specifying a relationship between governance and inequality. It might seem that the operation of governance modes produces a distributive outcome; but the ways in which the modes operate will be affected by the balance of power among interests in the society, which will be partly determined by the existing degree of inequality. Mutual influences are clearly at work in the influence between the two sets of variables. We therefore need to talk about 'associations' between them, rather than pronounce on causal directions.

OPERATIONALIZING INEQUALITIES OF POWER

A key variable for the study of policies and strategies around labour insecurity issue is therefore the balance of power between different class interests, as anticipated in the discussion in Chapter 1. We do not take up a position on whether it is a dependent or independent variable here; that issue will be addressed in Chapters 7 and 8. But if it is to be used as a variable of any kind it has to be operationalized. Dominant classes always have a capacity for action, because they are defined by property ownership and the occupation of dominant economic roles that automatically enable and entitle them to operate strategically. Challenges to inequality and the power differences it generates will be more varied and less systematic, depending on the capacity of non-dominant groups to organize themselves in order to participate in potential conflict with these dominant interests. Within the realm of work, that can only be interpreted in terms of the strength of autonomous trade unions. While these are not necessarily effective, there are no other potential candidates, at least not in the advanced economies. That strength can be operationalized as a combination of the sheer membership level of unions and some measure of their institutional capacity to affect outcomes.

Appendix Table A3.1 presents various data relevant to the calculation of trade union membership *c.*2001 and *c.*2011. The main data are based on the Institutional Characteristics of Trade Unions, Wage Setting, State Intervention and Social Pacts (ICTWSS) survey of the University of Amsterdam (Visser 2013), the most authoritative source that exists on industrial relations data. It covers all countries of interest to us except Croatia. A study by the European Industrial Relations Observatory (EIRO) 2012 cites Croatian national data that estimate union membership as having been 40 per cent of employees in 1999, dropping to about 34 per cent by the end of the next decade. This suggests a decline in line with that noted for several of our other CEE cases, though the overall figures seem high for the region. These data have been used here to enable us to include Croatia in the coverage, but there are doubts about comparability that will need to be borne in mind at various points in the analysis.

The ICTWSS survey follows the conventional practice of assessing union density as a proportion of people in dependent employment. However, here we need to gauge the strength of trade unions in an economy as a whole. Where self-employment or the shadow economy form a high proportion of employment, that strength is diminished in its overall impact on the economy. For example, imagine two societies, in both of which 50 per cent of dependent employees in the formal economy are members of unions, but where in the former all workers have that economic status, while in the latter 25 per cent of workers are either self-employed or working illegally. The impact of union membership is clearly higher in the former case. To give an impression of the power of unions across the workforce as a whole the ICTWSS should be deflated by the extent of self-employment, and by the size of the shadow economy. Data on the former are provided by the OECD and Eurostat. Estimates of the size of the shadow economy are by their nature always approximate, but Schneider and Buehn (2012) have made calculations from 2000 to 2010 for all countries we are attempting to cover except for Croatia and Russia. In an earlier World Bank paper, Schneider et al. (2010) provided data for a wider range of countries running from 2000 to 2006, including Russia and Croatia. Given that these numbers do not change dramatically from year to year, I have used the 2006 figure for Croatia and Russia.

The resulting patterns for all countries are shown in Figures 3.1a (*c*.2001) and b (*c*.2011), displaying the distributions around the means, as explained at the end of Chapter 2. Over the decade there was a considerable general decline in union density as here defined, the mean for European countries (less Croatia) on this measure dropping from 23.06 per cent of the total workforce at the start of the century to 19.94 per cent a decade

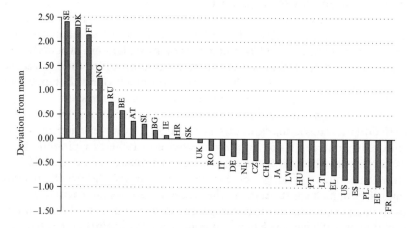

Figure 3.1a   Trade union membership density (adjusted), c.2000 (country scores in relation to standard deviation around mean)

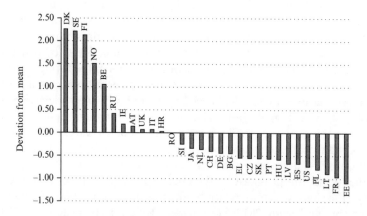

Figure 3.1b   Trade union membership density (adjusted), c.2011 (country scores in relation to standard deviation around mean)

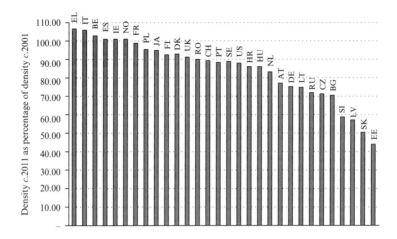

Figure 3.2   Union membership density (adjusted) c.2011 as a percentage of density (adjusted) c.2001

later. US density declined from 10.94 per cent to 9.62 per cent, Japanese from 15.82 per cent to 15.04 per cent, and Russian from 31.33 per cent to 22.58 per cent. Decline was concentrated in CEE countries and Russia, in which countries it had been dropping heavily since 1990, when it had been inflated by briefly continuing the high, virtually compulsory, union membership from communist times. However, the fall was also extensive in Austria, Germany and the Netherlands. As Figure 3.2 shows, only a very small number of countries saw increases in density, and in those cases the rise was very small and accounted for not by an actual increase in members, but by a general decline in the size of the estimated shadow economy, which has the effect of increasing union density in the approach to membership measurement adopted here.

By itself union membership strength does not tell us how that strength can be used. We are interested in unions as an indicator of the extent to which a challenge to propertied interests might be incorporated in the political and social structures that might share in determination of the labour security question. We must be clear that this formulation embodies a judgement that employees' influence can be exercised in this way, and that sheer membership strength and a capacity for militancy without incorporation do not constitute effective strength. Marxist theorists would contest this, and argue that it is only when working-class power takes this second form that it is really effective. The Marxist account of power is one that assumes irreconcilable conflict that can be resolved only through major confrontations of forms of society. Its concept of working-class power as embodied in organizational strength is therefore a transitory phenomenon, rising up at the moment of acute conflict, before being dissolved into a completely new society. In practice, in the known cases of Marxist revolutions, unions have been dissolved into the apparatus of a party-state and have lost their capacity to represent employee interests. That is however not our concern here. We are dealing with societies that have either experienced long periods of more or less stable capitalism (in which class organizations have been either too weak to raise a continuing serious challenge, or, being stronger, have accepted compromises that institutionalized their power), or have brief, post-communist periods of capitalism in which they have struggled with decline.

For the purposes of this study, therefore, we shall confine ourselves to institutionalized forms of union power. A relevant, though obviously not complete, measure of this is the presence of workers' interests within economic decision-making mechanisms in both political and corporate spheres. Of course, such inclusion could be merely formal, while informal mechanisms might be more important, and we shall need to confront that question at various points. But first, we can gain some idea of the extent and diversity of any conclusion by using some further indicators available in the ICTWSS database. These include the following, along with the scores attributed to them in ICTWSS:

- Existence of a standard bipartite council of central or major union and employers' organizations for purposes of wage setting, economic forecasting and/or conflict settlement: yes = 1; no = 0.
- Routine involvement of [both] unions and employers in government decisions on social and economic policy: full concertation, regular and frequent involvement = 2; partial concertation, irregular and infrequent involvement = 1; non-concertation, involvement is rare and absent = 0.
- Existence of works councils: existence and rights of works councils mandated by law or basic agreement = 2; works council is voluntary and/or no sanctions for non-observance of law or agreement = 1; no works council or similar institution = 0.
- Works council rights: economic and social rights, including co-determination on some issues = 3; economic and social rights, consultation only = 2; social rights [only] = 1; no rights (sanctions), only information = 0.

While it is difficult to say whether a unit of score on any one of these indicators is equal to another, we can use a cumulative score to provide a rough measure of the formal inclusion of unions and other forms of worker representation. The total scores possible on the ICTWSS scale would range from zero to eight points. Since we want to multiply the union density numbers by these scores we cannot have a zero. We therefore add an additional point to each country's score to indicate the initial step of inclusion, which is a legal right to exist, bringing the range on the ICTWSS scale to one to nine. If we were to extend our research to countries in which unions had no legal right to exist, their power score would be zero, however high membership might be. This is in line with the assumption set out above that we are counting only institutionalized forms as constituting union power. In the event of cases where union membership became very high, but governments refused to recognize it, we should predict extreme conflict, which would result in either the crushing of the union movement concerned, or its institutional recognition. At some point or other, this had indeed been the case in many of the countries being considered here, from the early struggles of British unions in the early nineteenth century to the struggles around Solidarność in communist Poland in the late twentieth century. In each case, however, by the time we reach the twenty-first century these struggles had been resolved into varying levels of incorporation of unions, even if in some cases this is no more than acceptance of their right to exist.

The scores are summarized in Appendix Table A3.1. In contrast with union membership, which declined, formal incorporation grew in European countries between 2001 and 2011, largely as a result of the inclusion of CEE EU member states in the formal provisions of EU treaties – though Meardi (2012) warns that formal requirements are often not implemented and that unions are usually too weak to enforce any legal rights. The European mean on the adjusted scale rose from 0.51 to 0.58, while the indicators for the US and Japan were static at 0.1 and 0.3 respectively, and that for Russia dropped from 0.2 to 0.1. According to EIRO reports (EIRO 2012), there has been a reasonably high level of union incorporation and works council activity in Croatia. It therefore seems reasonable to estimate this as having been similar to the level in Slovenia, with which the country had been joined in the former Yugoslavia – though like many other of the measures we shall use for Croatia, it has to be treated with reservation.

Figures 3.3a and b show the results of matching countries across these two indicators, measured in terms of distribution around the European mean, in *c.*2001 and *c.*2011 respectively. There is a modest positive correlation between the two indicators (for 2001, $r^2 = 0.2659$; for 2011 $r^2 = 0.2131$). At both periods a group of small north-west European countries – the Nordics, with Austria and Belgium – occupy the quadrant

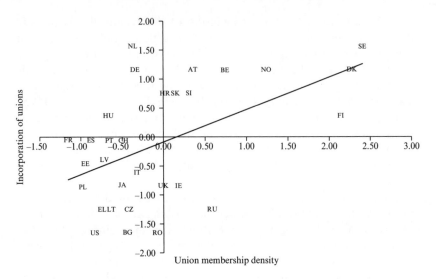

*Figure 3.3a   Union density by inclusion (distributions around means),
c.2001*

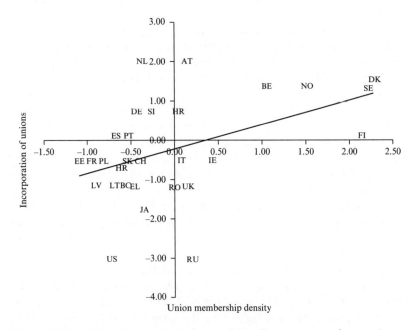

*Figure 3.3b   Union density by inclusion (distributions around means),
c.2011*

showing strength on both dimensions. In the earlier year Slovenia and (marginally) Croatia and Slovakia also occupy that quadrant, but by 2011 their relative union density has declined to push the former two towards the quadrant indicating high inclusion but weak membership, with Slovakia weaker still. Croatia remains the only CEE country marginally a member in the 'strong inclusion' quadrant, but we must remember the doubts over its statistics. At the earlier date Germany, the Netherlands and Hungary are the only occupants of this 'weak inclusion' quadrant. By 2011 Hungary has left it, being replaced by Slovenia and (marginally) Portugal and Spain. In 2001 non-incorporated (or excluded) positive union strength is displayed in Russia, and marginally Ireland. By 2011 Ireland and Russia remain in this quadrant, and Italy and the UK marginally join it. All other countries occupy the 'weak exclusion' quadrant, though some (France, Portugal, Spain, Switzerland) were only on the margins of exclusion in 2001.

Although for some purposes we shall consider countries as classified by their quadrants and their positions within them, we shall mainly make use of a combined indicator, deflating the membership density figure by the incorporation score. It must always be borne in mind that this is a dubious manoeuvre, as it produces an entirely synthetic indicator. In particular, it is often argued that French union strength is not appropriately measured by membership, but by various unions' capacity to mobilize strike calls or to attract votes in works council elections. It is also claimed that French unions' institutionalized power is mainly exercised through their role in *cogestion* of pension schemes – though this has declined in recent years. It is likely also that the incorporation of Austrian and German unions into their countries' governing institutions is underestimated by the elements included in the Visser index. On the other hand, it has been argued that unions in many parts of CEE are unable to use the rights formally accorded to them in the legislative changes necessary when their countries joined the EU (Ost 2000). In a comparative study of the kind being attempted here, one cannot make allowances for local variations of this kind. We must stay with standard terms and consistent statistics, and the term 'class challenge' will be used to refer to this combination of union strength and incorporation. The results are shown in Figures 3.4a and b. Using the nomenclature announced in the previous chapter, by around 2001 the four Nordic countries all demonstrated extremely or very strong relative class challenge, and Austria and Belgium demonstrated strong challenge – all based on both density and incorporation strength. Three CEE countries (Croatia, Slovakia and Slovenia) and the Netherlands showed moderately strong challenge, and Germany was marginally above the mean. The two western countries depended for their overall strength on a strong

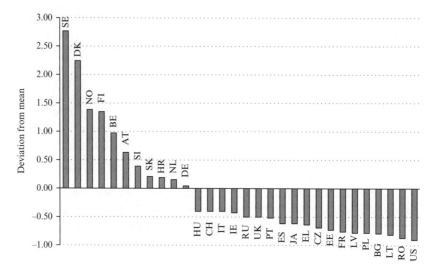

Figure 3.4a   Combined union power index, c.2001 (country scores in relation to standard deviation around mean)

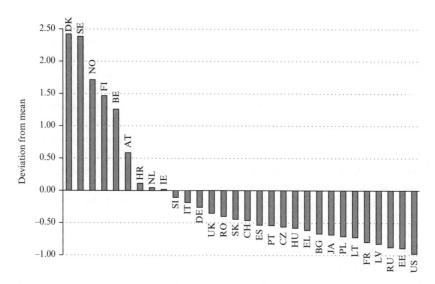

Figure 3.4b   Combined union power index, c.2011 (country scores in relation to standard deviation around mean)

incorporation score, compensating for membership density weakness. All other countries showed either moderately weak challenge (Hungary, Ireland, Italy, Switzerland, the UK) or weak challenge (Portugal, Russia, Spain, Japan, Greece, Czech Republic, Estonia, France, Latvia, Poland, Bulgaria, Lithuania, Romania and the USA).

These rankings show some affinity with the geo-cultural groupings of social policy regimes frequently encountered in the comparative literature. A comprehensive summary of these groupings, bringing together the findings of much of this literature, is to be found in the European Commission's (EC) report on industrial relations in Europe in 2008 (European Commission 2009). This is based on a number of studies of comparative European industrial relations and welfare states (Crouch 1993, 1996; Ebbinghaus and Visser 1997; Esping-Andersen 1990; Kohl and Platzner 2007; Schmidt 2002, 2006). It identifies the following:

- North (the Nordic countries)
- Centre West (Germany and the smaller countries of north-west Europe)
- South (the southern countries of the pre-enlargement EU)
- West (Ireland and the UK) and
- Centre East (the ex-communist EU member states).

This scheme appears purely geographical, as an official EC document presumably has to be, but the studies on which it was based were more political. Prominent among them are those that take a class relations approach similar to that being adopted in the current study (Esping-Andersen 1990), or one based on long-term state strategies towards organized interests (Crouch 1993, 1996; Schmidt 2002, 2006). This latter approach is also relevant to the question of the kinds of regime in which union incorporation takes place and on what terms. The EU authors then make some changes to their essentially geographical scheme, based on observations of major institutional differences in industrial relations organization. They allocate Slovenia outside the Centre East and put it with Centre West. They also put France with South. These are justifiable switches when the focus is on industrial relations systems alone and as they exist now, as opposed to social policy or earlier political development paths. The EU authors also express some doubt about the allocation of Finland (ambiguous between North and Centre West) and Hungary (ambiguous between Centre East and South).

Since this EU report was prepared, Bohle and Greskovits (2012) have provided a means of analysing differences among CEE countries, distinguishing among:

- the original Visegrád group of countries that first joined the EU (Czech Republic, Hungary, Poland, Slovakia), to which they provisionally add Croatia;
- the Baltic states, together with Bulgaria and Romania;
- and the lone case of Slovenia, which had been part of Yugoslavia and not the Soviet bloc.

We can now relate our class power account to these different forms of classification. Esping-Andersen's (1990) account was based on the strength of class challenge during industrialization, and saw the Scandinavian or 'social-democratic' group of countries as distinctively characterized by strong working-class challenge to capitalist rule during this period. Figure 3.4a fully corroborates this account for the years around 2001. He saw the Anglophone countries in general as having had industrialization controlled by liberal bourgeois elites, who were unwilling to compromise with labour movements. This is partly reflected in Figure 3.4a, in that the three Anglophone countries included (Ireland, UK, USA) all fell below the mean. However, the idea of an Anglophone group alone cannot account for the extreme gap between the two European cases and the USA. Figures 3.5a and b present a wider picture of the global Anglophone group, adding Australia, Canada and New Zealand, and showing union density (here unadjusted for self-employment and the shadow economy)

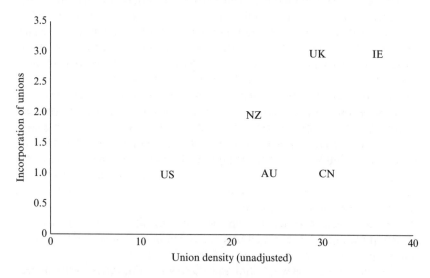

Figure 3.5a   Incorporation of unions by union density (unadjusted), Anglophone countries, c.2001

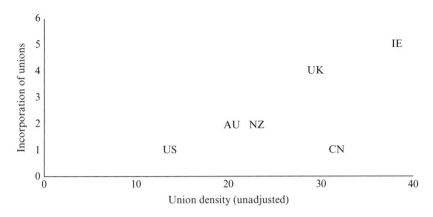

Figure 3.5b   *Incorporation of unions by union density (unadjusted),*
              Anglophone countries, c.2011

and the ICTWSS incorporation scores. Concentrating at present on the earlier year, it can be seen that the two European Anglophone nations had distinctly higher scores than the rest on incorporation, but were not so different from the three additional countries on union density. This is consistent with their being part of EU rules on union incorporation. The USA was extreme even within the Anglophone group.

Esping-Andersen's concept of 'Continental Europe' (i.e., all western countries from the Netherlands in the north to Greece in the south) as joined together by a history of industrialization by traditional elites, who eventually made compromises with labour movements by offering various conservative forms of incorporation, fares less well. These countries range all the way from the strong class challenges of Austria and Belgium to the weak class challenges of France and Greece. However, if we follow those writers (Ferrera 1996; Naldini 2003) and the EU report cited above, who have amended Esping-Andersen by making a separate group of the south-western European countries, we can make more sense of the data. The case for separating the south west in this context is usually made on the basis of the role of the family in their welfare states, rather than the nature of class challenge. This is an issue to be addressed more fully in a later chapter, but for the present we can point out that in three cases (Greece, Portugal and Spain) class challenge was particularly weakened by the existence of dictatorships into the 1970s. Italy has been democratic since 1945, but a majority of its labour movement was formally communist until the 1980s, and therefore excluded from most forms of incorporation even under democracy. The latter point also applies to France, perhaps even more strongly, and the question of whether France should be included as north- or south-western in these regime typologies is rightly debated. If typologies focus on the role of family in welfare states, then France belongs with the north west, if not with Scandinavia on some points such as state support for childcare; but if we focus on class challenge, there is a case for putting France with the south west. Certainly, the picture presented in Figure 3.4a suggests this. France, Greece, Portugal and Spain all had weak class challenge around 2001, though Italy ranked as only moderately weak. All other north-west European cases had higher levels of class challenge than these, but lower than the Nordics, located between strong (Belgium, Austria), moderately strong (the Netherlands), marginally strong (Germany) and moderately weak (Switzerland).

The central and eastern European cases present a more complex picture. Bohle and Greskovits (2012) put the Baltic states together as countries following particularly uncompromising neoliberal policies, which implies a very weak class challenge. They saw Bulgaria and Romania following a similar path. All countries had particularly weak institutional legacies from their communist periods. We should therefore expect to find these countries with particularly weak class challenge. Around 2001 this is more or less confirmed, as these countries as a group had the lowest scores in Figure 3.4a, interspersed with France, Poland and the USA at the lowest levels. The Visegrád group is seen by Bohle and Greskovits (ibid.) as pursuing compromises between neoliberalism and something approaching a western European concept of a welfare state and the protection of labour from insecurity. However, it is also important to their account that neoliberalism grows in strength over time, as the initial post-Communist role of Visegrád labour movements weakened. Hungary and the former components of Czechoslovakia had a similar history, in that they were the most industrialized within the old Soviet bloc, and with an historical orientation towards the west. Earlier, they had been part of the Austro-Hungarian Hapsburg Empire. They had thus had, until 1945, a shared legacy of class relations with the western countries of *Mitteleuropa*. Poland was more complex. It was less industrialized, and while a small region (Silesia) had been within Austro-Hungary and the rest of the western part had been incorporated within Prussia and then Germany until 1918, the eastern regions had been part of Russia until that time. It is notable that Poland's class challenge *c*.2001 was weaker than in the other Visegrád cases and closer to the other, 'non-Hapsburg' cases. Bohle and Greskovits (ibid.) saw Croatia adopting a similar class compromise in its social and economic policies, despite a rather different history.

These allocations are partly borne out by Figure 3.4a. Here Croatia and Slovakia score as having had moderately strong class challenge (but our Croatian data are suspect), and Hungary moderately weak, but ahead of several western European cases. Poland's considerably greater weakness can be explained as suggested, but the weakness of union power in the Czech Republic is more difficult to account for. Finally, Bohle and Greskovits (ibid.) identified Slovenia as a separate case, despite its very small size. Not only was it the most economically developed of the CEE states, but it had formed part of the ill-fated Yugoslav federation, which, though state socialist, had encouraged a form of worker participation in industry, giving it a considerably greater level of autonomous employee representation than in the Soviet bloc. That singularity is borne out in Figure 3.4a. If Croatian data are reliable, then it too corroborates the idea of a strong class challenge position deriving from the Yugoslav legacy.

All three non-European comparators had weak class challenge scores, but only the USA's score suggests overall distance from 'European' positions. It is however worth noting that, with the exception of France, the only other scores similarly low to those of the USA and Japan were of poor, CEE nations and Russia.

By the years around 2011 there have been some changes in relative rankings (Figure 3.4b). The Nordics still have exceptionally or very high scores, joined now by Belgium. The north west again occupies the expected mid-point positions, but now strung out from Belgium (very strong), Austria (strong), the Netherlands (marginally strong), Germany and Switzerland (marginally weak). The decline in Germany's relative position is notable, coming now below both Ireland and Italy. In its case and that of the Netherlands incorporation remains strong, and the decline is entirely the result of membership loss. The so-called Anglophone group is at least as dispersed as before, with Ireland's relative position rising. Figure 3.5b enables us to look again at a larger global Anglophone group. The gap between the two European cases and the others on incorporation has widened, suggesting a growing impact of EU and general European approaches differentiating these two from the other Anglophones. On union density, Canada scores more highly than the UK, but the Australasian pair have lower scores on both dimensions, and the USA appears as even more of an outlier. Ireland and the UK might constitute a small, distinctive 'European Anglophone' group, though on class challenge scores there is no need to distinguish them from the rest of north-west Europe. All south-west countries including France – but clearly excluding Italy – have distinctly lower scores than north-west European countries, and are indistinguishable from most of the Visegrád cases.

Among CEE countries, Romania now constitutes a partial exception to the putatively neoliberal group identified by Bohle and Greskovits (ibid.).

This results entirely from the implementation of strong works council legislation in the country on its accession to the EU in 2007. The three Visegrád countries (Czech Republic, Hungary, Slovakia) that we had before differentiated from Poland now cluster relatively close together, above the neoliberals, apart from Romania. Slovakia's membership has declined considerably from its exiguous position *c*.2001. Poland has the lower score anticipated, while Croatia appears with a moderately strong score. Slovenia has declined considerably in its relative position, but still has a stronger class challenge than the rest of CEE (apart from its fellow ex-Yugoslav neighbour, Croatia, if the latter's data are reliable). It is worth noting that absolute decline in union density was particularly strong in CEE countries and in Russia. This is partly concealed in the table by decline in western countries too, combined with increases in incorporation scores of EU accession states. These countries had very high union membership in state-dominated unions in the old state socialist systems. In several countries these unions played a role in the reform of communist movements that preceded the system's collapse – except in Poland, where it was the new, independent union Solidarność that did so. These factors enabled the unions to become accepted parts of the post-1989 regimes, initially inheriting their large and previously compulsory memberships. These drained away rapidly, but some decline has continued since 2001, proceeding at different times and speeds in different countries. This uneven process affects the statistics for both 2001 and 2011, making it difficult to compare density in CEE with that elsewhere.

Finally, Japan, Russia and the USA are all still found among the weak cases, with the USA touching on being very weak. Strong union power appears in all these data as a European phenomenon, as seen in the distinctiveness of Ireland and the UK within the wider Anglophone group. There is however too much diversity within Europe to enable us to speak of a single 'European social model'.

In subsequent chapters we shall pry open the content of social regimes, searching for more complex links and relationships, exploring the central hypothesis set out above.

4. Separating workers from consumers

Most of the analysis in the following chapters will be devoted to issues of internal distribution of risks, to inclusive strategies and to those that create outsiders. These discussions will take for granted that national societies are collectivities, potentially solidaristic. First, therefore, it is necessary to examine ways in which risk management might break the bounds of existing national societies, not only across space but also across time.

Wealthy people are able to invest their assets around the world and cut themselves off from the vicissitudes of their country of origin. They can live abroad and avoid fiscal and other obligations at home, even while continuing to intervene in domestic politics. As the income and wealth gap between very small, wealthy elites and the rest of a population increases in a context of growing global liberalization of the movements of capital and the increasing importance of secondary and derivative financial markets, this becomes an increasingly important feature of twenty-first-century politics. These elites are floating free from the rest of society, as Robert Reich (1991) anticipated over 20 years ago. Unfortunately, comparable data relevant to this aspect of the question are available for only a few countries, so we cannot carry out a systematic comparison, but for illustrative purposes Figures 4.1a and b present the statistics that the OECD was able to gather for its major study of income inequality (OECD 2011a). It seems that, at least among the wealthiest countries, it is in the US and to a lesser extent the UK that we would look to find the extremely wealthy most detached from their society, and least detached in north-west Europe (NWE) and Japan.

THE ROLE OF INTERNATIONAL TRADE AND SUPPLY CHAINS

But governments, even if heavily responsive to the demands of wealthy, internationalized elites, still have to be responsible for national economies. The separation of consumption from local workers is more difficult for them to achieve. Chapter 2 identified international trade and supply chains as means by which separations might be made across space, or rather across different jurisdictions.

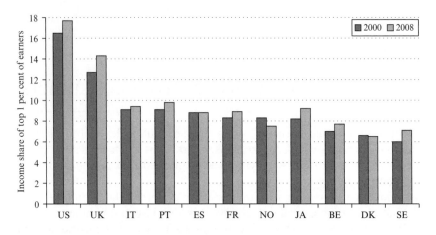

Source: OECD 2011a

Figure 4.1a   Income share of top 1 per cent of earners, 2000 and 2008

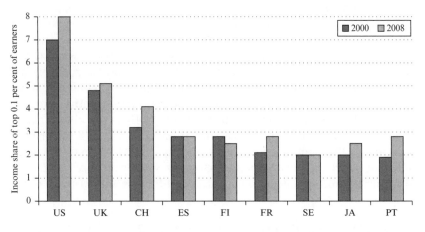

Source: OECD 2011a

Figure 4.1b   Income share of top 0.1 per cent of earners, 2000 and 2008

International Trade: Dependence on Export Consumption

Economic elites might resolve the problem of seeking flexible workers but confident consumers by depending on people in other countries consuming the goods and services produced by the capital they own, relieving them of any concerns about the security of their own working populations. Meanwhile, the mass of the domestic population would consume little overall, including little in the way of imports. This would typically be a strategy for wealthy elites in poor countries with weak solidarity. Bohle and Greskovits (2006) argue that this is the direction in which at least the foreign-owned sectors of the economies in central and eastern Europe are tending. This can be the case particularly in countries developing low-skill economies, where there is also no need for employers to bother with workforce cooperation and morale. They see this as characterizing the Baltic states, less so the Visegrád countries (see also Meardi 2012). Hermann and Flecker (2012) and Lehndorff (2012a) argue that, respectively, Austrian and German recovery from the crisis has been based on calculations of this kind, though that does not mean that overall living standards in these countries have become low. If such a strategy were being pursued systematically within an economy, we should see positive trade balances accumulating in countries with low GDP and high levels of inequality. Appendix Table A4.1 presents recent statistics on the data needed to make these calculations. Figures 4.2a and b respectively depict per capita GDP in terms of purchasing power parities for the start of the century and for the most recent year available at the time of writing, organized in terms of distribution around the mean as explained in Chapter 2.

The most generally accepted measure of income and wealth inequalities are Gini coefficients, which measure how far a given distribution departs from perfect equality. Perfect equality would receive a score of zero, while a society where one unit (individual or household) received all the wealth

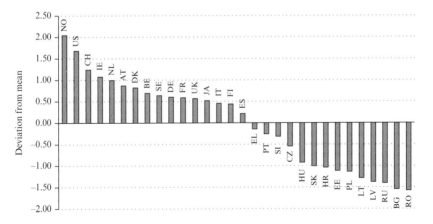

Figure 4.2a   GDP per capita, purchasing power parities, c.2001 (country scores in relation to standard deviation around mean)

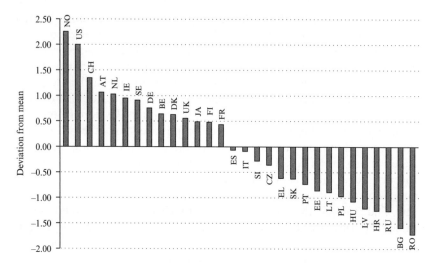

Figure 4.2b   GDP per capita, purchasing power parities, c.2012 (country scores in relation to standard deviation around mean)

or income would have a score of 100. Data are available for wealth distribution (Davies et al. 2010), but these are distorted by differences in the kinds of assets typically held in different societies, differences of household composition, and the uneven nature of data so dependent on self-reporting and taxation issues. Although wealth is the more fundamental inequality variable, we have to have recourse to data on income inequality, which are vulnerable to fewer (though still not zero) distortions. Figures 4.3a and b present the data as variations around the mean. For European countries Eurostat data have been used, as these give reasonable continuity over the period as well as between countries. For Japan, Russia and the USA, OECD and World Bank data have been used. These are less comparable both over time and with the European data, which limits the conclusions we can draw from them. All sources used claim to present the distribution of income after account is taken of taxes and transfers.

In 2001 we can label Slovenia, Denmark, Sweden and Austria as very egalitarian; Hungary, Germany, the Czech Republic, Bulgaria and Slovakia as egalitarian; and Norway, the Netherlands, France, Finland and Belgium as moderately egalitarian. Croatia, Italy, Ireland, Romania, Poland and Switzerland were moderately inegalitarian; Lithuania was inegalitarian; Spain, Greece, Japan, the UK, Estonia, Latvia, the USA and Portugal were very inegalitarian; and Russia was extremely inegalitarian.

Several changes took place in European inequality levels between 2001 and 2012, but the overall effect was to leave the mean unchanged at 29.0.

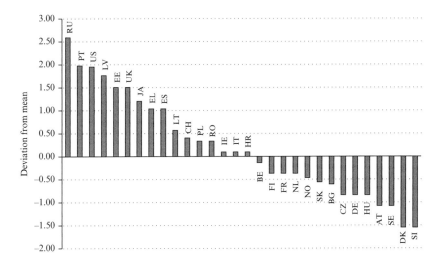

Figure 4.3a   *Household disposable income inequality index (Gini), c.2001 (country scores in relation to standard deviation around mean)*

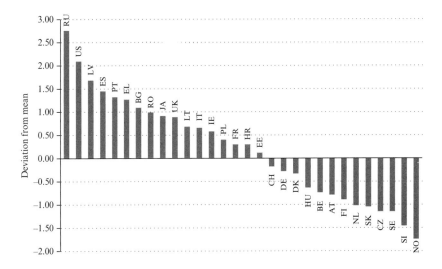

Figure 4.3b   *Household disposable income inequality index (Gini), c.2012 (country scores in relation to standard deviation around mean)*

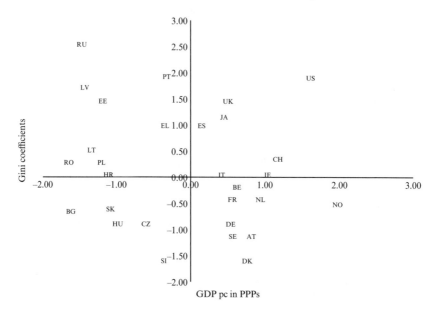

*Figure 4.4a   Income inequality (Gini coefficients) by GDP per capita,
                c.2001 (country scores in relation to standard deviations
                around means)*

Inequality in the USA rose slightly, from 36.9 to 37.5, and in Russia
from 39.6 to 40.1, but in Japan it fell slightly from 33.7 to 32.9. Overall,
the list of very egalitarian countries now comprises Norway, Slovenia,
Sweden, the Czech Republic, Slovakia and the Netherlands; the egali-
tarian countries comprise Finland, Austria, Belgium and Hungary; and
Denmark, Germany and Switzerland are moderately egalitarian. Estonia,
Croatia, France and Poland were moderately inegalitarian; Ireland, Italy,
Lithuania, the UK, Japan and Romania were inegalitarian; Bulgaria,
Greece, Portugal, Spain and Latvia were highly inegalitarian; and the US
and Russia were extremely inegalitarian.

Figures 4.4a and b combine the data on per capita GDP with those
for income distribution. The upper left quadrant of 'poor inegalitarians'
contains the potential candidates for dependence on foreign trade for
consumption of home-produced goods and services. In 2001 it contains
Russia, and to a lesser extent the three Baltic states, Croatia, Poland,
Romania, Greece and Portugal. By 2012 it also includes Bulgaria because
of its increasing reported income inequality. Russia again appears as an
extreme case.

Table 4.1 orders countries' rankings for foreign trade balances according

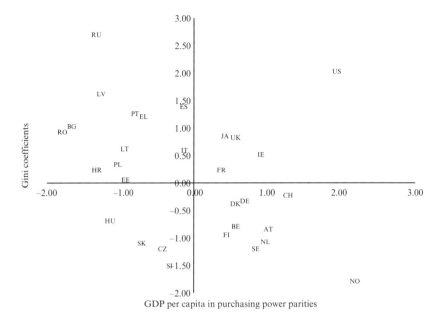

Figure 4.4b   Income inequality (Gini coefficients) by GDP per capita, c.2012 (country scores in relation to standard deviations around means)

to the quadrant in which they fell in Figures 4.4a and b. Countries with indifferent scores on any variable have been marked in parentheses and should probably be disregarded. Those falling into the upper left quadrant (I) in the figures and also falling into the positive side of the table for trade balances (tinted) would be those countries where the strength of foreign trade might enable elites to avoid dependence on domestic consumption. At both time points the only country that conforms to the hypothesis is Russia, and especially in 2001. Otherwise, it is largely most of the 'rich egalitarians' that have the best trade performances. Other countries resembling Russia in being relatively poor and inegalitarian had adverse trade balances. This implies that the economy as a whole is dependent on domestic consumption – but that does not refute the contention of Bohle and Greskovits (2006) that the transnational sector itself is independent. Nor does it refute what Hermann and Flecker (2012) and Lehndorff (2012a) claim about Austrian and German tactics during the crisis. But it is only in Russia that the possibility arises of local elites 'escaping' dependence on local populations' consumption. Below-mean trade performances were concentrated among poor CEE and middle-income south-western

Table 4.1   *Variations around trade balance means by relationship between inequality and per capita GDP*

Variation around trade balance mean	2001				2012			
	I	II	III	IV	I	II	III	IV
= >2.00 SD	RU	CH	NO				NO CH	
1.00 to 1.99 SD			FI				DE NL SE	SK SI
0.50 to 0.99 SD		JA	SE BE NL		RU	IE	DK	
0.10 to 0.49 SD		IE IT	DK FR	SI				
−0.09 to 0.09 SD			AT DE			JA	AT	HU
−0.1 to −0.49 SD		ES UK		SK	BG LT HR (IT)		BE	
−0.50 to −0.99 SD	EE LT PL RO HR	US		BG CZ	EE EL LV PT (ES)	US FR	FI	CZ
−1.00 to −1.99 SD	EL LV PT			HU	PL RO	UK		

Notes:
I   = high inequality, low GDP
II = high inequality, high GDP
III = low inequality, high GDP
IV = low inequality, low GDP

72

countries (SWE), with some interesting exceptions: the USA and (modestly) the UK in the earlier period, and the USA, France and (very low) the UK in the later one. All were examples of type II countries. Does this suggest an opposite process to the Russian one, with mass consumption being maintained unsustainably? This is a point to which we shall return.

Supply Chains

It is difficult to find aggregate comparative data on supply chains. A reasonable proxy can however be found in the level of net foreign direct investment (outward FDI) made by capital owners, as this indicates their use of returns from the products of labour in other countries. In principle, economic elites might in this way escape dependence on their domestic populations, either by investing in production facilities abroad or by sourcing many of their activities by subcontracting from locations abroad where workers have low wages and security. But neither direct investment nor outsourcing abroad necessarily hurt the domestic labour force. If cheaper operations are carried out abroad, with the result that more highly rewarded activities remain at home while overall price levels are kept down through the involvement of cheaper labour along the chain, domestic workers may gain. If only the first part (sending low-value-added operations abroad) succeeds but not the second (keeping overall prices low), domestic workers will maintain good pay and conditions, but at the expense of a loss of low-value-added jobs. Matters look different from the perspective of a country that is receiving the direct investment or is securing the supply contracts. There will be an increase in employment; whether this is poorly paid, insecure employment will depend on the supply of surplus labour in the country concerned.

UNCTAD (2013) has collected relevant data. It is important to consider figures for FDI in the context of the level of domestic employment. We can identify dependence on FDI at the expense of domestic labour only in those cases where the former is relatively high and the latter is relatively low. The basic statistics for these variables are given in Appendix Table A4.1, and Figures 4.5a and b relate outward FDI stocks to the level of employment. For outward direct investment to be undermining domestic employment – and thereby *easing* elites' need for internal solidarity – countries need to be found in the bottom-right quadrant. In 2001 the only potential candidate was Belgium, with outward FDI stocks amounting to over 78 per cent of GDP but with an employment rate of only 65 per cent. The greatest stress would have been placed on those countries with low employment and low outward FDI: Bulgaria, Croatia, Latvia, Lithuania, Poland, Hungary, Greece, Slovakia, Italy,

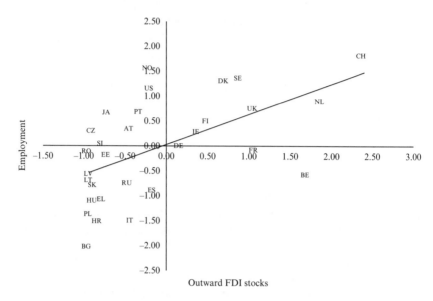

Figure 4.5a   Outward FDI stocks by employment, 2001 (country scores in relation to standard deviations around means)

Russia and to a lesser extent Spain. More generally, high FDI stocks were associated with high levels of employment ($r^2 = 0.3281$), so overall there is no evidence that high FDI was undermining domestic employment. By 2011, in the less benign post-crisis environment, the overall correlation had weakened considerably ($r^2 = 0.1753$), and Belgium is joined by Ireland as a country in the quadrant where direct investment might be undermining domestic employment. Under most stress are the same countries as in 2001.

Our concern here was with whether capital holders in particular countries might be using FDI to 'escape' their own workforces. We are not therefore particularly interested in inward FDI. This latter form can have two different motives: some countries attract investment because of the high quality of the labour skills and the infrastructure that they offer; others because of their low costs. This is relevant to our interest in whether investors try to escape, or are attracted to, particular kinds of workforce. The OECD has tried to collect data relevant to this for MNCs investing in various countries (OECD 2008). Unfortunately, only a few countries have provided data for this exercise, which prevents us from drawing confident conclusions. We also have figures only for around 2005, neither earlier nor later. One approach is to consider the proportion of a country's employees

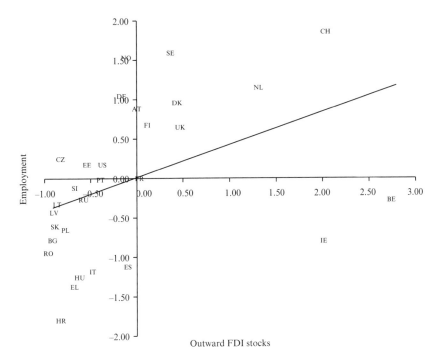

Figure 4.5b   Outward FDI stocks by employment, 2012 (country scores in relation to standard deviations around means)

of multinationals who are defined as research workers. This gives a broad estimate of the extent to which inward investors are locating high-value-added activities in a particular country. Here, Figure 4.6 shows particularly high levels in Germany and the Netherlands, followed by the US and UK, and shows particularly low levels in CEE countries. Unfortunately we do not have data from Belgium, the case where there might be some evidence of outward investment having significant implications for the domestic economy.

With various exceptions, there is a relationship of core and periphery between NWE, Japan and the USA on the one hand, and CEE on the other. The SWE countries stand somewhere between, as a semi-periphery. CEE countries have gained from inward investment, jobs being created which probably would not have existed given the low capital resources of these countries, but so far this investment has not produced the combination of high employment and high per capita national income (or GDP) found in the more advanced economies. Slovenia is the only one of these

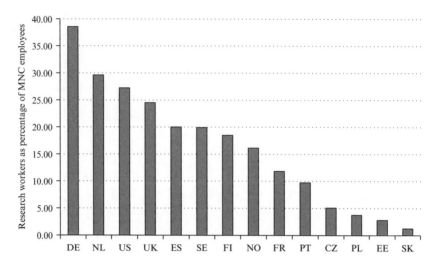

Figure 4.6   Research workers as proportion of MNC employees, c.2005

countries approaching both high employment and fairly high per capita GDP.

Overall, therefore, and with the exception of Russia on the issue of international trade balances, and possibly Belgium and now Ireland on outward FDI, these two hypothetically important variables are not significant for our purposes. In general, it does not seem that elites in European countries and our comparator countries are able to use dependence on external demand to protect economies from any implications of workers' insecurity. It is notable that Russia is the country under consideration where democratic accountability of governments is arguably lowest.

THE ROLE OF TIME

Societies that are wealthy today are able to ease dilemmas in the labour market by drawing on their stock of infrastructure and wealth accumulated in the past. These abiding legacies are evident in the data we have already discussed. The clusters of countries identified in the usual typologies are distinguished historically, as well as geographically, in their economic development. We see this most dramatically in the case of CEE. In Slovenia, the former Czechoslovakia, parts of Hungary and the Silesia region of Poland, the state socialist regimes built on the Austro-Hungarian legacy of strong industrial training (Keune 2006) and established some further infrastructural institutions. However, they neglected other aspects, including the development of marketing, and innovative and entrepreneurial capacities. The rest of the eastern part of Europe started from a far weaker base. Then, after 1989, the dismantling of the state socialist economy and its trading links left these countries with a considerable reduction in whatever capacities they had. They are clearly in a weaker position than most of their counterparts in the west, but there is partially a similar picture in those SWE countries where authoritarian right-wing regimes survived into the 1970s (Greece, Spain, Portugal). These dictatorships had also neglected development, though they had been more integrated than the CEE cases into the global capitalist economy.

It is difficult to measure inherited infrastructure on a comparable basis, as the nature and extent of past legacies of physical infrastructure are so dependent on geography; for example, Sweden necessarily has more kilometres of road and railway than Denmark. The best approximation we can get is by estimating total national wealth. This has been measured by the World Bank (World Bank 2011a). It is different from and more useful to us for this current purpose than household or individual wealth, as it includes all created national assets, though among these are transitory stock-market evaluations. The dataset does not include all countries of interest to us (Estonia and Slovenia are missing for both periods, Lithuania for 2000). Further, the Bank has not published data on this topic for any year later than 2005, so we cannot see any consequences of the 2008 crisis. Nevertheless, the results are summarized in Appendix Table A4.2 and depicted in Figures 4.7a and b. The stock of wealth increased in that pre-crises period between 2000 and 2005: by 7.08 per cent in Europe, 9.97 per cent in the USA, 7.79 per cent in Japan.

We should not anticipate any particular connection between national wealth and class challenge, measured by trade union strength as proposed in Chapter 3, but Figures 4.8a and b suggest an interesting relationship. Overall there was a positive statistical association between wealth and union power ($r^2 = 0.3506$ in 2000, declining slightly to 0.2821 five years later), but the quartile distribution is more worthy of attention. Around 2000, the wealthy/high class challenge quartile was occupied by the NWE countries identified in Chapter 3, while Croatia and Slovakia were the sole occupants of the quartile that combines strong class challenge with low wealth. (We do not have wealth data for Slovenia, but it is almost certain that it would also have occupied that space.) On the other hand, both low challenge quartiles are heavily occupied: the wealthy quartile with France, Ireland, Italy, Switzerland, the UK and two of the non-European

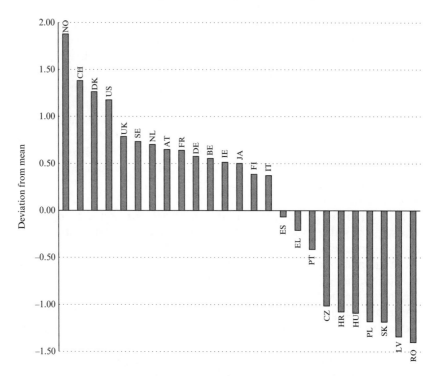

Figure 4.7a   Per capita wealth, c.2000 (country scores in relation to standard deviation around mean)

cases (Japan and the USA); and the poor quartile with primarily CEE countries and Russia, with Greece, Portugal and Spain coming closer to mean wealth. By the later period the strength of class challenge in Slovakia had weakened, that country joining the remaining CEE cases. This leaves Croatia (and probably Slovenia) as the sole occupant of the 'low wealth, strong class challenge' quartile, but there are doubts over Croatia's class challenge score. Whatever may have been the case in earlier decades, in today's advanced societies strong class challenge is almost wholly confined to wealthy countries, though by no means all such countries feature strong challenge. In later analyses particular interest will focus on any differences between wealthy countries with strong class challenge (most countries in northern Europe) and those where it is weak, especially the USA, also France and Japan, and to a lesser extent Switzerland, the UK, Germany and Italy.

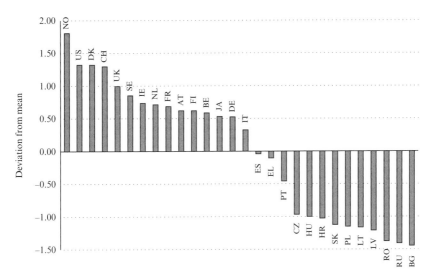

*Figure 4.7b   Per capita wealth, 2005 (country scores in relation to
standard deviation around mean)*

Sustainability

The more sustainable a society is, the less it exploits the future to help the
present. Therefore, a society's ability to survive in the present by displac-
ing its use of resources on to the future can be seen as the opposite of
sustainability. The simplest way of assessing financial non-sustainability
would be to examine the combined totals for public and private debt.
However, as noted in Chapter 2, it is difficult to distinguish between debt
as a postponement of problems on to future generations and a reorgani-
zation of the costs of consumption for an existing population. We shall
here treat public debt as a postponement over time, raising sustainability
issues, because repayment is not necessarily borne by the generation that
benefited from the debt. Private debt, although it might be passed on to
the children of the debtors, is experienced far more directly as a source of
consumption possibilities by individuals who, strictly speaking, also have
to repay it. We shall therefore deal with public debt here, but private debt
in Chapter 5.

Public debt
Statistics on public debt for all countries of interest to us except Croatia
are given in Appendix A4.2 and summarized in Figures 4.9a and b.

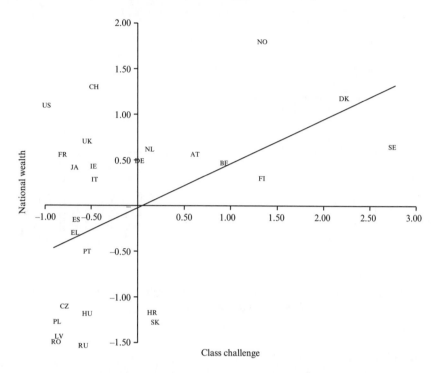

Figure 4.8a *National per capita wealth by class challenge, 2000 (country scores in relation to standard deviations around means)*

Because debt developed rapidly but at slightly different moments for different countries after the crisis, we have here calculated the average of two five-year periods, from 1996–2000 (fully pre-crisis) and from 2008–12 (the period of the crisis).

Overall, debt levels rose considerably after the crisis. The European average rose from 47.07 per cent of GDP in 1996–2000 to 59.46 per cent in 2008–12, in the US from 63.7 per cent to 94.4 per cent, and in Japan from 119.0 per cent to 212.1 per cent, while in Russia it fell from 79.42 per cent to 10.5 per cent. As Figure 4.10 shows, the European average conceals some wide fluctuations, with falls in some but rises in others. The largest absolute increases were in Portugal, Greece, Ireland and the UK, and the largest reductions were in Bulgaria and Sweden.

In neither period is there any statistical correlation between the class challenge index and the level of debt. There is certainly no evidence here for a hypothesis that strong trade unions push governments into spending programmes that involve incurring high debt. There is however an

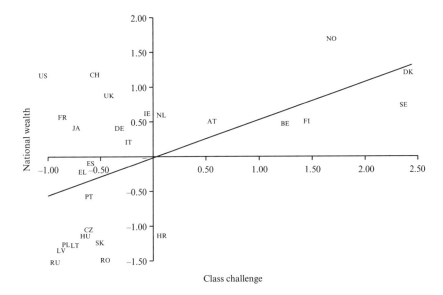

*Figure 4.8b   National per capita wealth by class challenge, mid-2000s
(country scores in relation to standard deviations around
means)*

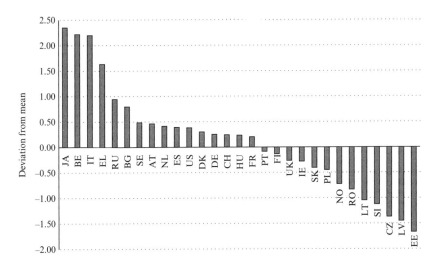

*Figure 4.9a   Government gross debt, average 1996–2000 (country scores
in relation to standard deviation around mean)*

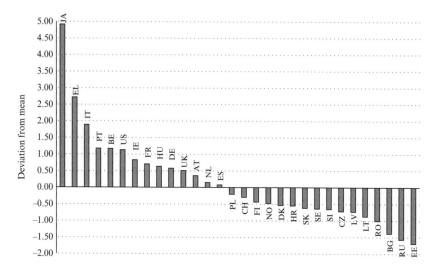

Figure 4.9b   Government gross debt, average 2008–12 (country scores in relation to standard deviation around mean)

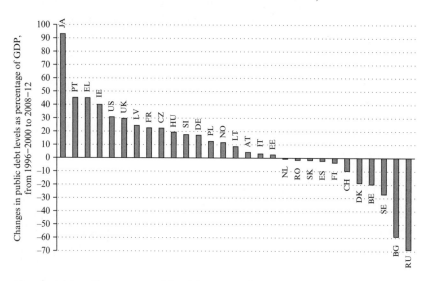

Figure 4.10   Changes in public debt levels, from 1996–2000 to 2008–12

interesting change over time (Figures 4.11a and b). In the earlier period, countries with strong class challenge had from high to moderately low public debt, while those with weak challenge divided as follows: low challenge wealthy countries (i.e., western countries and Japan) had debt

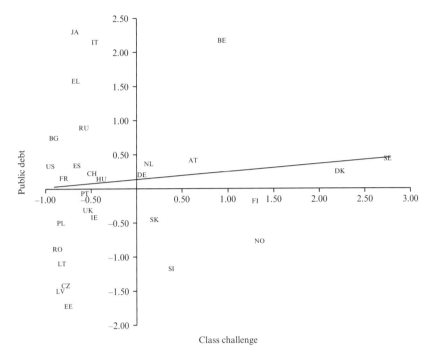

Figure 4.11a   *Public debt by class challenge, c.2000 (country scores in relation to standard deviations around means)*

levels ranging from moderately high to extremely high, with the exception of Ireland and the UK, which had low debt; with the exception of Bulgaria, Hungary and Russia, poorer countries had low debt. By the 2008–12 period there is a very slight negative relationship between debt and class challenge ($r^2 = 0.0142$), because debt levels have dropped in several, though by no means all, strong challenge countries, while rising in Ireland and the UK. With the exception of Belgium and (marginally) Austria, debt in high challenge countries ranged from moderately low to moderately high, while the only weak challenge countries with low public debt are found in CEE; all western weak challenge countries (and Japan) had public debt ranging from moderately high to extremely high by 2008–12.

Environmental sustainability
The use made of the future by a society to resolve current problems can also be assessed by considering environmental sustainability. While many factors enter into this, one variable that is both highly important and

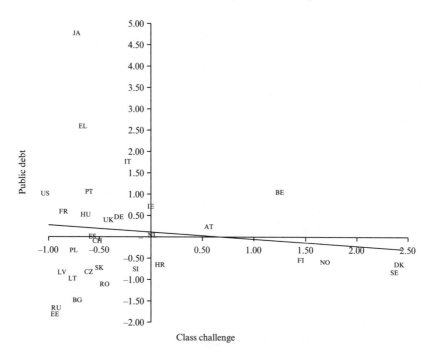

Figure 4.11b   Public debt by class challenge, c.2010 (country scores in relation to standard deviations around means)

measurable for all countries is the level of carbon dioxide emissions. Data for these in 2001 and 2010 are given in Appendix Table A4.2. Carbon dioxide emissions tend to vary with national economic activity. The data used here are therefore emissions at a rate of per capita GDP. This gives us the relative scale used in Figures 4.12a and b. The overall rate of emissions declined slightly in Europe over the period from 7.95 to 7.56 metric tons per capita, though this conceals larger reductions in some countries and increases in others. The average ratio to GDP fell more substantially from 0.43 to 0.26. During the same period, emissions declined in the USA from 19.7 to 17.6 (the ratio from 0.53 to 0.34), in Japan from 9.5 to 9.2 (0.36 to 0.26), while in Russia they increased from 10.7 to 12.2 (0.70 to 1.30). As the figures show, at both points in time the lowest emission rates per GDP come from a mixed group of countries from all regions.

The relationships to class challenge are shown in Figures 4.13a and b. In 2001 the overall relationship was weak ($r^2 = 0.1187$), sustainability increasing slightly with the strength of class challenge, but again we find almost all countries with above-mean class challenge having below-mean

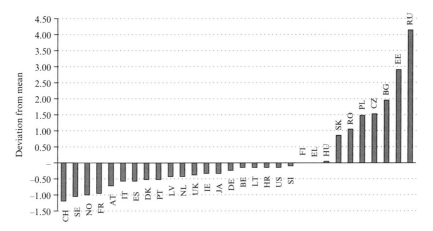

Figure 4.12a   Carbon emissions per GDP per capita, 2001 (country scores in relation to standard deviation around mean)

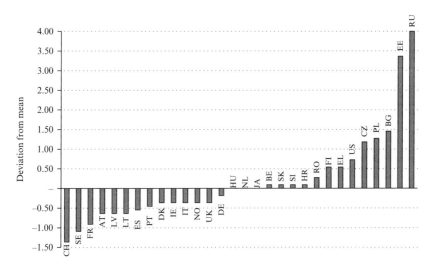

Figure 4.12b   Carbon emissions per GDP per capita, 2010 (country scores in relation to standard deviation around mean)

emissions, the only exception being Slovakia. There was no relationship at all between emissions and challenge strength in countries with weak challenge. By 2010 the relationship has weakened slightly to $r^2 = 0.1005$, but the same basic pattern is found, though Finland (and, marginally, Belgium) replace Slovakia as the only high challenge countries with above-mean emissions.

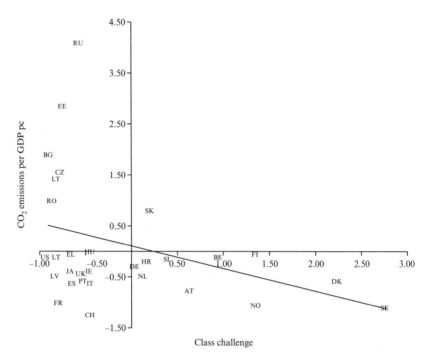

Figure 4.13a Carbon emissions by class challenge, 2001 (country scores in relation to standard deviations around means)

THE ROLE OF EXCLUDED FORMS OF LABOUR

Labour can finally be partially separated from consumption by having certain identifiable groups bear the main burden of labour-market risk. Their insecurity does not threaten the consumption standards of the rest of the working population. We shall consider this phenomenon again more directly when we examine the operation of labour market law and policy in Chapter 6. Here we are concerned not with policy but with the combined effects of various ways in which the labour market structures a population. Separation of sections of the workforce can mean a large gap between the lowest income groups and the rest, a labour-market segmentation according to ethnicity, gender, age or some other variable; or maintenance of a large shadow economy, whose workers necessarily are excluded from mainstream developments.

The simplest way to operationalize the first formulation of exclusion (a gap between the lowest income groups and the rest of the population) is

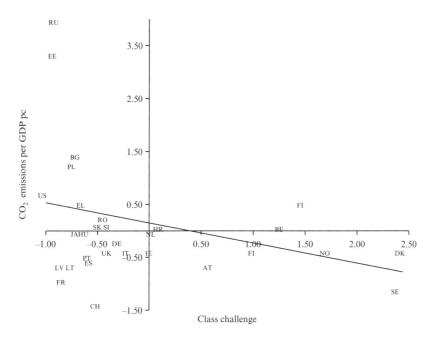

Figure 4.13b   Carbon emissions by class challenge, 2010 (country scores in relation to standard deviations around means)

to examine the difference in income between the poorest (say the bottom 10 per cent of the income distribution, or the first decile) and those around the median, or fifth decile. This does not take account of the distance between either of these groups and the very rich, but the purpose of our present search for the excluded is to explore the position of those who are excluded from standards of living enjoyed by the median citizen. For OECD member states we have these data for the late 2000s, but unfortunately not for the earlier period, and not for Bulgaria, Latvia, Lithuania, Romania or Russia. The basic statistics are given in Appendix Table A4.2, and the relativized details are shown in Figure 4.14. This shows an extreme exclusion level of the poor in the US; very high levels in Poland, Japan, Estonia, Greece, Ireland, Portugal and the UK; and a high level in Italy. There were modestly low levels of exclusion in Belgium, Finland, Germany, the Netherlands, Slovakia, Slovenia and Switzerland; low levels in Austria, France, Hungary and Norway; and very low levels in the Czech Republic, Denmark and Sweden.

As Figure 4.15 shows, there is a moderately strong negative relationship between class challenge and this measure of exclusion ($r^2 = 0.2683$), with

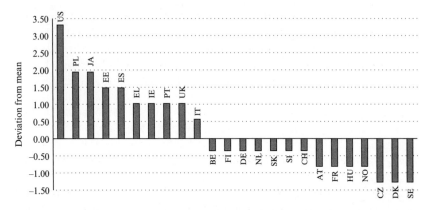

Figure 4.14   50:10 income decile ratios, late 2000s (country scores in relation to standard deviation around mean)

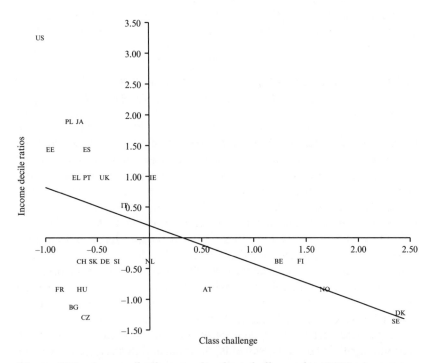

Figure 4.15   Income decile ratios by class challenge, late 2000s (country scores in relation to standard deviations around means)

an interesting spread across the quadrants. There are no cases of countries where relatively high levels of class challenge are associated with high levels of exclusion of the poor, while the majority of countries with weak class challenge have high levels of exclusion. Attention therefore concentrates on the exceptions, those with low exclusion but low challenge, especially Bulgaria, the Czech Republic, France and Hungary; exclusion is only moderately low in Germany, the Netherlands, Slovakia, Slovenia and Switzerland.

We can get some approximation of segmentation on the basis of outsider foreigner or ethnicity status by examining differences in the labour market experience of foreign-born and native workers. This will certainly not capture the full extent of ethnic segmentation, as it says nothing about the continuing disadvantages of second- and third-generation descendants of immigrants, or long-settled minority groups like the Roma in several CEE countries (Meardi 2012: 54, 55, 113–14); but comparable data are not easily found for these. Again we have data only for recent years, 2009 or a close year. These are Eurostat data, and therefore exclude our extra-European comparators, as well as Croatia, Norway and Switzerland. Appendix Table A4.2 provides (E(i)) the relative size of the foreign-born population of workforce age; (E(ii)) an estimate of difference in employment rate relative to that of the native workforce; and (E(iii)) their exposure to risks of poverty or social exclusion, again as a proportion of that of the native population.

The highest proportions of foreign-born are to be found in Estonia and Latvia (Figure 4.16). These are primarily Russians who comprised the dominant group in these countries during the Soviet period but who are now an outsider minority (Masso and Krillo 2011: 84). The immigrant

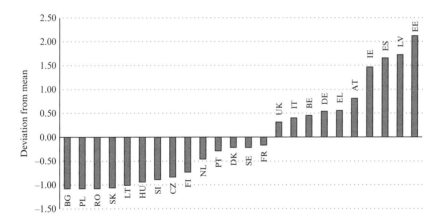

Figure 4.16   Foreign-born population, c.2009 (country scores in relation to standard deviation around mean)

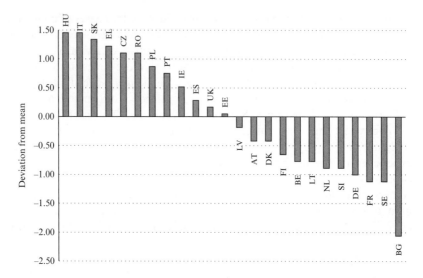

Figure 4.17   Foreign-born citizens' employment gap, c.2009 (country scores in relation to standard deviation around mean)

population is next highest in Spain and Ireland, then Austria, Greece, Belgium and Germany. Countries with the smallest foreign-born populations are Bulgaria, Poland, Romania and Slovakia, then Lithuania, Hungary, Slovenia, the Czech Republic, Finland and the Netherlands. CEE countries with less developed economies predominate here. The low level for the Netherlands is perhaps surprising, but that country (like France, Germany and the UK) has a large number of second- and third-generation ethnic minorities who may also be in problematic labour market positions. Unfortunately we cannot estimate this on a comparative basis. We know from other OECD data (OECD 2012) that the total foreign-born population of Switzerland is extremely high, of Norway and the USA very high (between those of Austria and Ireland), of Russia moderately high (similar to Italy), and of Japan low (similar to Hungary).

A first step to estimating whether these minorities are in inferior positions is to examine whether their employment level is below that of the native population. As Figure 4.17 shows, this gap is highest in Bulgaria, then in France, Sweden, Germany, Slovenia, the Netherlands, Belgium, Lithuania, Slovenia and Finland. Immigrants are not always found to be in inferior positions; in the Czech Republic, Greece, Hungary, Italy, Romania and Slovakia, and to a lesser extent in Poland and Portugal, immigrants are on the whole more likely to be employed than the host population.

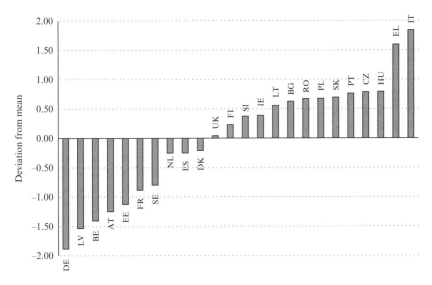

Figure 4.18   Immigrant employment by size of immigrant workforce,
c.2009 (country scores in relation to standard deviation
around mean)

But for any difference in immigrant employment levels to have an impact on the country's capacity to externalize risk on to this population, the employment gap has to be related to the overall size of the immigrant population. These data are shown in Figure 4.18. This shows Germany to have the largest aggregate immigrant employment gap, followed by Latvia, Belgium, Austria and Estonia, then France and Sweden.

The lowest gaps will represent a combination of countries with small immigrant populations and those where immigrants have better employment chances than natives. Countries making little use of immigrants for this purpose, either because their immigrant population is small or because they do not have specific employment problems, are Italy and Greece, and also Portugal and several CEE countries.

We can similarly consider any systematic poverty and social exclusion gap between immigrants and hosts by comparing their position on the EU poverty and exclusion index and again aggregating this by the size of the immigrant workforce (Figure 4.19). It is this measure that we shall use in later analyses, as it most accurately represents what we need: an indication of the extent to which an economy makes us of the disadvantaged position of immigrant workers.

This being a composite indicator, we should examine how the two components – size of immigrant workforce and extent of exclusion – relate

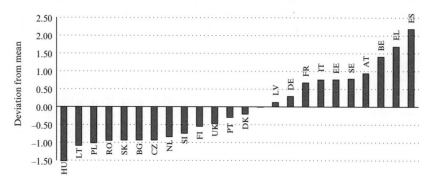

Figure 4.19   *Index of immigrants' relative poverty and exclusion by size of immigrant workforce, c.2009 (country scores in relation to standard deviation around mean)*

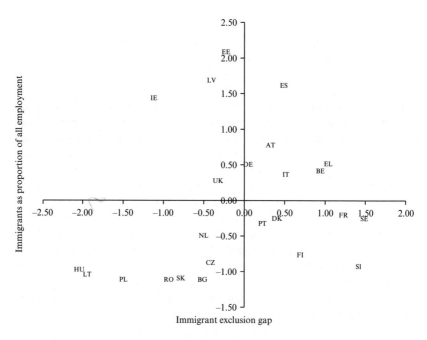

Figure 4.20   *Immigrants' relative poverty and exclusion by size of immigrant workforce, c.2009 (country scores in relation to standard deviations around means)*

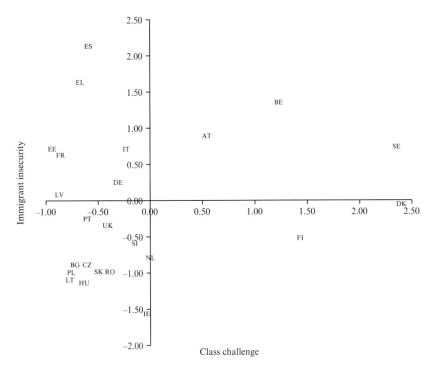

*Figure 4.21   Immigrant insecurity burden by class challenge, c.2009
(country scores in relation to standard deviations around
means)*

to each other. Figure 4.20 shows a number of countries where both elements are relatively high, a mixture of 'Bismarckian' NWE and SWE
cases: Austria, Belgium, Germany, Greece, Italy and Spain. With high
employment but a below-average gap are two Anglophone and two Baltic
cases: Ireland, the UK, Estonia and Latvia. With low immigrant employment but high exclusion are the three Nordic countries for which we have
data – Denmark, Finland, Sweden – as well as Slovenia, France and
Portugal. All remaining CEE countries plus the Netherlands had both low
immigrant exclusion and a low share of employment.

Figure 4.21 relates the overall exclusion indicator to that for class
challenge. There is no statistical significance ($r^2 = 0.0300$), but there is
a very slight positive association between class challenge and immigrant
insecurity. Immigrant insecurity also seems to be extensively used in the
weaker class challenge countries of SWE, and least used in Ireland, the
Netherlands and most CEE countries.

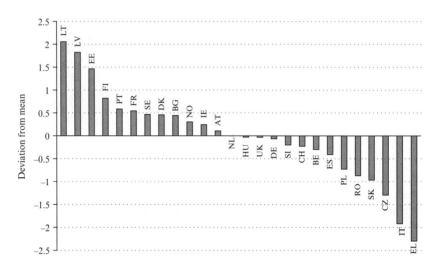

*Figure 4.22   Female employment as proportion of all employment, c.2011
(country scores in relation to standard deviation around
mean)*

We can do something similar in the analysis of female employment, but
again only for recent years. It is difficult to compare the idea of 'exclusion'
as applied to women and immigrants. A large majority of the former live
in partnerships with men and share a household income, whereas immigrants are likely to live in separate communities without additional access
to the standard of living of the majority population. On the other hand, if
women are systematically earning a lower hourly rate than men, then there
is a sense in which they are excluded from the dominant forms of income.
It is therefore appropriate to include this variable, provided we appreciate
the difference in the way in which the idea of exclusion is being used in
the two cases. Also, as with immigrants, our measure of exclusion will be
a combination of an income gap and the size of the workforce concerned,
not a measure of exclusionary practices per se. Appendix Table A4.2 contains the available data and Figure 4.22 shows the relativized female share
of all employment in European countries. This is highest in the Baltic
states, where it exceeds 50 per cent. It is also high in the Nordic countries
and some other western European cases. It is low in SWE and most CEE
countries.

Figure 4.23 shows the pay gap between men and women as the percentage gap between average male and female hourly earnings. This is undif-
ferentiated according to sector, job and whether full or part time. For our

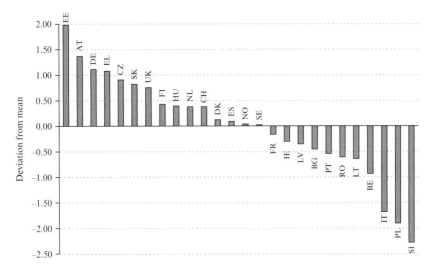

Figure 4.23   Gap between average unadjusted male and female hourly earnings, c.2011 (country scores in relation to standard deviation around mean)

purposes this is the relevant statistic, as we simply need to know whether women can be seen as a relatively excluded group, earning lower pay and 'protecting' the level of male earnings. It must be noted here that, whereas in the case of immigrants we had a statistic for actual deprivation, here it is only an earnings gap, and can apply throughout the income structure. The mix of countries is highly heterogeneous.

Combining the indices as was done for immigrants gives the array shown in Figure 4.24.

Figure 4.25 shows the composition of the combined index. Estonia is the country that combines most strongly a large female earnings gap with high participation. The only other countries with a broadly similar combination are Finland and Austria. The other Baltic states, and to a lesser extent Portugal, Bulgaria, France and Ireland, have high female employment, but a smaller earnings gap. Greece and the Czech and Slovak Republics have the opposite combination. Italy, Poland, Romania, Belgium and Slovenia have low scores on both variables.

As female labour-force participation becomes increasingly important to employment in post-industrial societies, the direction it will take will become a major defining criterion of future labour market arrangements. As Bosch et al. (2009a: 37) point out:

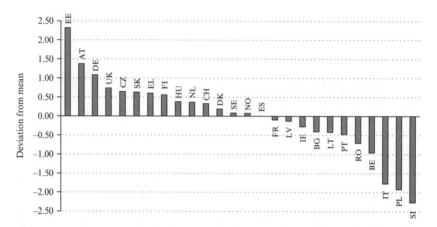

*Figure 4.24   Index of female hourly earnings gap by size of female
                workforce, c.2011 (country scores in relation to standard
                deviation around mean)*

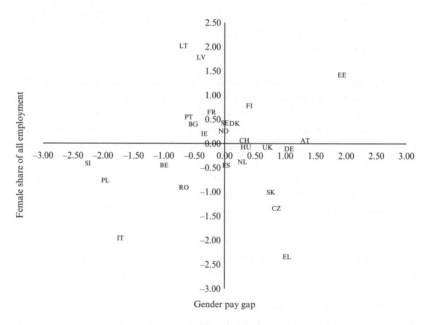

*Figure 4.25   Female hourly earnings gap by size of female workforce,
                c.2011 (country scores in relation to standard deviations
                around means)*

The integration of women could, under one scenario, be associated with a general pulling down of labour standards through competition between new forms of employment outside of protective regulation. Alternatively it could be associated with the development of more diversified but also more inclusive labour markets through the extension of protection to jobs and groups traditionally outside the core sectors.

One might quarrel with the emphasis they place on employment protection legislation alone, but their general argument indicates a major theme for the study of future labour market institutions.

Next it is necessary to explore the potential exclusion of young people. This cannot be done by examining either living conditions or incomes. Young people may live in their parental home; the ages to which they do this will be explored in the following chapter. Their incomes are also typically lower simply because they are at the early points of career tracks. It is possible to consider the differential extent to which they are found in precarious jobs, and it is certainly the case that most temporary posts are held by young people. But temporariness is important only in relation to the existence of permanent job contracts. In cases where there is no such thing as a permanent contract (as in the USA, outside a small number of occupations), should everyone be regarded as temporary? That would be unrealistic. An alternative approach to the specific labour-market insecurities of young people is to examine those who are not in work (whether unemployed or just inactive) nor in any education or professional training. This group, known as NEETs (Not in Employment, Education or Training), has been the object of considerable policy concern in recent years. As a result, useful statistics are produced on them. Eurostat collects data for the age range 15 to 24. The basic data for 2011 are given in Appendix Table A4.2, and the relativized data are shown in Figure 4.26. The highest numbers of NEETs were found in the countries caught up in the Euro crisis – except for Portugal – and in Bulgaria and Romania. The lowest numbers were found in NWE, the Czech Republic and Slovenia.

Figure 4.27 displays the NEETs data against class challenge. There was a moderate negative relationship, with $r^2 = 0.2314$. An examination of the quadrants shows that the great majority of countries fall into those rejecting the hypothesis that where class challenge is strongest young people will be most excluded. The quadrant that would contain high challenge with high exclusion is empty, and the only countries with low challenge and low NEETs are the Czech Republic, Germany and Slovenia, the last two of which had shown higher relative class challenge at the start of the century. Unfortunately we do not have data from Eurostat for non-member states, but the OECD produces statistics for its member states. These are based on the slightly, but importantly, different age range of 16 to 24, so we

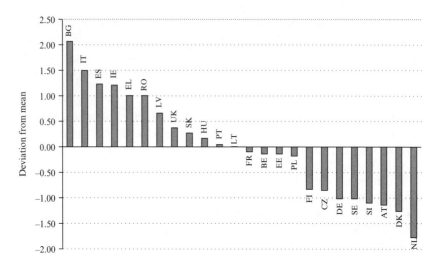

*Figure 4.26   Young people (aged 15 to 24 years) not in employment,
education or training (NEETs), 2011 (country scores in
relation to standard deviation around mean)*

cannot simply incorporate the OECD figures into the Eurostat data. However, by comparing the additional OECD countries to those near them and appearing in both sets of statistics, we can show where these would fall, except for Croatia and Russia, which are missing from both. In the OECD data, Norway and Switzerland had levels very similar to that of Sweden; we can therefore be confident that Norway would come in the same quadrant as the other Nordic countries, while Switzerland would be near Germany. Japan had a slightly higher level, but would also be in that bottom-left quadrant, further to the left on account of its very weak class challenge. The USA had the same level as the UK, and would therefore belong to the upper-left quadrant, combining a high number of NEETs and low level of class challenge.

Finally, in looking for indicators of exclusion, we can also examine the size of the shadow economy, where workers have no protection against labour-market fluctuations of a kind that might be enjoyed by the rest of the working population. The basic data for this were already discussed in Chapter 3, and the statistical base was listed in Appendix Table A3.1. Here we have data both for the beginning of the century and the end of its first decade. Figures 4.28a and b display the size of the shadow economy in all countries of interest to us in the years around 2000 and 2010. They suggest that this is primarily a phenomenon of the CEE countries

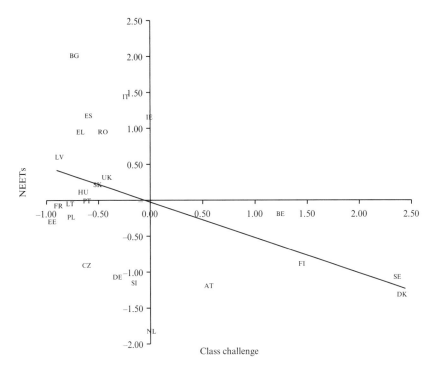

Figure 4.27 NEETs by class challenge, 2011 (country scores in relation to standard deviations around means)

(with the exception of the Czech and Slovak Republics) and of SWE (though not so much in Portugal) (for CEE see also Macovicky 2014 and Round 2013). This generalization remains true across the decade. There is no relationship at all between shadow economy and class challenge ($r^2 = 0.0110$, $r^2 = 0.0369$ respectively); the figure is not worth presenting.

EMPLOYMENT IN FAVOURED ECONOMIC SECTORS

Chapter 2 envisaged employment in favoured or protected sectors of an economy as a form of guaranteeing (implicitly or explicitly) the security of some workers, probably at the expense of others. There is ample evidence that this occurs. In their original forms, the European Common Agricultural Policy and the European Coal and Steel Community had this as a primary goal, easing workers through processes of change in these key

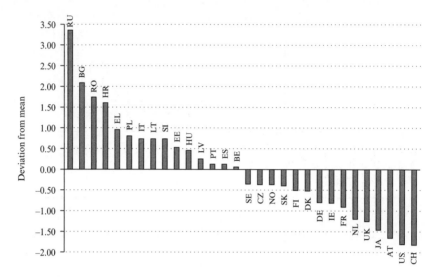

Figure 4.28a   Size of shadow economy, c.2000 (country scores in relation to standard deviation around mean)

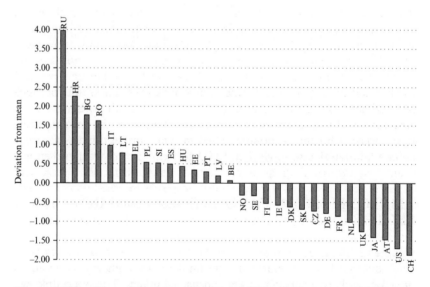

Figure 4.28b   Size of shadow economy, c.2010 (country scores in relation to standard deviation around mean)

sectors. Armaments, other defence-related industries like aircraft production, and finance have also been privileged in this way in many economies. 'National champion' firms have also been favoured in pharmaceuticals and other chemicals industries. It is also possible to identify sectors that rarely enjoy such status, as they are not seen as strategically important or as needing state support. Light industries and many private services sectors such as restaurants and hotels usually come in this category. Unfortunately, it is not possible to find studies that assemble data on a comparative basis across a range of countries for use in research of the kind being undertaken here, and we have to drop this part of the analysis. The only exception is the role of the public sector as a possibly protected form of employment, but this is a theme for the following chapter.

CONCLUSION

The purpose of this chapter was to identify to what extent various countries have a location in place, time and internal exclusion that might reduce dependence on internal solidarity mechanisms in their management of dilemmas of labour-market risk. The three possibilities have a very different political dynamic. The first would enable elites to detach themselves from the wider society within which they are primarily located; the second enables the resources of past and future to be used to ease conflicts across the whole society; the third places particular strain on particular groups within that society. We might expect the first to exist where domestic class challenge is weak, as it requires an elite able to ignore demands for compromise on security issues from the local population. On the other hand, the use of both time resources and exclusion of specific groups should be particularly favourable to the survival of class challenge, as these create space for compromises – in the latter case for favoured parts of the employed population.

Table 4.2 displays the spread of countries across these variables around the turn of the present century. Countries with extremely strong class challenge are indicated in underlined bold type, those with very strong challenge in bold, those with strong challenge in italics, those with medium challenge in italics and brackets, and those with only marginally above-mean scores in italics and square brackets. Unfortunately we lack important items of data on social exclusion for this period, having only the shadow economy. First, and outside the scope of the table but summarized in Table 4.1, we found little evidence of the use of place to provide escapes for elites from domestic labour forces through foreign trade, except for Russia, which conforms broadly to the hypothesis about the relation of

Table 4.2   Summary table: degrees of stress on internal solidarity, c.2000

	Wealth	Sustainability		Exclusion
		Public debt	CO² emissions	Shadow economy
		Reducing stress on internal solidarity		
Extremely high (= or > 2.00 SD)	**NO**	JA **BE** IT	RU EE	RU BG
Very high (1.00 to 1.99 SD)	CH **DK** US	EL	BG CZ PL RO	RO HR
High (0.50 to 0.99 SD)	UK **SE** [NL] AT FR [DE] BE IE	RU BG	(SK)	EL PL IT LT (SI) EE
Moderately high (0.10 to 0.49 SD)	JA **FI** IT	**SE** AT [NL] ES US **DK** [DE] CH HU FR	US	HU LV PT ES
Indifferent (−0.09 to +0.09 SD)	ES	PT	HU EL **FI**	**BE**
		Increasing stress on internal solidarity		
Moderately low (−0.10 to −0.49 SD)	EL PT	**FI** UK IE (SK) PL	(SI) (HR) **BE** LT [DE] JA IE UK	**SE** CZ **NO** (SK)

Table 4.2   (continued)

	Wealth	Sustainability		Exclusion
		Public debt	CO^2 emissions	Shadow economy
	Increasing stress on internal solidarity			
Low (−0.50 to −0.99 SD)		**NO** RO	LV [NL] PT **DK** ES IT *AT* FR **NO**	**FI** **DK** [DE] IE FR
Very low (−1.00 to −1.99 SD)	CZ (HR) HU PL (SK) LV RO RU BG	LT (SI) CZ LV EE	**SE** CH	[NL] UK JA *AT* US CH
No data	EE LT (SI)	(HR)		

'place escape' to weak class challenge, though it had by no means the weakest class challenge. Lack of democracy may be more relevant here. We also considered evidence of the existence of wealthy elites able to cut themselves off from an individual national economy, though this required data on the concentration of income among the top 1 per cent and 0.1 per cent of the distribution, which was available only for certain wealthy countries. This evidence suggested that such an ability to 'escape' might be available to the wealthy in the USA in particular, and also to the wealthy in the UK. The former country had the weakest class challenge of all, and the latter was among the weak. We also found the USA, and to a lesser extent the UK, as the exact opposites of Russia, to be the only wealthy countries with major trade deficits. Does this suggest a non-sustainable capacity to provide space for mass consumption despite labour flexibility? If so, why was this necessary, if class challenge was extremely weak in the

USA and relatively weak in the UK? Does the answer, like the opposite answer for Russia, lie in the strength of democracy in those countries despite the weakness of class challenge as such? It is difficult to pass beyond raising these questions on the basis of the data available.

There was also the possibility that FDI might be used to enable escape from local workforces, which was possibly relevant for Belgium. This certainly does not fit the hypothesis, as the country had one of the strongest class challenges.

Turning to the differential capacity of countries to create space for compromise through time, national wealth (the use of accumulations from past time) was strongly associated with class challenge on a 'necessary but not sufficient' basis. Strong class challenges exist only in countries with above-mean wealth, though by no means all wealthy countries have strong challenge. The only exceptions are the marginally above-mean challenge scores in Slovenia, Croatia and Slovakia. The perhaps unsurprising hypothesis that institutionalized class challenge thrives in societies with strong accumulations of past resources is supported. The same is the case for the role of public debt. All above-mean western European class challenge countries, and Switzerland marginally below mean, had above-mean levels of public debt, though only in Belgium was this level more than moderately above mean. The same resource was not available to the three CEE countries with above-mean challenge. Given that these are relatively poor countries, the stress hypothetically placed on their mechanisms for class compromise was strong.

The situation for the other less sustainable uses of future time, natural resource exploitation, here captured inadequately through data on carbon emissions, is however not consistent with the hypothesis. With the exception of the marginally strong class case of Slovakia, no country with above-mean class challenge, or even marginally below-mean challenge, had above-mean levels of emissions, though Finland and (among those with marginally low class challenge) Hungary had marginal emissions scores. High emissions were concentrated among poor countries and the USA.

A similar story applies to the role of the shadow economy, which is unfortunately the only means of assessing exclusion that we have for the turn of the century. This is heavily concentrated among poor and middle-income countries, with the marginal exception of Belgium, and as a result is not a resource available to strong class challenge countries, with the exception of the marginal cases of Croatia and Slovenia.

Turning to more recent years, Table 4.3 organizes countries on the same basis as for the earlier period in Table 4.2.

The place variables (again not included in the table) and the wealth

Table 4.3 Summary table: degrees of stress on internal solidarity, c.2010

	Wealth (NB 2005 data)	Sustainability		Shadow economy	Exclusion			
		Public debt	CO^2 emissions		Immigrants	Women	Young (NEETs)	General poor
Extremely high		JA	RU	RU *(HR)*	ES	EE	BG	US
Very high	NO US **DK** CH	EL IT PT **BE** US	EE BG PL CZ	BG RO	EL **BE**	*AT* DE	IT ES IE EL RO	PL JA EE ES EL [IE] PT UK IT
High	UK SE [IE] [NL] FR *AT* **FI** **BE** JA DE	[IE] FR HU	US **FI** EL	IT LT EL PL SI	*AT* SE EE IT FR	UK CZ SK EL **FI**	LV	

Reducing stress on internal solidarity

Table 4.3 (continued)

Wealth (NB 2005 data)	Sustainability		Shadow economy	Exclusion			
	Public debt	CO² emissions		Immigrants	Women	Young (NEETs)	General poor
			Reducing stress on internal solidarity				
Moderately high IT	DE UK **AT**	RO SK	ES HU EE PT LV	DE LV	HU [NL] CH **DK**	UK SK HU US	
Indifferent ES	[NL] ES	SI **BE** (HR) [NL] HU JA	**BE**	**DK**	<u>**SE**</u> NO ES	PT LT	
			Increasing stress on internal solidarity				
Moderately low EL PT	PL CH	DE IT [IE] **DK** UK NO PT	**NO** <u>**SE**</u>	PT UK **FI**	FR LV [IE] BG LT	FR **BE** EE PL	**BE** **FI** DE [NL] SK SI CH

Low CZ	**FI** **NO** **D̲K̲** *(HR)* SK **S̲E̲** SI CZ LV	ES LT *AT* LV FR	**FI** *[IE]* **D̲K̲** SK CZ DE FR	SI *[NL]* CZ BG SK RO PL	PT RO **BE**	**FI** *CZ JA* *NO CH*	*AT* FR HU NO
Very low HU *(HR)* SK PL LT LV RO RU BG	LT RO BG RU EE	**S̲E̲** CH	*[NL]* UK JA *AT* US CH	LT HU IE	IT PL	DE **S̲E̲** SI *AT* **D̲K̲** *[NL]*	BG CZ **D̲K̲** **S̲E̲**
Extremely low							
No data EE SI				*(HR)* NO CH JA RU US	*(HR)* JA RU US	*(HR)* RU	*(HR)* LV LT RO RU

Notes:
Countries with extremely strong class challenge are indicated in underlined, bold type.
Countries with very strong class challenge are indicated in bold type.
Countries with medium class challenge are indicated in italic and parentheses.
Countries with only marginally above-mean challenge are indicated in italic and square brackets.

variable operate as before, but there is a change in the public debt measure, which according to our hypothesis should be high, providing room for compromise, in countries with strong class challenge. Only Belgium and, to a lesser extent, Austria are countries with above-mean class challenge and above-mean public debt, though Ireland with high debt has a marginally above-mean challenge score. Following the crisis, debt is heavily concentrated among countries with weak class challenge, including all wealthy cases except Switzerland. Finland now appears as a country with above-mean carbon emissions, and some other high challenge countries have indifferent emissions scores, but overall the situation on emissions remains similar to that for the start of the century; they are concentrated among the USA and relatively poor countries. Overall, this means that countries with high class challenge are mainly making low use of non-sustainable time resources, which is contrary to our expectations. The reduction in most of these countries in the relative use of public debt through a crisis that elsewhere was often associated with a major increase is particularly interesting, as one might have expected such countries to need to find more 'room' in which to make class compromises.

For these more recent years we have richer data on the issue of exclusion, enabling us to add to the inadequate measure of the size of the shadow economy general exclusion of the poor, of immigrants, of women and of young people. We can therefore test the hypothesis that countries with strong class challenge might see higher levels of exclusion than those with low challenge. The shadow economy continues to be concentrated among poor and middle-income countries, and therefore does not affect the situation. Where immigrants, women, young people and the general poor are concerned, however, there are clearer patterns. Not one above-mean class challenge country, with the exception of marginal Ireland, practises general exclusion of the poor through a large income gap separating the lowest earners from the median; nor do they have high numbers of NEETs. This is compatible with expectations, if we assume that unions are likely to represent the lowest income groups, which should be the case where membership is high, as by definition it is in the high challenge cases. On the other hand, all such cases make some use of exclusion of immigrants or women; and in the case of Austria, of both. The only exception is Croatia (if its union data are accurate), but it sustains a large shadow economy. Among countries with relatively low class challenge, the only countries for which we have data and which do not discriminate against the poor are Slovenia, Germany, Slovakia, Switzerland, Bulgaria, the Czech Republic, Hungary and France. This is an interesting group, as it includes countries where relative decline in class challenge has occurred since 2001 (Slovenia, Germany, Slovakia, Switzerland), the three most advanced Visegrád economies (Slovakia again, Czech Republic and Hungary), Bulgaria, and the frequently exceptional France. The only countries to practise no relatively high exclusion of women (Romania, Portugal, Bulgaria, Lithuania) all maintained large shadow economies. It is in this context that the relative exclusion of immigrants and/or women in all wealthy countries, whether with strong or weak class challenge, needs to be seen. The case of young people was somewhat different, with the high class challenge countries, along with a small number of others, least excluding young people. It must be noted however that NEET status refers to exclusion from education as well as from employment; as we shall see in the following chapter, a high level of spending on education characterizes many of our high class challenge countries.

We shall return later to some of the implications of these findings, including their paradoxes, particularly the changing relationship between class challenge and public debt during the crisis, and the complex patterns of exclusion, after we have examined the other forms of managing the dilemma between labour flexibility and confident consumption.

5. Separating consumption from labour income

We now move to considering ways in which the need for solidarity within the labour market might be reduced by shifting risk on to other areas of life: workers are here consumers, but they do not necessarily depend on their labour income for their consumption. Some of the available strategies redistribute the burden of solidarity; others resemble some of the elements considered in the previous chapter, reducing the need for solidarity at all. The basic data on which discussion in the chapter is based will be found in Appendix Tables A5.1–3, and presentation of statistical material within the chapter will be based on relative distributions around means as described in Chapter 2 and practised in Chapters 3 and 4.

SEPARATION BY PLACE: REMITTANCES AND EARNINGS FROM WORKERS ABROAD

Returning to the scheme set out in Chapter 2 (Table 2.1), separation by place here has the limited application of remittances from emigrant workers. While workers who emigrate reduce the quantity of (usually skilled) labour at a country's disposal and thereby its GDP and value added, to the extent that they send money back home, they also provide their families who remain behind with sources of income that do not make use of the domestic labour market and its institutions. Emigration shrinks the domestic collectivity around which issues of flexibility and security need to be reconciled, in the same way that we have hypothetically seen occur for high levels of net outward investment and for high sustained trade deficits. A strong emphasis is placed on solidarity within families, but this relieves the burden of solidarity from the society as a whole.

A study by the International Monetary Fund (IMF) (Chami et al. 2005) provided data on average annual remittances across the world for the 1970–98 period. This is useful for western European countries, but far less so for CEE, as it was only during the final decade of the period that people were permitted to leave those countries. For western Europe these data show remittances to have been important only for Portugal and to a lesser extent Greece. Figures were also provided on the proportion of exports constituted by emigrant remittances for the same period, which indicates to what extent countries' ability to participate in the international economy was provided by remittances. Again only Portugal, Greece, and to a lesser extent Spain and Italy, had more than very small proportions. Poland also showed more than a miniscule level, for after 1989 Poles were able to emigrate legally. The main concern of the IMF report was to discover whether these remittances were important for providing investment resources in the home countries; their findings were negative, and they argued rather that such an effect was observable only in richer countries, where it took the form of capital investment, not remittances. They did however make a finding of considerably more interest to us here: remittances were used by emigrants to compensate people at home for bad economic outcomes and correlated negatively with economic growth back home. Their findings related mainly to developing countries, but they have some implications over the longer historical period for southern European and, more recently, for some CEE countries (Meardi 2012).

A further guide to the potential importance of emigration in CEE countries and the former Soviet Union comes from data on population loss in a World Bank Report (Mansoor and Quillin 2006). This showed that emigration was important for some, though not all, CEE countries, at least during the 1989–2003 period, with several countries seeing population losses through emigration of 2 or 3 per cent, though the Czech Republic saw a slight increase. This report also contained data on remittances for the single year 2003 or 2004 for CEE countries, but unfortunately without comparative material for the west. The percentage of GDP involved was significant only for Hungary and to some extent Lithuania; the percentage of export earnings from emigration showed Latvia and Poland with important levels. A similar pattern was also shown for a datum that is most central to our interests: the contribution of remittances to household expenditure. Only Hungary, and to some extent also the Baltic states, had more than very small figures.

Strictly speaking, the term remittances refers to money sent back to their home country (usually to relatives) by people who have fully emigrated to another country. There are in addition earnings and other benefits received by employees working temporarily in countries other than those in which they are resident, in other words temporary migrants (World Bank 2011b). Both are relevant for our purposes, without a need to distinguish, and inclusion of these foreign earnings gives us a larger supply of data. We shall henceforth call them both remittances. Sums for the two combined are included in Appendix Table A5.1. It is not possible to get full data for years earlier than 2003. The figures shown are the net

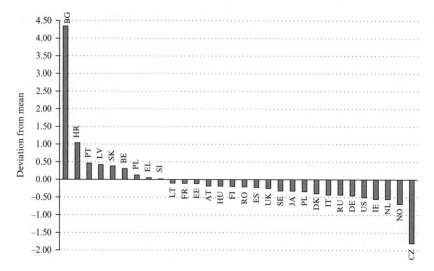

Figure 5.1a   Net emigrant remittances, 2003 (country scores in relation to
*   standard deviation around mean)*

balances, most countries receiving remittances from emigrants and 'losing'
payments from immigrants. Although we shall pursue our usual methodology of considering countries in terms of deviations from means, it is also
important for this and the other variables being discussed in this chapter
that we take account only of money flows above a certain size in terms
of proportions of GDP. In general we shall pay serious attention only to
amounts above 5 per cent and no attention at all to those below 1 per cent.

According to the available figures, which might not always be accurate, at the start of the twenty-first century only Bulgaria depended in
an important way on remittances as a contribution to GDP, at the high
level of 10.25 per cent (the relative scores around the mean are presented
in Figure 5.1a). No other country came near that at all, though the level
in Croatia was nearly 3 per cent, and Portugal, Latvia, Slovakia and
Belgium came above 1 per cent (Poland coming marginally below that
level). Of these, only Bulgaria and Croatia came above the threshold of
more than 0.5 SD – Bulgaria considerably so. At the other end of the scale,
Switzerland 'lost' around 3.26 per cent of its GDP in remittances out of the
country, Norway being the only other country to experience a comparable
loss at −0.52 per cent.

By 2010 the average net flow of remittances to European countries had
declined from 0.69 per cent to 0.47 per cent of GDP. Japan and the USA

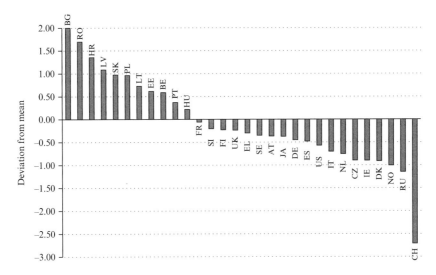

Figure 5.1b   Net emigrant remittances, 2010 (country scores in relation to standard deviation around mean)

also showed very small reductions. However, the European decline is primarily accounted for by the diminished dependence of Bulgaria (from 10.25 per cent to 3.24 per cent). Croatia also saw a slight decline to 2.34 per cent. Meanwhile, absolute levels increased in a number of other countries, bringing Romania to 2.81 per cent, and some others to more than 1 per cent of GDP: Belgium, Estonia, Latvia, Lithuania, Poland and Slovakia. These rises, combined with the decline in Bulgaria, bring a number of cases above the new 0.5 SD threshold (Figure 5.1b).

We can note Bulgaria, Romania, Croatia, then Latvia, Slovakia, Poland, Lithuania, Estonia and Belgium, as all gaining some serious relative assistance from remittances. With the exception of Belgium, these are of course all CEE countries. There is no relationship between these statistics and class challenge measures.

SEPARATION BY TIME: PENSIONS AND INSURANCE

Protection of income from labour market insecurity over time can in principle be achieved by making private insurance arrangements to protect oneself from potential job loss, injury, sickness or disability. Here again no demand is made on the solidarity of the national society, and not necessarily on family either. The burdens are borne by the individual, who purchases security at a future point of time by making payments in the present. In practice private insurance is very rarely used for income protection purposes, and it is impossible to separate out life insurance policies that might incorporate such a component. There are however various items of private social expenditure concerned with income security, primarily but not solely private pensions. Although those making use of such pensions might not realize it, they are accepting risks of failure of investment schemes and of their own life chances that are not part of a pooled risk system (Ebbinghaus 2012). Unfortunately no data are available on this variable for non-OECD countries, but the OECD does publish data for its member states. 'Private' spending takes a wide variety of institutional forms, some of them as collective funds and not individual market expenditure; these are however the nearest estimates available for such spending. The data are shown in Figures 5.2a and b for 2000 and 2010 respectively. There are no particular patterns in these groupings of countries. Between the two dates, spending increased slightly as a proportion of GDP in many countries, but declined very heavily in the USA and to some extent also in Austria, France, Greece, the Netherlands, Switzerland and the UK.

According to the model set up in Chapter 2, collective, i.e. public, insurance and pension schemes should also be seen as means of dispersing labour market risk over time. These place a higher burden on national or work-group solidarity than private schemes. In purely private insurance, premiums are based on an assessment of individual risk, and pension returns are based on the stock-exchange valuation of one's personal contributions. No demands are made on the solidarity of a wider group. This is different for typical occupational schemes, whether or not they form part of a national system. Here, contributions are fixed on a per capita basis, and the wider membership group bears the burden of unanticipated changes in risk (such as increased longevity). In recent years the insurance quality of many national social protection systems has been considerably diluted, as employer and employee contributions have been supplemented by government funding not established on an insurance basis. As this occurs, the solidaristic community changes from being the occupational group to being the taxpayers of the national society. As part of this process the once highly important distinction between social insurance and general funds used for protection has been diluted (Palier 2010b), though strictly speaking these differ from insurance-based systems in that they are part of a national solidarity system (that is, they internalize risk within the current generation). The distinction may still be important, for example

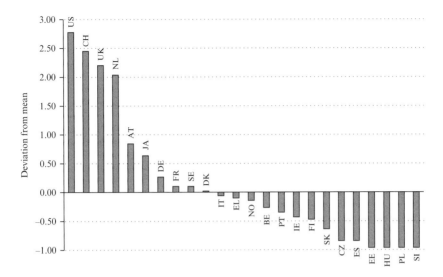

Figure 5.2a   Private social spending, 2000 (country scores in relation to standard deviation around mean)

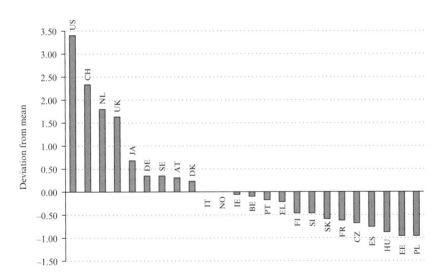

Figure 5.2b   Private social spending, 2010 (country scores in relation to standard deviation around mean)

in establishing concepts of entitlement, in organizing the governance of schemes, and in determining to what extent solidarity is limited to specific groups within a society. However, in practice it is difficult to disinter these differences in the available comparable statistics, so we shall here consider a combined gross figure for all publicly funded social protection. This includes insurance schemes and others alike, and seems the best way to get at the underlying reality of contemporary means for dispersing labour-market risk over time, whatever the formal differences between different kinds of scheme – differences which will have important implications for other kinds of research (e.g., Palier 2010c). These data (based on Eurostat statistics) are shown in Figures 5.3a and b for 2001 and 2010 respectively. Unfortunately we have no evidence for Bulgaria, Croatia or our three extra-European comparators for the earlier year.

As can be seen from Figure 5.4a, the data for 2001 correlate positively moderately strongly with the class challenge scores ($r^2 = 0.3928$). All high challenge cases except for Slovakia are among the highest providers of social protection; the majority of weak challenge countries are found in the opposite quadrant, providing low levels of social protection. But there are important exceptions that lead us to conclude that class challenge is not the key variable. Apart from Ireland, all wealthy west European states have high levels of social protection irrespective of the strength of their class challenge; the overall wealth of the society is more important than the challenge variable. All low spenders apart from Ireland are from CEE or SWE. By 2010, during the first stage of the financial crisis and with pressure on some previous low spenders on social protection to compensate for rising levels of unemployment, the European average rose from

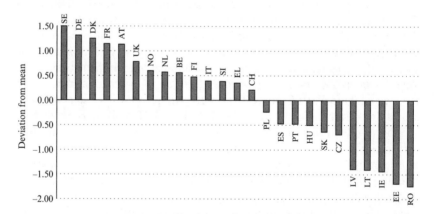

Figure 5.3a   Public social protection spending, 2001 (country scores in relation to standard deviation around mean)

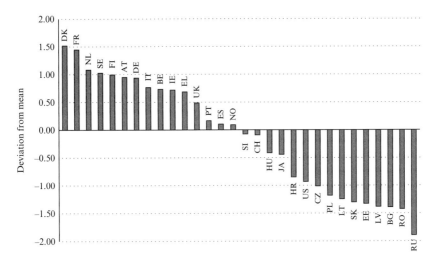

Figure 5.3b   Public social protection spending, c.2010 (country scores in relation to standard deviation around mean)

21.74 per cent to 24.83 per cent of GDP. The rise was nearly universal, only Poland and Slovakia seeing very small reductions. The rise in Ireland was particularly large. We can now add statistics for Bulgaria and the three extra-European comparators, but not Croatia. The statistical correlation with class challenge is slightly lower, at $r^2 = 0.3510$, marginally because of the addition of Bulgaria to calculation of the mean, but mainly because expenditure rose considerably in some weak challenge countries worst affected by the crisis (Ireland, Italy, Portugal, Spain). It had already been fairly high in Greece and the UK. Otherwise the relative positions of countries remain very much as before. Japan, Russia and the USA appear as low spenders; Japan and the USA giving us cases where the weakness of class challenge better 'predicts' their spending level than their identity as wealthy countries.

Special attention should be paid to the particular case of unemployment benefit among social protection expenditures as it is the element most directly related to providing security from labour market disturbance. We can avoid repeating material already covered in the discussion of social protection spending by looking at the question in a different way: in terms of the level of replacement for employment income, and the duration for which it is offered. Statistics have been collected on this, with the construction of an index known as the unemployment replacement rate (URR) by the OECD (2013a). The maximal statistic they calculate is the percentage

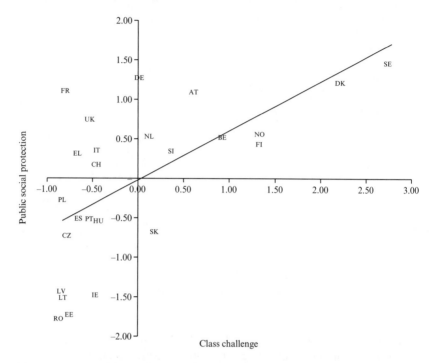

*Figure 5.4a   Public social protection spending by class challenge, c.2001
(country scores in relation to standard deviations around
means)*

of average in-work earnings that is replaced by unemployment benefit
over five years of unemployment. They calculate for different family
types – single person, one-earner couple without children, lone parent
with two children, one-earner couple with children – and offer an overall
average for them, assuming that the family qualifies for cash housing
assistance and social assistance 'top-ups'. For the earlier period (2001)
the statistics cover the then members of the OECD alone, i.e. excluding
Bulgaria, Croatia, the Baltic states, Romania, Slovenia, Russia. For 2011
they include all these except Croatia and Russia.

Figure 5.5a presents the data for the earlier year. The most generous
supporter of the unemployed at that time was Slovakia, followed by the
Nordic countries and Switzerland. By far the least generous was Italy,
where the system of maintenance for the unemployed is shared among
various uncoordinated funds. Between 2001 and 2011, as unemployment
rose as a direct consequence of the banking crisis, European states (with
the exception of Austria, Belgium, Italy, the Netherlands, and to a minor

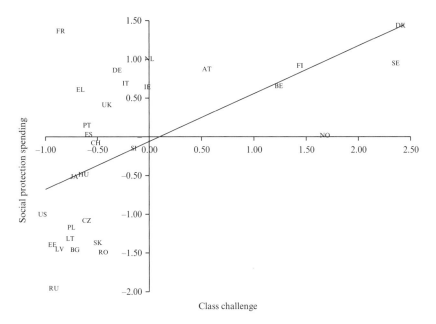

Figure 5.4b   *Public social protection spending by class challenge, c.2010 (country scores in relation to standard deviations around means)*

extent Portugal and the UK) responded by withdrawing financial support from those who lost their jobs or were unable to find one. The average replacement rate for those countries that we are able to cover across the decade dropped considerably from 63 per cent to 55 per cent. In the US it rose from 29 per cent to 36 per cent, and in Japan from 70 per cent to 75 per cent. Figure 5.5b presents the data for the larger group of countries for which we now have data. Japan has become the most generous provider; Slovakia has dropped considerably to a place among most other CEE countries.

The relationship between unemployment support and class challenge follows a pattern familiar from some other variables. In 2001 the overall statistical correlation was modest ($r^2 = 0.2389$) (Figure 5.6a), but within that there was a strong association between a high level of class challenge and generous unemployment support: the quartile that would show strong class challenge but weak unemployment support is empty (with the very marginal exception of Belgium). Also, the majority of weak challenge societies have below-average unemployment support, irrespective of whether they are wealthier western countries from various regions or from CEE.

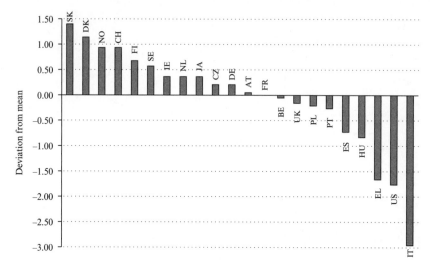

*Figure 5.5a   Generosity of unemployment replacement pay (URR), 2001
(country scores in relation to standard deviation around
mean)*

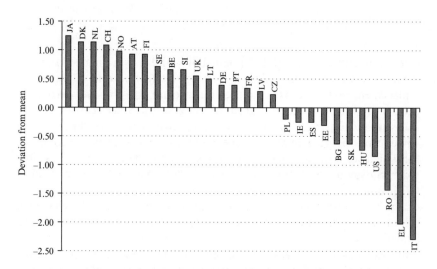

*Figure 5.5b   Generosity of unemployment replacement pay (URR), 2011
(country scores in relation to standard deviation around
mean)*

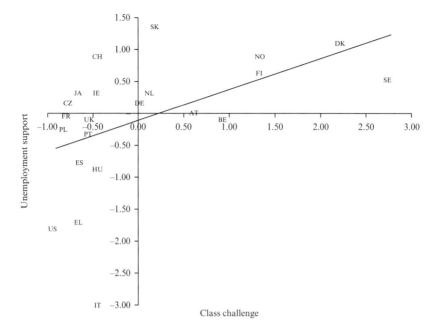

Figure 5.6a   Unemployment replacement pay (URR) by class challenge,
2001 (country scores in relation to standard deviations
around means)

The exceptions lie in those cases that combine relatively weak class challenge with generous unemployment support, in particular Switzerland,
but more modestly the Czech Republic, Ireland and Japan. By 2011 the
overall correlation is weaker at $r^2 = 0.1897$ (Figure 5.6b). Data are available for several more countries, but the basic pattern remains the same.
More countries with low class challenge have joined Switzerland as strong
supporters of the unemployed, though only Japan and to a lesser extent
Slovenia score more than modestly high in relative terms.

OTHER MEANS OF SEPARATING SECURITY FROM THE LABOUR MARKET

Table 2.1 identified three forms of protecting economic security and
consumption possibilities from the vagaries of the labour market that
depended on arrangements made within national societies and time
periods: intra-family transfers, household debt and public services.

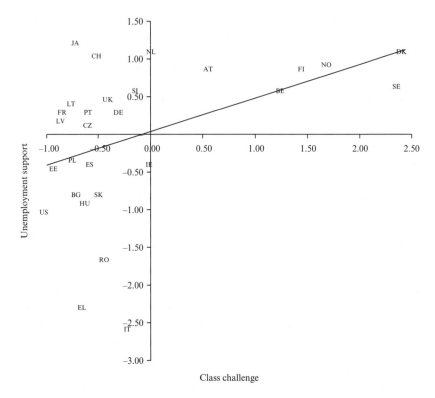

Figure 5.6b   *Unemployment replacement pay (URR) by class challenge,*
                 2011 (country scores in relation to standard deviations
                 around means)

There are unfortunately insufficient data available to enable us to measure
the impact on inter-generational transfers of income, wealth and services
on protecting working families from the market. This would, like remittances, constitute a form of solidarity at the family level, sparing demands
on national solidarity. The only comparative study conducted to date is
very useful, but it deals only with certain western European countries,
and it does not enable us to judge the size of flows as proportions of GDP
(Attias-Donfut and Ogg 2009). Some central findings of this research are
summarized in Table 5.1. A main datum reported is the proportion of
persons over 50 years of age giving at least €250 per annum to younger
family members. Another is the proportions of grandparents giving help
in looking after grandchildren. It is notable that these do not follow familiar patterns of the social models found in the literature. One might have

Table 5.1   Cross-generational support given within families, c.2006

Country	Percentage giving aid to younger family members	Percentage of grandparents helping to care for grandchildren
Austria	12.1	29.9
Belgium	7.5	46.8
Denmark	10.9	45.7
France	8.7	40.1
Germany	12.6	38.4
Greece	15.2	36.5
Italy	11.3	32.2
Netherlands	7.9	48.4
Spain	2.1	22.1
Sweden	14.7	43.0
Switzerland	13.1	37.7

Source: Based on Attias-Donfut and Ogg 2009

expected levels of family help to be highest where public social services are least provided, but this is by no means the case. If one examines help given with grandchildren, Denmark and Sweden, where public childcare services are particularly strong, have higher scores than Greece or Spain, where it is usually argued that, in the absence of public childcare, the main burden falls on families. The authors of the study point out certain north–south differences: families in northern Europe are more likely to give care to family members not living with them, those in southern Europe are more likely to provide the probably more intensive care of sharing a home with an elderly relative.

Given the small number of countries covered, it is difficult to incorporate the findings of this research into our general data, except to conclude: (1) that inter-generational transfers play a part in stabilizing the living conditions of younger generations; (2) that the financial and services flows concerned may be substantial; and (3) that these activities are to be found in strong welfare states as much as in weak ones.

Another way of considering cross-generational support is the age at which young people leave the parental home and set up their own households (Iacovou and Skew 2010, 2011). The later this takes place, the more a young generation is depending on support from their parents for their consumption standards rather than on their own labour-market position or other institutions. Unfortunately, comparable data based on Eurostat sources are available only for the year 2007, which does not enable us to assess whether the crisis has had any effect in itself. We have to assume

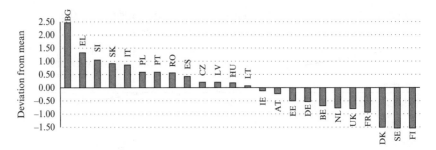

Figure 5.7a   *Age of leaving parental home, males, 2007 (country scores in relation to standard deviation around mean)*

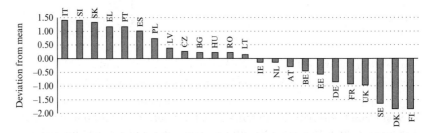

Figure 5.7b   *Age of leaving parental home, females, 2007 (country scores in relation to standard deviation around mean)*

that the situation around that year tells us something about the situation across the decade. Figures are also limited to EU member states at that time. In several countries there is a clear difference between the ages at which men and women leave home (see Figures 5.7a and b). There is also a fairly clear geographical pattern: young people stay at home longest in southern European countries (whether south-eastern or south-western), and in Poland, and leave home earliest in NWE. The pattern for central and north-east Europe is closer to the mean. These generalizations apply for both men and women, even though the rankings of individual countries differ for the genders.

In fact, the major geographical difference also holds for the gender difference in the age of leaving home (Figure 5.8). Exceptionally so in Bulgaria, but also more generally, the gender gap is biggest in the south (where sons stay at home far longer than daughters) and much lower or non-existent in NWE (where, if anything, daughters leave home later). Iacovou and Skew point out the clear links between leaving home and overall prosperity, and this is reinforced by the gender difference finding. It is when sons in particular cannot support themselves economically that

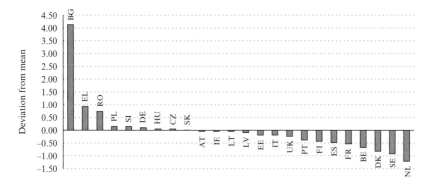

Figure 5.8 Age of leaving parental home, gender differences (sons' age minus daughters'), 2007 (country scores in relation to standard deviation around mean)

they remain with their parents; daughters leave home to marry (or form partnerships), not necessarily entering the labour-force. It is in these same southern countries that female labour-force participation is lowest.

It is therefore the male statistic that we should use as an indicator of family protection against labour-market insecurity. Figure 5.9 matches these data against the class challenge statistics. The correlation is relatively high ($r^2 = 0.3860$), sons' age at leaving home declining with the strength of class challenge. Clearly, there can be no direct relationship between trade union strength and the age at which young males leave their parental home, and if we had been able to include data from the USA the relationship would certainly have been weaker. However, it does hint at some important linked characteristics of what used to be called 'modernization' in at least European societies. It is a theme to which we shall return in Chapter 8.

UNSECURED HOUSEHOLD DEBT

A major means through which consumption has been protected from the labour market has been through household debt, as explained in Chapter 2. The extent of household indebtedness can be measured as the amount of debt net of assets held by households as a percentage of average disposable income. Figures for this for 2000 and 2010, based on Eurostat and OECD data, are given in Figures 5.10a and b respectively. At the start of the century the lowest levels were without exception held by citizens in CEE countries. This is not surprising, as private home purchase through

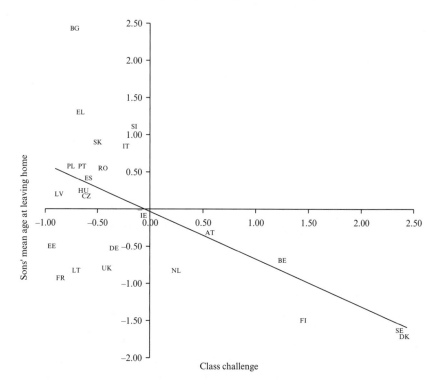

*Figure 5.9   Sons' age at leaving home by class challenge, 2007 (country
            scores in relation to standard deviations around means)*

mortgages was in its infancy in that part of Europe. The highest levels of
debt were held in the Scandinavian countries and some other NWE ones,
including Ireland and the UK, though not in France, Austria or Belgium.
There was no profile for SWE countries. There was a considerable increase
in European household debt over the succeeding decade, from 71.73 per
cent of disposable income in around 2000 to 118.05 per cent by 2010. In the
US it rose from 100.5 per cent to 122.5 per cent, though in Japan it dropped
from 130.4 per cent to 121.3 per cent. In fact, in most countries the peak
came in 2008; by 2010 the banking crisis had started to have its effect on
borrowing. There was not much change in relative positions during that
time, except that relative debt levels in Germany fell considerably, while
those in Estonia began to exceed those in some western economies.

Our concern here is not with household debt as such as with its role in
supporting labour income as a means of access to consumption, and it
is difficult to determine whether or to what extent aggregate borrowing

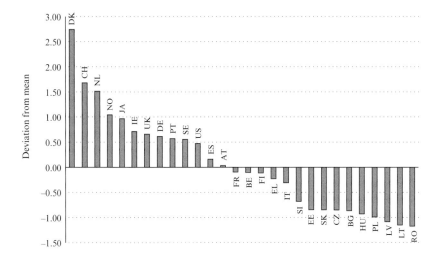

Figure 5.10a   Household debt, c.2000 (country scores in relation to standard deviation around mean)

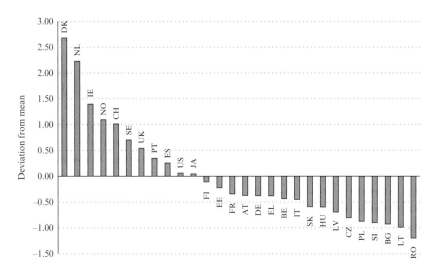

Figure 5.10b   Household debt, c.2010 (country scores in relation to standard deviation around mean)

is being used to fund consumption rather than to acquire assets, such as residential property, financial investments or the funding of small business ventures. We know that most household borrowing is for mortgages, but there do not seem to be statistics that would enable us to determine

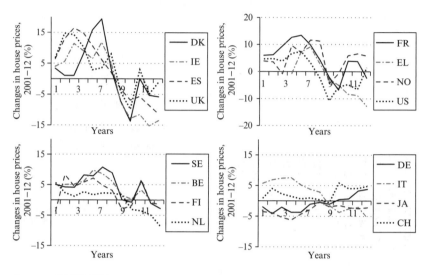

Source: OECD 2014

Figure 5.11   House price fluctuations, 2001–12

whether mortgages are also being used to fund consumption. We know, for example, that in the run-up to the banking crisis many low-income US households had mortgages of more than 100 per cent of the value of their homes, indicating that they were borrowing money on the collateral in order to fund consumption (the sub-prime mortgages) – or even as a form of unemployment insurance (Mulligan 2008). But how extensive were such practices across Europe?

We can examine OECD statistics (2014) on fluctuations in house prices, to examine where mortgages might have been used actively in unstable housing markets. Only western economies are covered, but the results are presented in Figure 5.11. This groups countries in fours according to the size of their house-price fluctuations between 2001 and 2012. Denmark and Ireland appear as countries with particularly high household debt and wide house price fluctuations; as to some extent do Spain and the UK.

There have also been several attempts by economists and others to establish whether indebtedness has become 'excessive'. The European Commission Social Situation Observatory (2010) has calculated levels of consumer credit outstanding as percentages of household disposable incomes, for the years around the start of the century and for 2009. The Eurostat data available covered only then EU member states, and is therefore less extensive than the above discussion of overall debt levels. The results are shown in Figures 5.12a and b for the years around 2000 and 2009 respectively. Those for the start of the century show some differences from the overall debt situation shown in Figure 5.10a. Austria, which had low overall debt, appears here second only to the UK, while Sweden, which had high overall levels, appears with the lowest outstanding consumer credit of all. The Netherlands also drops from its earlier high position. CEE countries tended to have low outstanding credit levels, except for Bulgaria, Slovenia and Poland.

The level of outstanding consumer credit in Europe, like the overall level of household debt, rose heavily over the following decade, from 8.22 per cent of disposable income to 13.81 per cent. As Figure 5.12b shows, there was considerable change in countries' relative positions, certain CEE countries (Bulgaria, Hungary, Romania, Poland) joining the UK, Ireland and Greece with particularly high levels. Although at neither period was there any statistical relationship between consumer debt and class challenge, as with public debt by 2009 there was a slight tendency for countries with strong challenge to have lower debt levels than wealthy countries with weak challenge – with the exception of France.

Another means of assessing potential over-indebtedness is to consider the extent of debt among lower-income households. Normally debt is concentrated among wealthier families, who use it to finance the acquisition of a variety of assets. Lower-income households are less likely to acquire assets, even residential accommodation. The European Commission Social Situation Observatory (ibid.) also collected information on this datum, concerning the proportions of households living on below 60 per cent of median national income who had debts of more than 100 per cent of disposable income. Unfortunately they could find data for only one time point, 2008, the year of the crisis itself. The findings are presented in Figure 5.13. Again the UK heads the list, and the level in Greece was also high; next come Austria and Germany. The lowest levels were found in a mix of countries.

Finally, IMF researchers (2012) have used a different method of assessing the relationship between debt levels and consumption, by relating changes in debt levels between 2002 and 2006 (the years when pre-crisis household debt was rising particularly sharply) with the changes in consumption levels that took place in 2010. They examine the latter by comparing actual 2010 consumption levels with those that would have been expected had past trends continued. Their main aim was to discover if rising household debt was responsible for a subsequent collapse of consumption (in most countries debt was rising fast and consumption declined). This would indicate excessive indebtedness had been incurred during the years of acceleration. They found a clear statistical relationship,

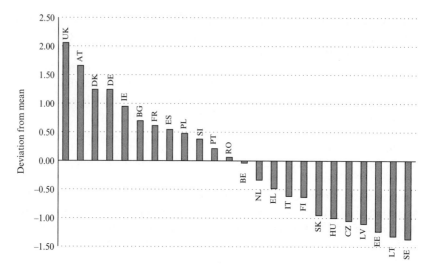

*Figure 5.12a   Outstanding consumer credit as a percentage of disposable
income, c.2000 (country scores in relation to standard
deviation around mean)*

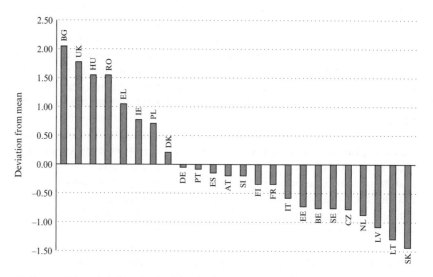

*Figure 5.12b   Outstanding consumer credit as a percentage of disposable
income, c.2009 (country scores in relation to standard
deviation around mean)*

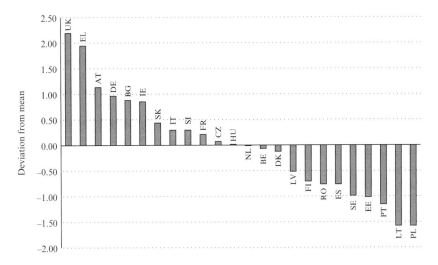

Source: European Commission Social Situation Observatory 2010

Figure 5.13 *Percentage of households below 60 per cent of median income with debts of more than 100 per cent disposable income, 2008 (country scores in relation to standard deviation around mean)*

though they did not explore the several non-conforming cases that their data produced. But the same data can also be used to enlighten our own search for the role that debt might play in sustaining consumption rather than in funding the acquisition of assets. The findings, as they relate to the countries of interest to this study, and expressed in terms of relations to means and standard deviations, are presented in Figure 5.14. This demonstrates the overall relationship that the IMF study found (for the countries depicted here the correlation is only $r^2 = 0.2276$), but we can also explore the distribution across quadrants. The combination of an above-average rise in household debt followed by an above-average collapse of consumer spending was concentrated in the three Baltic states, Romania, Ireland, and (though only marginally) in Spain and the UK – a mixture of particularly poor CEE countries and three western European countries that had experienced very strong mortgage-based booms. Other countries that experienced a strong increase in debt had a more robust 2010 consumption experience, Denmark actually experiencing an increase in consumption; the strong class challenge cases of all four Nordic countries and (marginally) the Netherlands are found here. With the exception of Greece, Croatia and, in particular, Hungary, which had consumption falls despite

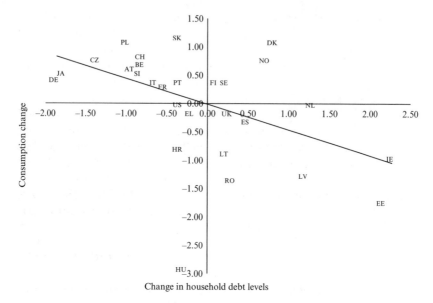

Source: IMF 2012

Figure 5.14   *Household debt change 2002–06 by estimated consumption level change 2010 (country scores in relation to standard deviations around means)*

only moderate debt increases, all remaining countries combined below-average declines (or, in Poland and Slovakia, increases) in consumption with below-average rises in debt.

It is time to draw some conclusions from these various debt statistics. For the earlier (*c.*2000) period we have only two data points from which to draw conclusions about the use of debt to support consumption: overall household debt expressed as the debt to income ratio, and the burden of outstanding credit (Figure 5.15a). There was a moderately positive relationship between the two variables, i.e., the higher the household debt the higher the level of outstanding consumer credit, but only at $r^2 = 0.2305$. Concentrating on cases that are at plus or minus at least 0.5 SD on both counts enables us to identify four countries where debt may have been used to finance consumption to an important extent: Denmark, the UK, Ireland and Germany. We lack data on certain potential cases: Japan, Norway, Switzerland and the USA, though we know from various studies that the USA has been a further case of debt-supported consumption. At the other extreme, countries where debt seemed to play no part at all in

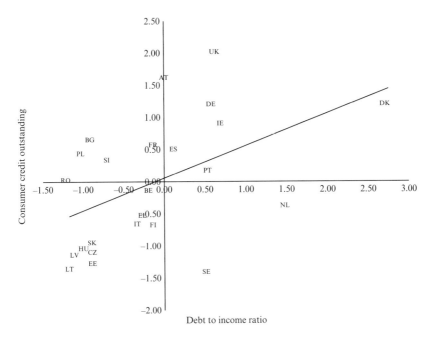

Figure 5.15a *Consumer credit outstanding by debt to income ratio, 2000*
(country scores in relation to standard deviations around
means)

the maintenance of consumption included all CEE cases except Bulgaria, Romania and Slovenia. Only one country combined high overall debt with very low outstanding consumer credit (Sweden), while Bulgaria had the opposite combination of high credit but low debt. The use of household debt for consumption was primarily a feature of wealthy countries; neither the countries of CEE nor the middle-income countries of SWE made much use of it. There were no other discernible patterns among 'types' of society.

As Figure 5.15b shows, by the time of the crisis and its immediate aftermath, any relationship between household debt and outstanding consumer credit had disappeared ($r^2 = 0.0018$). Only Ireland and the UK continue to occupy the quadrant of more than moderately high debt and outstanding consumer credit, and Denmark is the only other inhabitant of the quadrant, with more modest outstanding credit. Sweden has been joined by the Netherlands with 'more than moderately high debt, less than moderately low consumer credit', while the quadrant of less than moderately low debt with more than moderately high outstanding

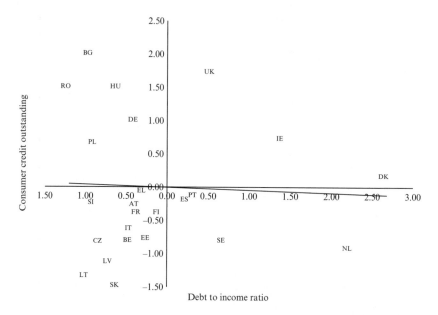

Figure 5.15b   *Consumer credit outstanding by debt to income ratio, c.2009*
                   (country scores in relation to standard deviations around
                   means)

consumer credit now has four CEE cases: Bulgaria, Hungary, Poland, Romania, plus Germany.

For this more recent period we can add the additional information from Figure 5.13 on the extent to which low-income families experienced heavy debt, and from Figure 5.14 on the differential impact of changing debt levels in the 2002–06 period on consumption in 2010. Table 5.2 summarizes this information and ranks countries by their strength of class challenge score for the period, to enable us to test the hypothesis that countries with strong class challenge would make more use of household debt for consumption than those with weak challenge. This hypothesis, similar to that concerning public debt in Chapter 4, is based on the assumption that countries with strong class challenge need to draw on additional resources, even non-sustainable ones, to finance class compromises. Table 5.2 organizes countries into a number of categories of debt management, with the use of debt for consumption, and particularly among the relatively poor, increasing as one moves from left to right across the table. Contrary to the hypothesis, it is notable that the three countries with strongest class challenge (Denmark, Sweden and Finland) were the only three to have

Table 5.2   Private debt profiles by strength of class challenge, c.2010

I	II	III	IV	V	VI	VII	No data
					DK*		
	SE*						
							NO
FI*							
BE							
			AT				
							HR
	NL						
						IE**	
			SI				
			IT				
			DE				
						UK**	
		RO**					
			SK				
							CH
	ES**						
	PT						
			CZ				
		HU***					
				EL			
				BG			
							JA
		PL					
LT**							
			FR				
LV**							
							RU
EE**							
							US

Notes:
I   = Relatively low debt, low outstanding credit, low burden on poor
II   = Relatively high debt, low outstanding credit, low burden on poor
III   = Relatively low debt, high outstanding credit, low burden on poor
IV   = As II, but high burden on poor
V   = As III, but high burden on poor
VI   = Relatively high debt, high outstanding credit, but low burden on poor
VII   = As VI, but high burden on poor
*   = Relatively good 2010 consumer performance; relatively high rising debt 2002–06
**   − Relatively poor 2010 consumer performance; relatively high rising debt 2002–06
***   = Collapse of consumption 2010; relatively low rising debt 2002–06

relatively good consumer performance in 2010 despite earlier high debt. Four of the countries with the strongest class challenge also fall into the two categories making least use of debt for consumption, especially by the relatively poor (Sweden, Finland, Belgium, Netherlands). However, Austria and Denmark, the two other countries with above-mean class challenge scores in 2011, were cases with high reliance on debt. Denmark, the country with the strongest class challenge, made particularly heavy use of debt, but it is notable that the burden of debt on the Danish poor was low, and it was one of the countries where consumption was sustained despite high debt.

The countries relying most on debt, particularly for the poor, were Ireland and the UK. These have moderate class challenge, but they are distinguished by being the only two Anglophone cases among those for whom we have adequate detail to complete Table 5.2.

While the class challenge variable makes some limited sense of the diversity among the wealthier countries (though in a way that confounds any particular hypothesis), it is of no help in understanding that among the poorer and medium-income countries. The Baltic states share with some of the strongest class challenge cases a profile of making little use of debt, though all three were distinctively associated (alongside Romania, Ireland and the UK) with deteriorating consumption following growing debt in the run-up to the crisis.

DIRECT PROVISION OF PUBLIC SERVICES

A very different way in which living standards, and therefore consumption security, can be removed from the fluctuations of the market economy is through the direct provision of public services, funded either fully by government or at least at subsidized prices. Today these services are often provided by private firms, hence the official renaming by the European Commission of public services as services of general interest. The central point here however is the source of funding and the question of the insulation of prices from the full force of the market, rather than the institutional form of the provision. The full range of such services might be included here, including the provision of public administration, transport, military and security services. However, we are interested in services that individuals would have to find for themselves from market resources if there were no public provision, and where public provision might protect consumption standards for other, usually less basic, goods and services in a context of labour-market insecurity. This applies primarily to health, education, social care, and a large proportion of housing and cultural services. It is

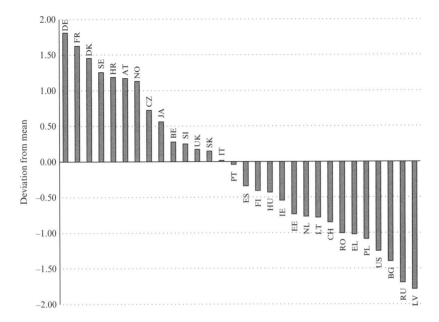

Figure 5.16a   Public spending on health (deflated), c.2000 (country scores in relation to standard deviation around mean)

not easy to separate the provision of care (apart from healthcare) from social protection budgets, which we have already discussed, or the provision of transport subsidies from infrastructure provision in transport budgets. These therefore have to be left out, but the main constituents of these direct services in cost terms are in any case education and health.

Figures 5.16a and b present the relevant data for health around the years 2000 and 2011. The extent to which citizens' concerns about health security are alleviated by public spending is a product of two factors: the overall level of public spending on health (as expressed by public health spending as a proportion of national income) and the proportion of total health spending represented by that proportion. If we consider only the former factor, we fail to take into account the overall costs of receiving healthcare in a particular country; if health costs are very high, citizens might still be left with a high personal bill even if the government were spending a relatively large sum on health. The World Bank data (website) on which the current analysis is based enable us to distinguish these two factors. In Figures 5.16a and b they have been combined by deflating total public health spending by the proportion of total health spending represented by this sum. Ideally we should want to break down these raw

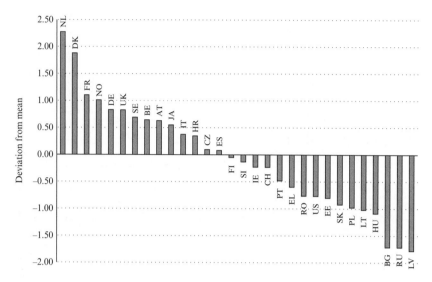

Figure 5.16b   *Public spending on health (deflated), c.2011 (country scores in relation to standard deviation around mean)*

data by different income levels within the population, but the data do not enable us to do this.

Around the year 2000 the highest levels of health cost support were given to citizens of the Scandinavian countries, also Germany, France, Croatia, Austria, the Czech Republic and Japan. The lowest levels were found in a number of CEE countries, the USA, Greece, Switzerland, the Netherlands and Ireland. There was a modest positive correlation between public health spending and class challenge ($r^2 = 0.3131$) (Figure 5.17a). Only two high challenge countries came below the European mean (Finland and, in particular, the Netherlands). The majority of countries with weaker challenge, from all regions, had below-mean health spending, the most outstanding exception being France, but also Japan, the Czech Republic and, marginally, the UK.

By 2011 there had been an overall increase in public support for health costs across Europe, the deflated average rising from 4.18 per cent to 5.02 per cent. There were similar rises in Japan (from 4.93 per cent to 5.92 per cent), Russia (from 1.92 per cent to 2.21 per cent) and the US (from 2.51 per cent to 3.76 per cent). The correlation with class challenge (Figure 5.17b) rises very slightly ($r^2 = 0.3322$), largely because of major changes in the funding of Dutch healthcare in 2006, which have brought the country from being among the lowest to the very highest public

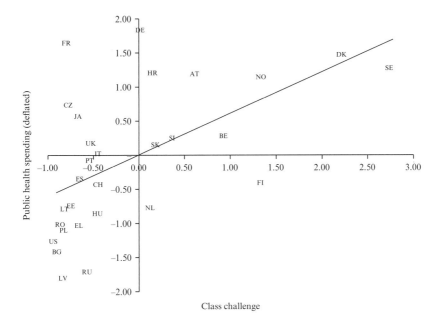

Figure 5.17a   Public health spending (deflated) by class challenge, c.2000 (country scores in relation to standard deviations around means)

spenders; otherwise the pattern was rather similar, with high spending concentrated among the strong class challenge cases, with the marginal exception of Finland. Italy joins France, Japan and the UK as high-spending cases with less strong class challenge. No CEE country now features among the highest spenders, but instead CEE countries and Russia occupy all positions at −1.00 SD or below, and all at −0.5 SD or below except for the USA and Greece.

For education spending we do not have the same capacity to consider public spending as a proportion of all spending as we had for health, and must be content with the statistics for public education spending as a proportion of national income. This matters less, as education is a more generally publicly provided service in advanced economies than is healthcare. The relevant data are shown in Figures 5.18a (*c.*2000) and b (*c.*2010). At the earlier date the Nordic countries clearly dominate, with spending also high in Belgium. The lowest spenders are a combination of CEE countries, but also Japan, Greece, Spain, Ireland, Italy and Germany.

The correlation with the class challenge index (Figure 5.19a) is fairly

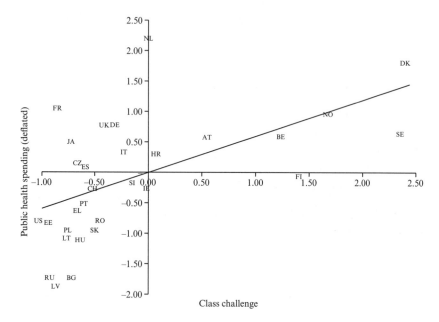

Figure 5.17b *Public health spending (deflated) by class challenge, c.2010 (country scores in relation to standard deviations around means)*

strong ($r^2 = 0.4864$). The high challenge countries (with the exception of Croatia and Slovakia) spent considerably more than others. Elsewhere there is the familiar mixed situation among low challenge countries, though with unfamiliar constituents of the respective quadrants. It is notable that the USA and the Baltic states here appear above the mean – though in no case by as much as 0.5 SD. No relatively low challenge country comes above this level, and the great majority fall below the line, except France and Switzerland.

By 2010, overall spending levels rose slightly: in European countries on average from 5.40 per cent to 5.56 per cent, in Japan from 3.6 per cent to 3.8 per cent, in Russia from 3.8 per cent to 4.1 per cent, and in the USA these were stable at 5.6 per cent. It might seem surprising that both health and education public spending rose in most countries during the first years of the recession. This is probably a reflection on how cuts in public budgets respond more slowly to crisis than private spending, constituting one of the ways in which public spending protects a population's standard of living from labour market flexibility. There was also little change by 2010 in countries' relative positions, except a major upward shift in the

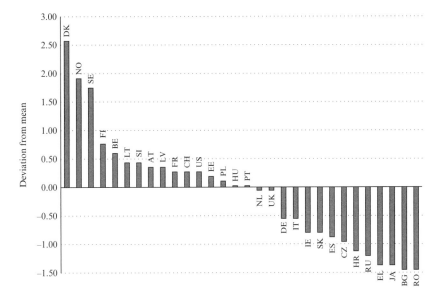

*Figure 5.18a   Public spending on education as a percentage of GDP,
c.2000 (country scores in relation to standard deviation
around mean)*

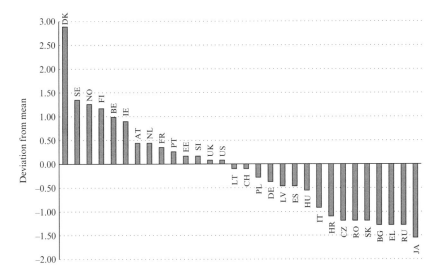

*Figure 5.18b   Public spending on education as a percentage of GDP,
c.2010 (country scores in relation to standard deviation
around mean)*

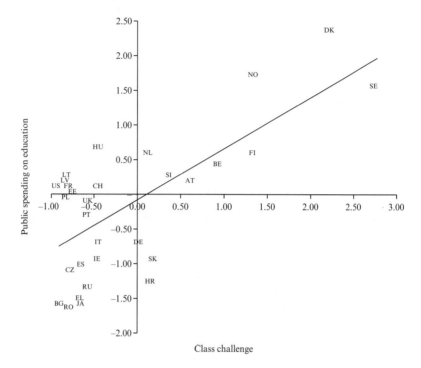

Figure 5.19a   Public education spending by class challenge, c.2000
            (country scores in relation to standard deviations around
            means)

position of Ireland, and decline in Hungary. The correlation with the class challenge index rises further (Figure 5.19b), to $r^2 = 0.5879$.

INTERNALIZING OR EXTERNALIZING PUBLIC SPENDING

According to Table 2.1, we must next examine whether public spending is playing an inclusive or exclusionary role. We can calculate this by considering the effect of government taxing and spending activities on the Gini coefficient of income inequality. If the net effect of government actions were to increase the Gini coefficient, the ratio of change in the Gini coefficient to the pre-tax and spending coefficient would be high and negative, a score of −100 indicating that income had been completely redistributed towards the rich. High negative scores would therefore indicate that public

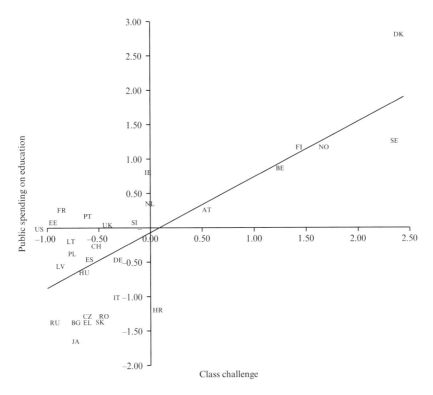

Figure 5.19b *Public education spending by class challenge, c.2010*
(country scores in relation to standard deviations around
means)

social policy was an instrument of exclusion. Against this, a high positive
ratio would indicate an impact of taxation and spending to spread burdens
more evenly, a score of +100 indicating total redistribution; state social
policy would be facilitating social inclusion. Unfortunately pre-tax and
spending Gini data are available only for OECD countries, excluding
Hungary and Switzerland and only since 2004, which limits the scope of
our analysis, and prevents us from using the post-tax and spending Gini
data for a wider range of countries and for the start of the century applied
in the previous chapter. Figures 5.20a (*c*.2000) and 5.20b (*c*.2010) present
countries' relative positions in our normal way.

In every country for which we have data, tax and spending had
some redistributive effect towards lower-income households, there
being no negative scores; so in no case can we talk of an exclusionary
impact of government intervention, its role everywhere being to reduce

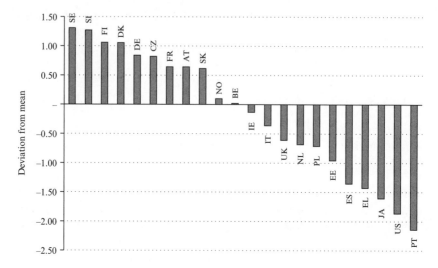

Figure 5.20a   Ratio of Gini reduction effected by taxes and spending to pre-tax and spending Gini, c.2004 (country scores in relation to standard deviation around mean)

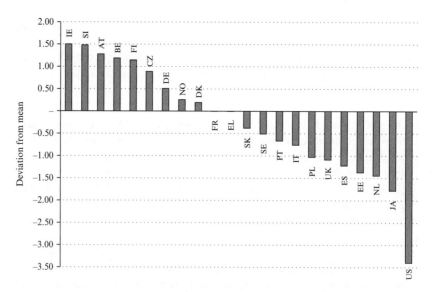

Figure 5.20b   Ratio of Gini reduction effected by taxes and spending to pre-tax and spending Gini, c.2011 (country scores in relation to standard deviation around mean)

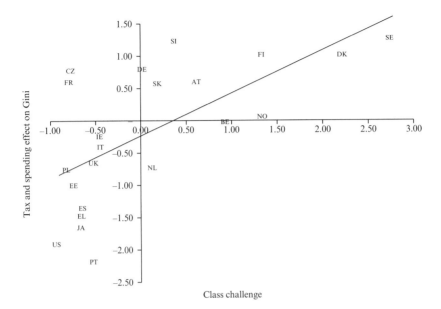

Figure 5.21a   Effect of taxation and spending on Gini coefficient, by class challenge, c.2000 (country scores in relation to standard deviations around means)

inequality and enhance inclusion. However, the degree of redistribution varies widely. Around 2004, the most redistributive were most of the Nordic countries, along with the Czech Republic, Germany and Slovenia, followed by France, Austria and Slovakia. The least redistributive and therefore the least inclusive were Japan, the UK, the USA, three SWE countries, Estonia and Poland. These data provide a positive correlation with the class challenge index ($r^2 = 0.4085$) (Figure 5.21a). The only exceptions to the overall relationship are the Netherlands (marginally above-mean class challenge but weakly redistributive), and the Czech Republic and France (below-mean challenge but redistributive).

The average rate of redistribution rose among European countries between 2004 and 2011 from 37.62 per cent to 39.66 per cent, and in Japan from 27.54 per cent to 31.15 per cent, while in the USA it declined from 25.93 per cent to 23.43 per cent. There was some change in countries' relative positions, with Ireland, Slovenia, Austria, Belgium and Finland now achieving most redistribution, followed by the Czech Republic. The least redistributive were the USA by a large degree, followed by Japan, the Netherlands, Estonia, Spain, the UK and Poland. The correlation

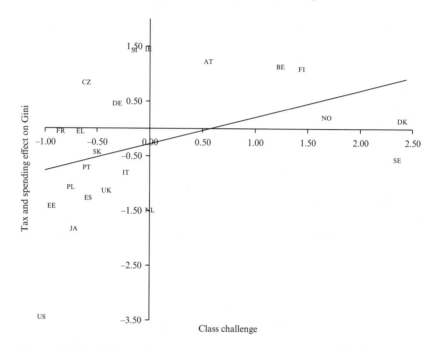

Figure 5.21b   *Effect of taxation and spending on Gini coefficient, by class challenge, c.2010 (country scores in relation to standard deviations around means)*

with class challenge (Figure 5.21b) declined very considerably over the period to $r^2 = 0.1749$. Sweden now appears as a country with relatively strong class challenge but redistribution below the mean, while the Czech Republic, Germany, Ireland and Slovenia were countries with weak challenge but strong redistribution.

CONCLUSION

The purpose of this chapter was to identify to what extent various countries might resolve the central dilemma of labour market uncertainty by having recourse to various non-labour supports for security. Unlike the issues considered in Chapter 4, by no means all of these alternatives involved the avoidance of dependence on a wider internal social solidarity. What is here being displaced on to other times or socially excluded groups is the role of the labour market as a provider of consumption; for some topics this involves avoidance of wider social solidarity, but for others it involves intensified dependence on that solidarity. Avoidance of wider solidarity takes the form of the use of individualized market governance, represented here by such resources as private social spending and/or dependence on private debt. We shall here use as the main indicator of the use of private debt as a means of assisting consumption the statistics on outstanding consumer credit, as it relates most directly to our central idea of supporting consumption. It also corresponds fairly closely to the more complex qualitative ranking displayed in Table 5.2.

There is then a distinction in forms of solidarity between those based on public services and transfers (state governance) and those rooted in family (community governance), captured in our variables through remittances and adult children living at home. Finally comes the question of the extent to which any action of the state operates by social inclusion.

We proceed, as in Chapter 4, with a spread of countries across these variables, starting around the turn of the present century (Table 5.3). In doing so, we should pay attention to the different importance of the variables. This can be done only for those that can be compared as a result of their being expressed as percentages of national income (i.e., not to unemployment support rate or age of males on leaving the parental home). Remittances accounted for 10 per cent of national income in Bulgaria, 3 per cent in Croatia, and levels between 1 per cent and 2 per cent in Portugal, Latvia, Slovakia and Belgium. Everywhere else they were smaller. Private social spending accounted for 9.1 per cent of GDP in the USA, 8.3 per cent in Switzerland, 7.7 per cent in the UK, 7.3 per cent in the Netherlands and below 1 per cent everywhere else. Social protection expenditure ranged between 15 per cent and 30 per cent. Outstanding consumer credit (the indicator of household debt dependence that we shall use initially) accounted for 20.6 per cent of GDP in the UK, but for the Baltic states and Sweden it was below 1 per cent. Expenditure on health ranged from more than 1 per cent to 6.6 per cent everywhere; that on education ranged from 3.6 per cent to 8.4 per cent. To deal with this variety, we might ignore all absolute scores of less than 1 per cent, even if these would show a country as having relative scores high above the standard deviation for the variable in question. In practice this would apply only to Poland, which counts as moderately high for remittances, though these amounted to 0.97 per cent of GDP.

We can cluster countries on the following basis (see Table 5.4 for the years around 2000):

- A (use of private means): Countries are counted as making use of means that avoid dependence on internal solidarity if they score relatively highly on private social spending and consumer credit.

Table 5.3 Summary table, separation of consumption from labour market, c.2000

	Market			State			Family		Inclusion
	Private pensions	Consumer credit	Social protection	URR	Health	Education	Remittances	Home leaving	Tax and spending redistribution
Extremely high	US CH UK NL	UK				DK	BG	BG	
Very high		AT DK DE	SE DE DK FR AT	SK DK	DE FR DK SE HR AT NO	NO SE	HR	EL SI	SE SI FI DK
High	AT JA	IE BG FR ES	UK NO NL BE	NO CH FI SE	CZ JA	FI BE		SK IT PL PT RO	DE CZ FR AT SK
Moderately high	DE FR SE	PL SI PT	FI IT SI EL CH	IE NL JA CZ DE	BE SI UK SK	LT SI AT LV FR CH US EE PL	PT LV SK BE [PL]	ES CZ LV HU	NO
Indifferent	DK IT	RO BE		AT FR BE	IT PT	HU PT NL UK	EL SI	LT	BE

Reducing stress on social solidarity (spanning the State, Family and Inclusion columns)

148

Increasing stress on social solidarity

Moderately low	EL NO BE PT IE FI	NL EL	PL ES PT	UK PL PT	ES FI HU	LT FR EE AT HU FI RO ES UK SE JA DK IT RU DE US	IE AT	IE IT
Low	SK CZ ES EE HU PL SI	IT FI SK	HU SK CZ	ES HU	IE EE NL LT CH	DE IT IE SK ES CZ	EE DE BE NL UK FR	UK NL PL EE
Very low	HU CZ LV EE LT SE	LV LT IE EE RO	EL US	RO EL PL US BG RU LV	HR RU EL JA BG RO	CH	FI SE DK	ES EL JA US
Extremely low				IT			PT	
No data	HR BG LV LT RO RU	HR NO CH US JA RU	BG HR JA RU US	BG HR EE LV LT RO SI RU			HR NO CH US JA RU	BG HR HU LV LT RO RU CH

Note: [ ] = a score of < 1 per cent GDP

Table 5.4   Clusters, c.2000

Cluster		(i) Inclusive variant	Inclusion uncertain	(ii) Less inclusive variant
A	Dependence on private means only			IE (US) (JA)
A/B	Dependence on private and public means	AT DK FR DE	(CH)	NL UK
A/C	Dependence on private and family means		(BG)	
B	Dependence on public means only	FI (NO) SE	BE	
B/C	Dependence on public and family means	SK SI		
C	Dependence on family means only	CZ	(HR) (HU) (LV) (RO)	EL IT PL PT ES
D	No means		(LT) (RU)	EE

Note: ( ) signifies that there are some missing data for the country concerned

> They are counted as not making use of means that avoid solidarity if they score low on these variables.
>
> • B (use of public means): Countries are counted as making use of means that imply dependence on internal public solidarity if they score relatively highly on public spending on social protection, unemployment support, health and education. They are counted as avoiding that dependence if they score relatively low on those variables.
>
> • C (use of family means): Countries are counted as making use of means that imply dependence on internal family solidarity if they score relatively highly on remittances and mean age of males leaving home. They are counted as avoiding that dependence if they score relatively low on those variables. If scores are contradictory, the age of males leaving home is deemed to be more important, on grounds that low remittances do not necessarily indicate low family strength.
>
> • D (use of no means): Countries are counted as being in this cluster if they have net positive scores on none of the previous groups of variables.

- Sub-clusters (i) and (ii) indicate degree of inclusion: In each cluster, countries are listed under (i) and counted as having strong inclusion in their internal solidarity if they score relatively highly on redistribution through the tax and spending system. They are listed under (ii) and counted as not having strong inclusion if they score low on this variable. Given the lack of data for several countries on this variable we also need an intermediate 'unknown' category.

If, in A and C, a country's scores on the two variables are contradictory, the allocation is based on the variable in which it scored more heavily in either direction. If it is not possible to discriminate between these scores, or if the scores are indifferent, the country is classed as indifferent on that variable. If data are available for only one variable, the allocation has to be based on that one alone. If, in B, a country's scores are contradictory across the four components, the allocation is based on the balance of relative scores across them. If this produces an unclear result, or if the scores are indifferent, the country is classed as indifferent on that variable. If data are unavailable for one or more variables, the allocation has to be based on those that are available.

On this basis we can identify the following broad clusters among our countries *c*.2000:

- Cluster 5 (2000) A(ii): Predominant use of private means (public and family means low), with low inclusion: Ireland, Japan, USA.
- Cluster 5 (2000) A/B(i): Predominant use of both private and public means (family means low), with high inclusion: Austria, Denmark, France, Germany.
- Cluster 5 (2000) A/B(ii): As Cluster 5 A/B(i), but with low inclusion: Netherlands, UK, possibly Switzerland if we knew the degree of fiscal redistribution.
- Cluster 5 (2000) A/C: Public means low, but with high use of family: possibly Bulgaria (inclusion unknown).
- Cluster 5 (2000) B(i): Predominant use of public means only (private and family means low), with high inclusion: Finland, Norway, Sweden, partially Belgium, which has indifferent inclusion.
- Cluster 5 (2000) B(i)/C: As Cluster 5 B(i), but with high use of family: Slovakia, Slovenia.
- Cluster 5 (2000) C(i): Predominant use of family means (private and public means low), with high inclusion: Czech Republic; possibly Croatia, Hungary, Lithuania, Romania, with unknown inclusion.

- Cluster 5 (2000) C(ii): As Cluster 5 C(i), but with low inclusion: Greece, Italy, Poland, Portugal, Spain; possibly Croatia, Hungary, Lithuania, Romania (unknown inclusion).
- Cluster 5 (2000) D: No predominant means, low inclusion: Estonia; possibly Latvia, Russia (unknown inclusion).

Table 5.5 shows the distribution across these paths of countries ranked according to strength of class challenge. For simplicity, countries with high inclusion have been indicated in bold type; those with unknown or indifferent inclusion are in italics; and those with low inclusion are given in normal type. While for most of the individual indicators discussed in this chapter regional groupings often made more sense of the diversity of positions, when we bring the material together in this synthetic way, class challenge acquires an autonomous power, largely in relation to the role of state governance, in line with the hypothesis set up in Chapter 3. Of the 11 countries with the strongest class challenge, only Croatia (whose challenge statistic is in any case somewhat doubtful) did not have a relatively high score on items in B, i.e. in making important use of public policy measures for protecting labour from insecurity. Further, of these 11 only the Netherlands, possibly Switzerland, and to some extent Belgium, were not among the strongest users of fiscal redistribution. Of the 15 countries with the weakest challenge, only France made strong use of state governance. The majority of countries with weak class challenge were dependent solely on family means, or on nothing at all, to protect consumption in the face of eventual labour market instability. Although a large number of countries made use of market governance, the majority of these used state governance too, leaving just the USA (with particularly weak class challenge), Ireland and Japan, using above-mean market governance alone, and with a low level of fiscal redistribution and therefore of inclusion. Class challenge was not important in distinguishing levels of exclusion among countries depending primarily on community governance, though it is notable that all four medium-wealth SWE countries made high use of exclusion, while the pattern in CEE was more varied.

As we have already noted, the geo-cultural regimes identified in much of the literature overlap with the class challenge variable, because the Nordic or social-democratic group is defined in terms of greater class challenge than the others. In Table 5.5 these regimes can be seen to have some further independent effect in addition to class challenge, mainly in uniting France with the other northern 'Continental' cases despite the weakness of its class challenge. Those geo-cultural arguments that separate the SWE, 'familistic' cases from the northern members of the 'Continental' regime, also find strong justification here, though that

Table 5.5 *Different patterns of governance of separation of consumption from labour market by class challenge,* c.*2000*

Clusters 5 (*c.*2000)						
A	A/B	B	A/C	B/C	C	D
		Sweden				
	Denmark					
		Norway				
		Finland				
		Belgium				
	Austria					
				Slovenia		
					Croatia	
				Slovakia		
	Netherlands					
	Germany					
					Hungary	
	Switzerland					
					Italy	
Ireland						
						Russia
	UK					
					Portugal	
					Spain	
Japan						
					Greece	
					Czech Republic	
						Estonia
	France					
						Latvia
					Poland	
			Bulgaria			
					Lithuania	
					Romania	
USA						

Note:
Countries with high inclusion are indicated in bold type
Countries with unknown or indifferent inclusion are indicated in italic type
Countries with low inclusion are indicated in normal type

also corresponds to the findings of class challenge analysis. The failure of Table 5.5 to distinguish SWE from CEE is not accounted for in the standard literature, because this does not embrace central and eastern Europe. The discrimination among CEE countries proposed by Bohle and Greskovits (2012) is partly borne out, with Slovenia more closely associated to NWE, and with two of the three Baltic states distinct from the Visegrád group, but Slovakia is an anomaly in belonging with Slovenia.

Moving to the period around 2010, Table 5.6 presents data on the same basis as Table 5.3 for the earlier years. First, we should again examine the relative size of the different variables. Remittances declined considerably as a percentage of national income in Bulgaria (from 10 per cent to 3.24 per cent) and declined slightly in Belgium, Croatia and Portugal, but rose in some other countries. Hungary and Portugal are both rated medium strong in the remittance table, but had scores of less than 1 per cent GDP. Private social spending was stable at around 2.3 per cent of GDP across Europe, and in Japan at around 4.0 per cent, but fell heavily in the USA from 10.6 per cent to 3.0 per cent. It accounted for 8.0 per cent of GDP in Switzerland, 6.7 per cent in the Netherlands, 6.3 per cent in the UK and less everywhere else. Social protection expenditure continued to range between 15 per cent and 30 per cent. Consumer credit rose generally, accounting for 26.5 per cent of GDP in Bulgaria, and no lower than 15 per cent for any country counting as at least moderately high. Expenditure on health ranged from more than 1 per cent to 6.6 per cent everywhere; that on education from 3.6 per cent to 8.4 per cent. Ignoring all absolute scores of less than 1 per cent again has only a minor effect, and on remittances alone.

On the basis of an analysis similar to that for 2000 in Table 5.4, Table 5.7 allocates countries to clusters in the more recent period. This enables us to identify the following broad clusters among our countries:

- Cluster 5 (2010) A(ii): Switzerland, the USA. Switzerland has moved to this cluster from the mixed cluster A/B, as its former relatively strong use of state measures is overtaken by a growth in state action elsewhere. On the other hand, Ireland and Japan have left this cluster because of a relative rise in the role of state action.
- Cluster 5 (2010) A/B(i): Denmark, Belgium, Ireland, possibly France (indifferent inclusion). Austria, Germany and Norway leave this cluster for B(i) as a result of a relative decline in their use of household debt as other countries saw increased debt.
- Cluster 5 (2010) A/B(ii): Japan, the Netherlands, the UK, possibly France (indifferent inclusion).

Table 5.6 *Summary table, separation of consumption from labour market, c.2010*

	Market governance			State			Family		Inclusion
	Private social spending	Consumer credit	Social protection	URR	Health	Education	Remittances	Home leaving	Tax and spending redistribution
Extremely high	US CH	BG		*Reducing stress on social solidarity*			BG	BG	
Very high	NL UK	UK HU RO EL	DK FR NL	JA DK NL CH	NL DK FR NO	SE NO FI	RO HR LV	EL SI	IE SI AT BE FI
High	JA	IE PL	SE FI AT DE IT BE IE EL	NO AT FI SE BE SI UK LT	DE UK SE BE AT JA	BE IE	SK PL LT EE BE	SK IT PL PT RO	CZ DE
Moderately high	DE SE AT DK	DK	UK PT	DE PT FR LV CZ	IT HR CZ	AT NL FR PT EE SI	[PT HU]	ES CZ LV HU	NO DK
Indifferent	NO	DE PT	ES NO		ES FI	UK US		LT	FR EL

Table 5.6 (continued)

	Market governance			State			Family		Inclusion
	Private social spending	Consumer credit	Social protection	URR	Health	Education	Remittances	Home leaving	Tax and spending redistribution
				Increasing stress on social solidarity					
Moderately low	EL SI PT FI	ES AT SI FI FR	SI CH HU JA	PL IE ES EE	SI IE CH PT	LT CH PL DE LV ES	FR SI FI UK EL SE AT JA DE ES	IE AT	SK
Low	SK FR CZ ES HU PL EE	IT EE BE SE CZ NL	US	BG SK HU US	EL RO US EE SK PL	HU IT	US IT NL CZ IE DK	EE DE BE NL UK FR	SE PT IT
Very low		LV LT NO SK CH	CZ PL LT SK EE LV BG RO RU	RO	LT HU BG RU LV	HR CZ RO SK BG EL RU JA	NO RU	FI SE DK	PL UK ES EE NL JA
Extremely low				EL IT			CH		US
No data	HR BG LV LT RO RU	HR JA RU US		HR RU				HR NO CH US JA RU	BG HR HU LV LT RO RU CH

Note: [ ] = a score of < 1 per cent GDP

Table 5.7   Clusters, c.2010

Cluster		(i) Inclusive variant	Inclusion uncertain	(ii) Less inclusive variant
A	Dependence on private means only		(CH)	(US)
A/B	Dependence on private and public means	AT DK DE IE		(JA) NL PT (also family) UK
A/C	Dependence on private and family means		EL (BG) (HU) (RO)	
B	Dependence on public means only	BE FI NO	FR	SE
B/C	Dependence on public and family means	SI		
C	Dependence on family means only		(HR) (LV) (LT)	PL SK
D	No means	CZ	(RU)	EE IT ES

Note: ( ) signifies that there are some missing data for the country concerned

- Cluster 5 (2010) B(i): Austria, Finland, Germany, Norway. Sweden has left this cluster to form B(ii) by itself, following the dramatic decline in its redistributive fiscal activity.
- Cluster 5 (2010) A/C(ii): Bulgaria, possibly Greece (indifferent inclusion) and Hungary, Romania (level of inclusion unknown). Spain has left this cluster for D as a result of relatively declining family role. Greece, Hungary and Romania have joined it from C(ii) as a result of increased use of consumer debt.
- Cluster 5 (2010) B/C(i): Slovenia.
- Cluster 5 (2010) B/C(ii): Portugal.
- Cluster 5 (2010) C(ii): Poland, Slovakia (moved to here from B/C(i) as a result of a relative decline in its state action), possibly Croatia, Latvia, Lithuania (unknown inclusion). Italy and Portugal leave this cluster as a result of declining relative family role in the former and rising state role in the latter.
- Cluster 5 (2010) D(i): Estonia, Hungary and Italy; Hungary and Russia (with unknown inclusion), Spain. Deviant case, with high inclusion: Czech Republic.

There are important changes in these configurations, which it must be remembered are based on changes in relative rather than absolute scores. The relative decline in the use of consumer credit in some of the countries that previously had been relatively high users leads to a decline in the role of market governance and therefore a shift of countries from the hybrid Cluster 5 (2000) A/B to the clearly public-means oriented Cluster 5 (2010) B. A rise in the use of remittances in some countries but a decline in others leads to more of the latter moving into Cluster D, though it is doubtful whether this has important substantive implications. Meanwhile, the rise in the role of consumer credit in some of the family-dependent countries sees a growth in Cluster 5 A/C.

As with Table 5.5, Table 5.8 shows the distribution across these paths of countries ranked according to class challenge. As in the earlier period, of the 11 most egalitarian countries, only Croatia does not make important use of public policy measures for protecting labour from insecurity, and only the Netherlands and (less so) Belgium are not among the strongest users of fiscal redistribution. In the wake of the crisis a larger number of countries overall are now relatively high users of public means – though most of these are not highly inclusive. Again, the great majority of countries with weak class challenge were dependent solely on family means, or on nothing at all, to protect consumption from labour insecurity. Although a large number of countries made use of private means, the majority of these used public means too, leaving just the USA, now joined in part by Switzerland, as the sole cases placing relative emphasis on private means alone, and with a low level of fiscal redistribution and therefore of inclusion.

The relation between these variables and geo-cultural clusters remains similar to the earlier period. Although the SWE countries are no longer so homogenous, there is further absorption of them among the CEE cases, and among the latter the earlier anomalous position of Slovakia is partly resolved, as its earlier union strength has declined. Europe increasingly seems to have a north-western core where strong social policy protects from potential vagaries of the labour market, flanked to the west by Ireland and the UK where market support (including high consumer debt) is far stronger, and to the east and south a periphery where market and state are both weak, and only family is relatively strong.

Table 5.8 *Different patterns of governance of separation of consumption from labour market by class challenge, c.2010*

	Clusters 5 (*c.*2010)					
A	A/B	B	A/C	B/C	C	D
	Denmark					
		Sweden				
		Norway				
		Finland				
		Belgium				
	Austria					
					Croatia	
	Ireland					
	Netherlands					
			Slovenia**			
						Italy
	Germany					
	UK					
			Romania			
					Slovakia	
Switzerland						
						Spain
						Czech Republic
				Portugal		
						Hungary
			Bulgaria			
			Greece			
	Japan					
					Latvia	
					Poland	
	France					
						Lithuania
						Russia
						Estonia
USA						

Note:
Countries with high inclusion are indicated in bold type
Countries with unknown or indifferent inclusion are indicated in italic type
Countries with low inclusion are indicated in normal type

6. Integrating consumption and labour income

The classic arena for coping with labour market uncertainty in post-war twentieth-century societies was the national welfare state and system of labour law and industrial relations. In the scheme set out in Table 2.1 (see p. 27) this is the area covered primarily by Approach III, 'Integrating consumption and labour income', though the welfare state also includes item 14 (Public services and transfers as decommodifying) from Approach II, which we have already discussed in the previous chapter.

Welfare states try to reduce uncertainty in three different ways. First, macroeconomic policy may make use of large public budgets to act counter-cyclically to stabilize demand, reducing fluctuations. Second, large parts of those large spending budgets are used to provide both welfare services and financial transfers that further reduce uncertainty in the lives of workers and their families. Transfers do this obviously by raising the incomes of people unable to find work or too old or too sick to do so. Public services, normally provided free at the point of use or at subsidized prices, reduce uncertainty by making capacity to enjoy basic facilities independent of fluctuating incomes. Third, the provision of these same services creates public-service employment that is itself protected from fluctuating demand because it is not purchased in the market. This does not mean that it is immune from uncertainty, because demand management sometimes requires governments to reduce spending and therefore create some unemployment among public employees. But this is expected to happen rarely and with extensive warning. Public service workers' incomes also tend to fluctuate less (in either direction) than those in the private sector, because they are less exposed to the market. This makes public employment something of a privileged insider corner of the labour market, though in exchange for this stability public service incomes often tend to be lower than those of their private sector counterparts. Also, once public employees have become a large part of the workforce, the stability of their employment and incomes contributes to a general stability in consumption, particularly in local economies subject to decline in the market sector.

Labour law typically prescribes the ways in which workers can be disciplined and dismissed, protects their health and safety in the workplace, sometimes prescribes minimum rates of pay, and often provides for rights to consultation and sometimes co-decision-making, usually by providing rights to join and be represented by trade unions. Trade unions have in turn been embedded in systems of industrial relations, the character of which has been determined partly by provisions of labour law and partly by unions' own internal structures and those of their counterparts among employers' associations. Industrial relations systems have contributed to the reduction of uncertainty in so far as they have stabilized the process of wage determination and provided procedures for the resolution of disputes and processing individual workers' grievances against employers. On the other hand, they can also provide the means through which conflict is waged and disagreements exacerbated. The system of industrial relations is always relevant to the issue of uncertainty, whether by reducing or worsening it.

The neoliberal challenge towards the end of the twentieth century produced considerable changes in existing sets of arrangements. (For a more detailed account of these arguments, see Crouch 2012a.) The economy in general and labour in particular were considered to have become overburdened with mechanisms trying to protect the population against the uncertainties of market forces, with the result that European economies were becoming sclerotic, unable to innovate, with the eventual consequence that they would become incapable of providing prosperity – or could do so for parts of the labour force only by excluding others (OECD 1994; World Bank 2004–2009). In other words, integrative strategies could work only in their exclusionary form. The timing of this debate is important, as major structural changes were taking place in the advanced economies of the capitalist world as a result of globalization and technological change. Systems of labour protection that had taken for granted a basic continuity of types of economic activity, interrupted only by conjunctural trade fluctuations, did not seem appropriate to a world where entire occupations and indeed sectors were undergoing radical change. Paradoxically but logically, it followed from this that labour-market uncertainty could not be reduced through labour protection laws and collective agreements, as these would be unable to stem the underlying processes of change; also, by inhibiting radical adjustment they would end only by creating more insecurity and unemployment. For neoliberals the conclusion to be drawn from this was that, given that perfect markets were self-correcting, it was only if markets were liberated that adjustments could take place in a way that smoothed disruptive forces, in the long run reducing uncertainty. The 'post-war' paradigm and the neoliberal paradigm therefore differed radically on the kinds of social policy that would maximize economic success.

In the former case, a combination of state and associational governance, depending on individual cases; in the latter, the market alone. Neither found any space for community governance.

The issues that receive attention in this chapter provide evidence only for state and community governance. They have to be combined with elements of Chapter 5 to give us a rounded view of the other governance forms. A further important point, discussed in Chapter 2, is that there are two variants to all integrative approaches: inclusive integration of everyone within the national labour market concerned; and exclusionary integration that provides security for the majority at the expense of 'outsider' groups. As in Chapters 4 and 5, this element needs to be considered separately.

To explore further we need to provide indicators for the various elements under consideration. In appraising whether a country's level is 'high' or 'low' on a particular dimension we shall adopt the methodology used in the previous chapters. Positions are expressed in relation to the standard deviation for the European cases, and the data are standardized as ratios to the standard deviation in order to enable eventual comparison of the different indicators being used. The basic data on which calculations are based will be found in Appendix Tables A6.1 and A6.2.

INTEGRATING CONSUMPTION AND LABOUR INCOME OVER TIME: DEMAND MANAGEMENT

The first item in this part of the scheme set out in Table 2.1 concerns government demand management (or Keynesian policy as this approach is usually known). The overall share of government revenue in GDP stands as the best proxy for a government's potential capacity to manage demand, whether it uses that power or not. We are using revenue rather than spending, because it better measures a government's capacity to control its fiscal interventions. Spending can, for a while, continue at an irresponsible level, that is without government being able to fund it, and is therefore a less good indicator of potential capacity to manage demand. By the same token, it is the revenue variable, and not the actual size of public debt, which is the appropriate indicator of Keynesian demand management, which, correctly understood, uses debt only at periods when it is necessary to stimulate demand. At times of inflation, government budgets should be in surplus. Over an economic cycle government spending should be matched by taxation and public finances should be balanced. A high and persistent level of debt, which we have already considered in Chapter 4, indicates a government unable or unwilling to raise taxes to meet its spending commitments. Against the high government revenues that characterize a strong government capacity for managing demand, under a neoliberal policy regime the overall level of both government revenue and spending should always be low, as they are considered to interfere with markets, in terms of both the substance of the interventions and their use for demand management. The aggregate role of government revenue acts generally on the economy, and therefore does not raise questions of exclusion.

Because government revenues fluctuate more widely from year to year than most of the variables we have been considering, a 'snapshot' of one year is not appropriate. To secure data we shall take means of runs of five years: 1996–2000 for the start of the century, 2007–11 for the later years. Unfortunately we have no comparable data for Russia.

During the earlier period, high government revenues were concentrated in NWE countries and Croatia, while the lowest spenders were found among the Anglophone countries, the Baltic states, Japan and Switzerland (Figure 6.1a). Government revenue correlated highly with the class challenge indicator (Figure 6.2a), at $r^2 = 0.6696$. Apart from some marginally low levels among the moderately strong class challenge cases of Slovakia and Slovenia, and a marginally high one in moderately weak challenge Italy, the only real exception to the relationship was France, where weak class challenge was nevertheless associated with strong government revenues. Otherwise, wealthy western countries with weak challenge are found

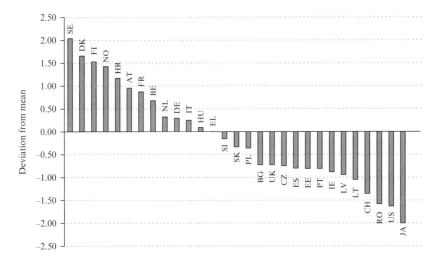

Figure 6.1a   Government revenue, 1996–2000 (country scores in relation to standard deviation around mean)

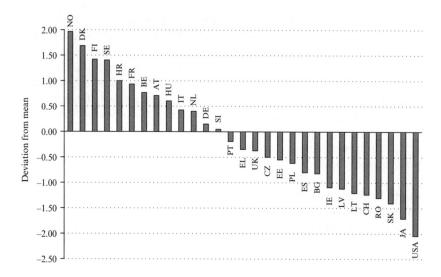

Figure 6.1b   *Government revenue, 2007–11 (country scores in relation to*
standard deviation around mean)

alongside poorer countries also with weak challenge. Class challenge is
here more important than national wealth.

Between 1996–2000 and 2007–11 the level of government revenue
declined slightly as governments moved into deficit to meet the crisis – the
European mean falling from 44.0 per cent to 43.0 per cent of GDP, with a
slight fall in the standard deviation (from 7.38 to 7.25). Revenue declined
more strongly in the USA, from 31.81 per cent to 28.23 per cent, but rose
slightly in Japan, from 29.06 per cent to 30.69 per cent. Most individual
European countries saw only minor fluctuations, but there were reductions of at least 0.5 per cent of GDP in Ireland and Italy, and similar
increases in the Baltic states, Romania and Spain. There was not much
change in countries' relative positions (Figure 6.1b), apart from a rise in
Hungary's ranking and a decline in that of Slovakia. The correlation with
the class equality indicator (Figure 6.2b) has declined to $r^2 = 0.5875$, still
high. There are now no cases in the high challenge/low revenue quadrant,
but France and Italy are joined by Hungary to increase slightly the population in the low challenge/high revenue quadrant. It is again notable that
for both periods, with a small number of exceptions, the class challenge
indicator works independently of geo-economic factors: most low challenge countries, whatever their wealth and regime type, are found together
in the low challenge/low revenue quadrant.

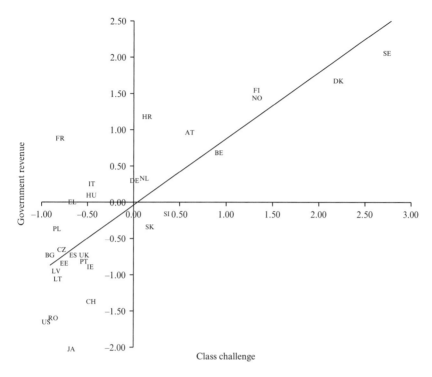

Figure 6.2a   Government revenue by class challenge, 1996–2000 (country scores in relation to standard deviations around means)

INTEGRATING CONSUMPTION AND LABOUR MARKETS

The remaining items from Table 2.1 all concern the 'manner' of integrating consumption and labour income within the current time period. In each case we have to examine to what extent measures are universal (within a nation state) and to what extent they make use of outsiders.

Collective Bargaining

The level of organization of an industrial relations system is measured by the extent of coverage of collective bargaining (indicating to what extent the labour force is part of the system), and the degree to which it is coordinated. Coverage is clearly relevant in indicating the overall significance of bargaining, and its inclusiveness. But coordination is important in indicating the extent to which bargainers have a capacity for strategy.

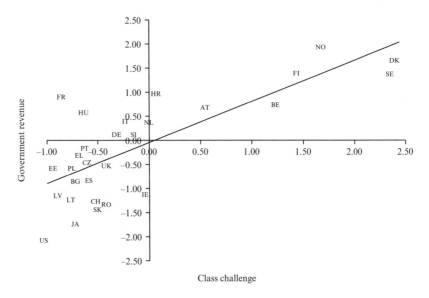

Figure 6.2b   Government revenue by class challenge, 2007–11 (country scores in relation to standard deviations around means)

The two variables interact to produce the overall level of encompassment of the bargaining system. A high level of coordination with low coverage (i.e., that reaches only a small proportion of the workforce) is clearly limited in its macroeconomic importance. As numerous researchers have shown (Calmfors and Driffill 1988; Crouch 1993; Traxler 2003; Traxler et al. 2001; Traxler et al. 2008a), the more bargainers coordinate their actions so that they cover either a whole national economy or key parts of it, the less they can externalize the consequences of their actions on to other parts of the economy (see also the pioneering theoretical work of Olson 1982), and the more they are pressured to acting in a neo-corporatist way, that is both to represent their members and have regard to the wider (usually national) entity to which their actions relate. Bargainers in such situations are forced to be aware that their bargaining could have negative outcomes for their own constituencies if they price themselves out of markets. But if coordination extends over only a small part of the economy, it will fail to achieve encompassment. Those covered by the coordination will be sensitive to the impact on their own members, firms or industries of forcing wages up to uncompetitive levels, but they might well reach deals that privilege insiders, externalizing negative consequences to outsiders in the workforce. On the other hand, high coverage without coordination suggests an economy in which a large amount of bargaining takes place, with little capacity to ensure competitiveness. Outsiders might also be created if bargaining strength varies considerably across the uncoordinated groups. We are therefore interested in the relationship between coordination and coverage, and this will be considered below.

Broadly and paradoxically, high coordination with high coverage is often seen to produce outcomes that conform more to market forces than low coordination with high coverage (Traxler et al. 2001). As was argued in Chapter 2, the more extensive and coordinated that collective bargaining is, the more it is likely to reconcile labour flexibility with high consumption. In an ideal neoliberal economy there are no trade unions; but there is a paradox here in that neoliberalism has to accept the general liberal principle of freedom of association. In a neoliberal world, therefore, unions can exist provided they can have no effect on wages and conditions. This means that in such an economy there should be no institutions for organized industrial relations; that is, no arrangements for collective bargaining. If bargaining does exist, then the smaller the proportion of the workforce involved, the better. Also, it should be as close to market as possible; that is, highly fragmented, uncoordinated, preferably limited to individual firms with no cross-firm linkage. The perfect neoliberal economy would therefore have zero scores on both coverage and coordination. Flexibility is achieved by pure market means, but maintaining consumption standards is also left to market forces.

Details of coordination and coverage are given in Appendix Table A6.1. These are based on the Amsterdam ICTWSS database (Visser 2013) that was also used to derive union membership density data in Chapter 3. The measure of coordination given in the database that most corresponds to our needs is that which combines a measure of the degree of authority in the union movement and the degree of external and internal unity, with a measure of union concentration that takes into account the multiple levels at which bargaining takes place. The combined score is expressed as an index where 1 would equal total coordination on both components. The ICTWSS statistics for coverage calculate that variable in relation to the number of workers in dependent employment, that is excluding the self-employed. For most purposes that is appropriate, as unions can do little for self-employed workers. However, we are here concerned with the whole-economy role of industrial relations systems. In Appendix Table A6.1 the available data for coverage have therefore been recalibrated to take account of the self-employed. The change has important implications for those SWE economies with particularly high levels of self-employment.

The state of encompassment derived by combining the scores for coordination and coverage (amended to take into account the self-employed) is shown in Figures 6.3a and b for the years around 2001 and

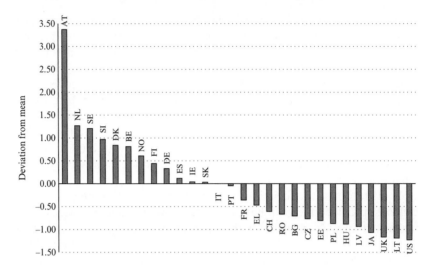

*Figure 6.3a   Bargaining encompassment, deflated for self-employed,
c.2001 (country scores in relation to standard deviation
around mean)*

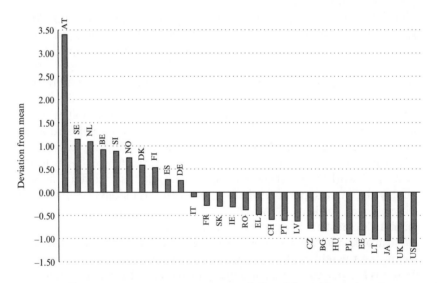

*Figure 6.3b   Bargaining encompassment, deflated for self-employed,
c.2011 (country scores in relation to standard deviation
around mean)*

2011 respectively. Unfortunately no comparable data are available for Croatia or Russia. The level of encompassment of the Austrian system is extraordinary, being the most outlying characteristic of any country in any variable considered in this study. Around 2001, high levels were also achieved in the Nordic countries, Slovenia and the Low Countries. It was particularly low in the USA, the UK, Japan, the Baltic states, most other CEE countries and Switzerland. There was a general decline in the overall encompassment of corporatist collective bargaining institutions in Europe, Japan and the USA between 2000 and 2010, but little variation in the position of individual countries. The European mean for encompassment *c.*2001 was 0.23 (where 1.00 = total encompassment); by 2010 it was 0.22. The standard deviation was stable at 0.17. In Japan it fell from 0.05 to 0.04, and in the USA it was stable at 0.02. These figures also give an indication of the extent to which encompassing collective bargaining is a 'European' phenomenon. Only in the UK and the Baltic states did it reach levels approaching those as low as in Japan and the USA.

Workers in the shadow economy are of course also excluded from the reach of unions, and, as we saw in Chapter 3, in some European countries this accounts for large numbers of workers, while in others it accounts for only a few. For an accurate comparative account of the actual scope within an economy of the bargaining system, especially if we want to take into account issues of inclusion and exclusion, we need to reduce the measure of encompassment accordingly, as was done for the self-employed. Revised estimates of encompassment on this basis, using the data presented for the shadow economy in Chapter 3, are shown in Figures 6.4a and 6.4b for *c.*2001 and *c.*2011 respectively. They make little difference to overall rankings, but obviously reduce the overall scores of all countries. The European mean of encompassment on this count was 0.18, with standard deviation stable at 0.15 at both time points. The Japanese and USA figures were stable at 0.04 and 0.02 respectively. These countries have very small shadow economies. Henceforth, we shall use bargaining coverage data that take into account the size of the shadow economy.

It should not be surprising that bargaining encompassment (doubly deflated) would correlate positively with degree of class challenge, as the latter variable includes union membership density, which is not entirely independent of encompassment, though it is by no means the same. Figure 6.5a presents this relationship for *c.*2001, when the correlation was $r^2 = 0.4225$. There are no exceptions to the relationship, apart from the extreme position of Austria, again the class challenge data being more important than any regional or wealth groupings. By 2011 (Figure 6.5b) the correlation was lower ($r^2 = 0.3893$), though here again there were no true exceptions.

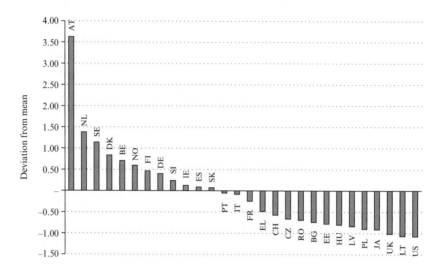

*Figure 6.4a   Bargaining encompassment, deflated for both self-employed
              and shadow economy, c.2001 (country scores in relation to
              standard deviation around mean)*

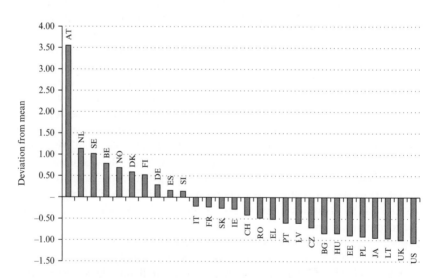

*Figure 6.4b   Bargaining encompassment, deflated for both self-employed
              and shadow economy, c.2011 (country scores in relation to
              standard deviation around mean)*

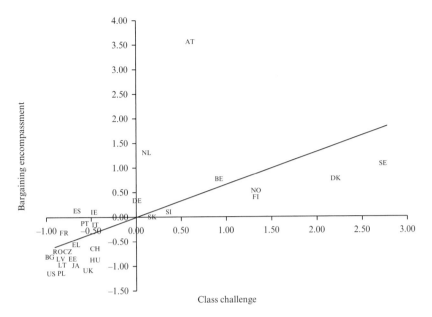

Figure 6.5a   *Bargaining encompassment (deflated) by class challenge,*
c.2001 (country scores in relation to standard deviations
around means)

By definition, the higher the encompassment of an industrial relations system, the fewer workers are excluded by it. Exclusion through the operation of collective bargaining should also be low where the two components of encompassment (coordination and coverage) are both low, as this indicates a bargaining system incapable of having much effect. On the other hand the two remaining opposed quadrants might indicate potential exclusion. Where coverage is high but coordination low, individual groups of bargainers in sectors of high coverage might be able to secure privileges. But this might also be the case where coverage is low (indicating few sectors covered) but coordination high (indicating bargaining strength). Figure 6.6a plots coordination against coverage for *c*.2001, to enable us to explore these relationships. We are here again using calculations of coverage that take account of both the self-employed and the shadow economy, as workers in these employment forms are particularly vulnerable to exclusion. According to the hypothesis, the top-right and bottom-left quadrants of Figures 6.6a and b are those where bargaining is, respectively, either too coordinated or too weak to make exclusion a problem. Where there is high but uncoordinated coverage there might be exclusion. Around 2001

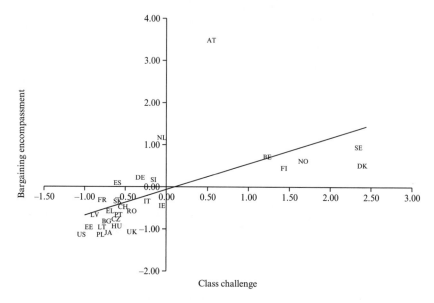

Figure 6.5b *Bargaining encompassment (deflated) by class challenge,*
            c.2011 (country scores in relation to standard deviations
            around means)

this would apply mainly to France, and possibly to Greece and Portugal. There are no clear cases of high coordination and low coverage, except perhaps Latvia.

We might consider that absolute levels of coverage are more important to possibilities of exclusion. As an arbitrary rule of thumb, we might surmise that once bargaining coverage comes below two-thirds of the workforce there is a danger that a minority starts to be excluded from any benefits from bargaining. Once coverage goes below 50 per cent, it might be a majority that is excluded. Below one-third coverage bargaining, if effective at all, will probably be defending a small group of privileged insiders. Figures 6.7a and b enable us to identify potential candidates for this. We might regard those in the first group, from Austria to Belgium, as being fully encompassing – though there are doubts about the effectiveness of encompassment in Belgium given governments' frequent resort to state intervention to resolve impasses in collective bargaining coordination (Hemerijck and Marx 2010: 148); those from Finland to Germany as potentially excluding a minority; those from Italy to Greece as excluding the majority (i.e., defending a minority); and those from the Czech Republic to Lithuania as defending small insider groups.

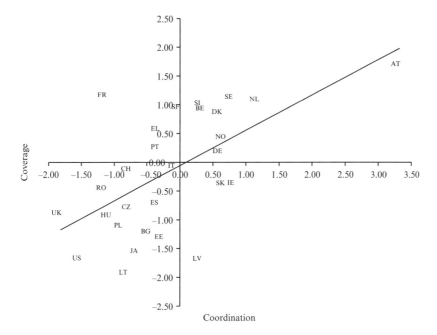

Figure 6.6a   Bargaining coordination by coverage, c.2001 (country scores in relation to standard deviations around means)

Figure 6.6b presents the same comparison of coordination and coverage for c.2011 as Figure 6.6a did for c.2001. There has been little change: France again appearing as potentially practising exclusion, but possibly also, through the opposite mechanism, Latvia, Slovakia and Ireland. Figure 6.7b does the same for c.2011 as Figure 6.7a did for c.2001. The Netherlands has dropped from the ranks of those with over two-thirds coverage, and, following the general decline of bargaining coverage, there has been an increase in the number of cases where bargaining might protect small groups of insiders.

Public Employment

The role of public employment as a labour-market stabilizer is not easy to assess without detailed information on how public sector pay is determined. All we can do is examine the relative size of public sector employment in a country. Data are available on this variable from the International Labour Organization (ILO annual) (see Appendix A6.1), but several countries do not provide their data on a comparable basis and

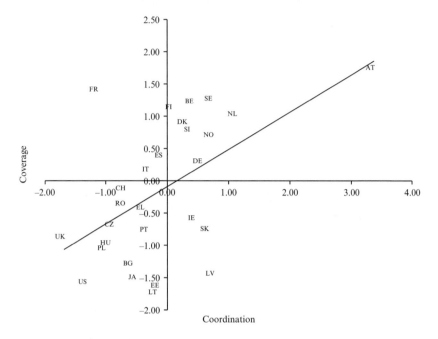

*Figure 6.6b	Bargaining coordination by coverage, c.2011 (country scores in relation to standard deviations around means)*

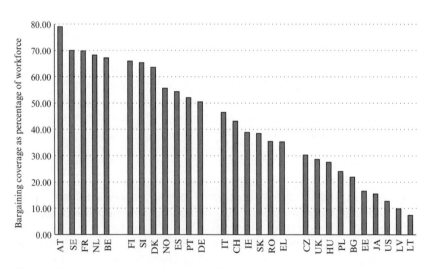

*Figure 6.7a	Bargaining coverage, c.2001*

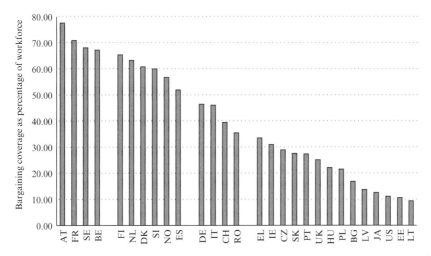

Figure 6.7b   Bargaining coverage, c.2011

therefore have had to be excluded: Austria, Czech Republic, Hungary, Italy, Netherlands, Portugal and the USA. (For evidence of the way in which public employment serves as both a stabilizer and a source of privilege in Hungary, see Köllő 2011.)

The data for 2000 (Figure 6.8a) show extremely high levels of public employment for Croatia, and high levels for Russia, Norway, Denmark; and moderately high levels for Lithuania, Latvia, Sweden, Slovakia and Bulgaria. This is the first time we have encountered such a Nordic and CEE grouping. Extremely low levels were found in Japan, very low levels in Switzerland, Spain, Germany and Ireland, and low levels in the UK, Greece and Belgium. There was a low positive correlation with the class challenge indicator (Figure 6.9a), $r^2 = 0.073$. The cases are scattered around the quadrants, though Belgium is the only case of a strong challenge country with low public employment.

Data were not available at the time of writing for 2010 for several countries, so data for 2008 have had to be used. Figure 6.8b presents the results. The overall European mean for public employment had declined from 26.6 per cent to 23.05 per cent, that for Japan from 8.1 per cent to 7.0 per cent, and for Russia from 37.5 per cent to 30.3 per cent. Much of the European (and Russian) decline resulted from the major gradual dismantling of the large state sectors in CEE countries. As a result, the relationship between this variable and class challenge (Figure 6.9b) shows a fortuitous rise, with $r^2 = 0.2235$. The quadrant of strong class challenge and weak public employment is now empty.

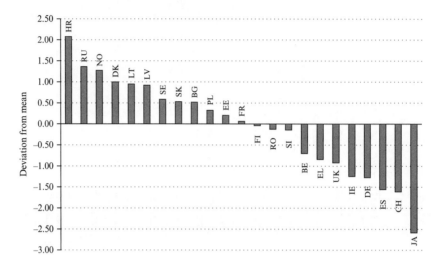

*Figure 6.8a   Public employment as a proportion of all employment, c.2000
              (country scores in relation to standard deviation around
              mean)*

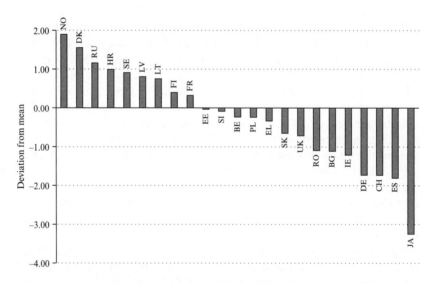

*Figure 6.8b   Public employment as a proportion of all employment, 2008
              (country scores in relation to standard deviation around
              mean)*

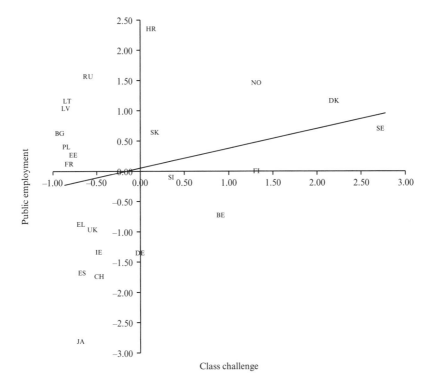

Figure 6.9a   Public employment by class challenge, c.2000 (country scores in relation to standard deviations around means)

It is difficult to determine the extent to which public employment has a stabilizing effect or creates privileged insider groups among public employees. We can examine this in part by examining the difference in collective bargaining coverage between the public and private sectors. Where coverage in the former is considerably higher, we might presume that certain insider effects are at work. Figures 6.10a and b enable us to examine this on the basis of information in the ICTWSS database (see Appendix A6.1), although unfortunately for only a few countries. Around 2001 there were grounds for suspecting extremely strong public sector insider status in Ireland, very strong public insider status in the UK, and strong public insider status in Norway, the USA and Germany; but that there was none in Slovenia, Austria, Hungary, Sweden and France. By *c.*2011 Spain had joined the list of potentially protected. At the other end Hungary had become the extreme case, being the only country where bargaining levels in the private sector had actually become higher than in the public.

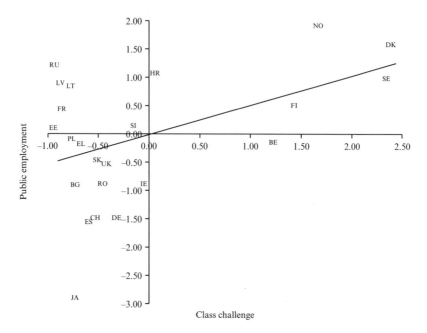

Figure 6.9b   Public employment by class challenge, 2008 (country scores
            in relation to standard deviations around means)

However, these figures do not enable us to judge whether remuneration actually increased faster in the public sector, justifying the potential label of 'privileged'. Some light is thrown on this by a European Central Bank Study (Giordano et al. 2011), which compared changes in wages and salaries and in total compensation packages in the private and public sectors in certain countries between 1999 and 2007. The coverage was limited to Austria, Belgium, France, Germany, Greece, Ireland, Italy, Portugal, Slovenia and Spain. It showed total compensation improving faster in the public sectors in Belgium, France, Greece, Ireland, Italy and Spain, though in Belgium and France by only very small amounts. The pattern was similar for wages and salaries considered alone, except that there the French private sector advanced clearly more than the public sector. In the remaining countries both total compensation as well as wages and salaries alone advanced more strongly in the private than in the public sector. With the exception of Belgium, all cases where the private sector advanced more rapidly had levels of bargaining encompassment in 2010 above the mean, while all those where the public sector advanced more rapidly had levels below the mean. This limited evidence suggests that (apart from Belgium)

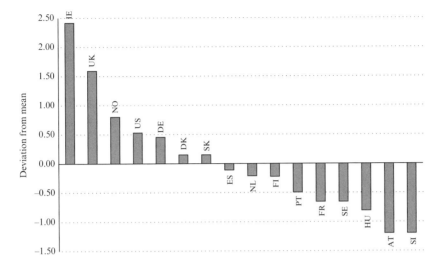

Figure 6.10a   Differences in bargaining coverage, public over private
(excluding self-employment and shadow economy), c.2001
(country scores in relation to standard deviation around
mean)

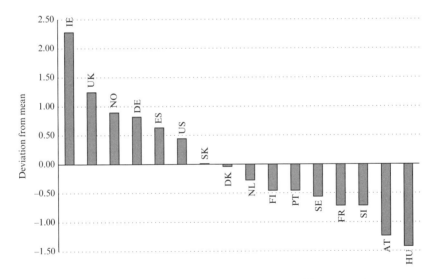

Figure 6.10b   Differences in bargaining coverage, public over private
(excluding self-employment and shadow economy), c.2011
(country scores in relation to standard deviation around
mean)

encompassing bargaining tends to operate on this specific question in the way predicted for it in general by collective action theory: it tends to limit the protection of privileged groups.

Active Labour Market Policy

ALMP seeks to equip people with labour market problems with skills and other attributes that would facilitate their entry into the labour market (Van den Berg and De Gier 2008). Eurostat usefully defines these problems as possessed by the unemployed, those whose employment is at risk (mainly through imminent redundancy), and those outside the labour market (such as the disabled) but who wish to enter it. Included in the calculations are: publicly financed training, job rotation and sharing schemes, employment incentives for potential employers, supported employment and rehabilitation, direct job creation, and start-up incentives to encourage self-employment. We are not including here the so-called 'passive' policies of unemployment benefits, as these were considered in the previous chapter as examples of policies that separate standard of living from labour force participation. Presumably the data include spending on 'workfare' policies, which are not covered by our own concept of ALMP as protecting people from insecurity, and it is difficult to disentangle these. In general, however, the more 'positive' measures are more expensive, so the more a country is spending on ALMP, the more it is likely to be using these policies to integrate consumption and labour income; the less it is spending, the more likely it is to be using 'workfare' only.

Figures 6.11a and b show the percentage of GDP spent by countries on ALMP *c.*2000 and *c.*2010 respectively. Data are missing for Croatia, Switzerland and the three non-European comparators. There is so much variation around the mean that all of our cases (except Denmark) fall within the 0.5 SD range. If we adjust to take 0.2 SD as a threshold, we can regard spending levels in Denmark, Sweden, Germany and France as being high, and those in the UK, Estonia, Latvia and Slovakia as being low. The mean fell very slightly between 2000 and 2010, from 0.56 per cent to 0.53 per cent. Only Denmark and Belgium had particularly high levels, while no countries came above the −0.2 SD threshold at the lower end.

It might be expected that ALMP spending would increase with the size of the population in need. This possibility is explored in Figures 6.12a and b, which relate the spending level to the proportion of the population aged 20–64 not in work. In fact, some countries with the highest proportions of their workforces in work also spend high sums on ALMP, while some with low levels of activity spend small amounts. In 2000, Denmark and Sweden were extreme outliers with high spending on this measure. The

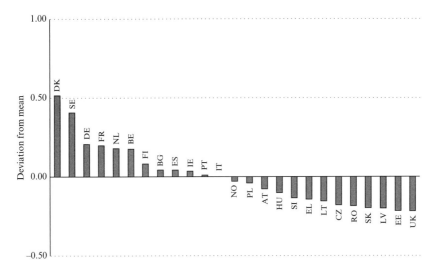

Figure 6.11a   ALMP spending as a percentage of GDP, c.2000 (country scores in relation to standard deviation around mean)

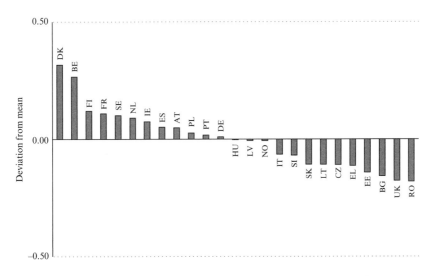

Figure 6.11b   ALMP spending as a percentage of GDP, c.2010 (country scores in relation to standard deviation around mean)

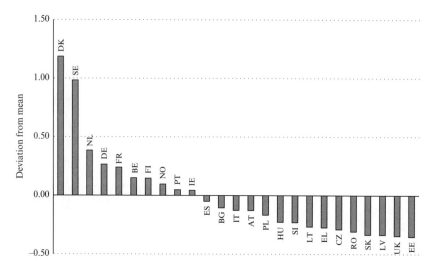

Figure 6.12a   ALMP spending per working-age population not in
*   employment, as a percentage of GDP, c.2000 (country*
*   scores in relation to standard deviation around mean)*

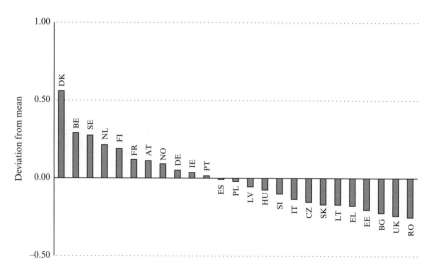

Figure 6.12b   ALMP spending per working-age population not in
*   employment, as a percentage of GDP, c.2010 (country*
*   scores in relation to standard deviation around mean)*

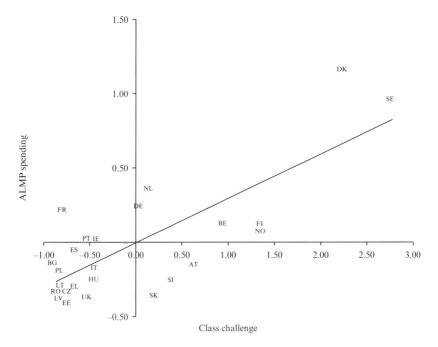

*Figure 6.13a   ALMP spending per working-age population not in
employment by class challenge, c.2000 (country scores in
relation to standard deviations around means)*

correlation with the class challenge indicator (Figure 6.13a) was high at
$r^2 = 0.6029$. France is the only country with weak class challenge spending
above the mean, while only three countries (Slovakia and Slovenia, and to
a lesser extent Austria) with strong class challenge at that time spent below
the mean. The lowest spenders were certain CEE countries and the UK.
By 2010 Denmark had become the most strongly performing country. A
similar combination of countries as in 2000 has the stronger performances,
and again some CEE countries and the UK perform weakest. The relationship between ALMP spending per non-working population and class
challenge (Figure 6.13b) has strengthened slightly to $r^2 = 0.6302$.

Employment Protection Law

Legal measures to protect workers from losing their jobs as the result of
market fluctuations consist mainly of employment protection laws (EPL)
of various kinds. The OECD has developed an EPL indicator, which

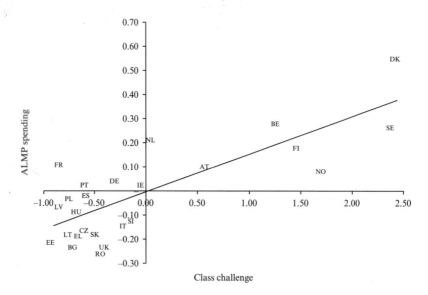

*Figure 6.13b   ALMP spending per working-age population not in
              employment by class challenge, c.2010 (country scores in
              relation to standard deviations around means)*

assesses the strength of a number of legally mandated employee rights to
protect workers with open-ended contracts against individual and collective dismissal. It makes a separate calculation for protections for temporary workers (i.e., those on fixed-term contracts), which of course take a
different form. Questions can be asked about the aggregation procedure;
why assume that, say, protections from redundancy and against unfair
dismissal have the same importance? It is difficult to resolve such issues,
and here we are using the simple OECD measures, so the criticism remains
valid in relation to that use.

There is also the same problem that we considered in connection with
collective bargaining coverage: assessment of employment protection
leaves out the self-employed and the shadow economy. Also, although
the OECD has a specific indicator for assessing protection of temporary
workers, their rights clearly have a very different basis from those of
permanent employees. The self-employed are always more exposed to
the market than employees, even where the latter have few forms of legal
protection. What became the normal work form of the twentieth-century
economy – employment on an ongoing, indefinite contract by a firm or
other employing organization – is rarely fully exposed to the market, as
workers are to some extent protected from its rigours by the fact that

employers do not normally have routine recourse to market testing, laying-off existing staff every time they find they can find better or cheaper employees. Workers in the shadow economy are the most exposed of all to pure market insecurity. We can take all these factors into account by appropriately deflating the EPL indicator.

Appendix Table A6.2 (see p. 275) demonstrates successive stages of this process. Unfortunately data are available only for OECD member states, so we cannot consider Bulgaria, Croatia, Lithuania, Romania, Russia – or, in 2000, Latvia. The table first shows the original OECD scores for the strength of employment protection for employees with open-ended contracts. The relative scores around the mean using these basic data are summarized in Figures 6.14a and b for *c*.2000 and *c*.2010 respectively. The OECD updated its EPL scores in 2013. Turning first to *c*.2000, we see Portugal with a far higher level than anywhere else, followed by a varied group of countries. There is more obvious coherence in the lowest scores, where the three Anglophone countries are clustered together, followed by Japan, but then by a more mixed group. By 2010 there had been some major changes. Overall there is a slight decline in the European mean (from 2.65 to 2.49), no change in the already extremely low US score, and some reduction in the standard deviation (from 0.49 to 0.31), indicating some convergence on deregulation. There has been some considerable deregulation in Portugal, and also in Greece, leaving Germany, Latvia and the Netherlands with the highest levels.

However, in order to assess the amount of legal protection of employment rights within the workforce as a whole represented by EPL, we need to deflate the index to take account of the size of various excluded groups: workers on temporary contracts; the self-employed; those in the shadow workforce. Details of the first are given in Appendix Table A6.2;

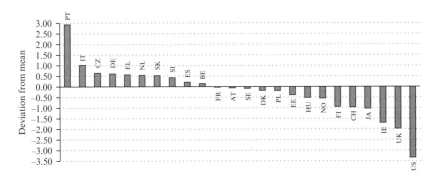

Figure 6.14a   *EPL (permanent workers), basic data, c.2000 (country scores in relation to standard deviation around mean)*

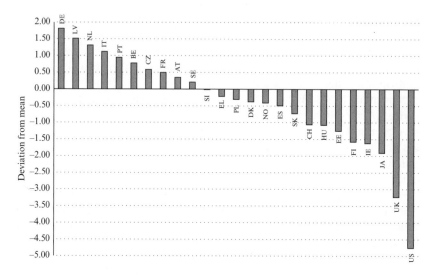

Figure 6.14b　EPL (permanent workers), basic data, c.2010 (country scores in relation to standard deviation around mean)

those for the self-employed and shadow economy are given in Appendix Table A3.1 (see p. 263). These data are usually for 2010, but have been applied here to the OECD's EPL index for 2013. This does not exhaust the real limitations that might reduce the impact of EPL. For example, the model assumes equal efficacy of law enforcement across countries, which we know is not the case. However, it is the best we can do. In the following analysis we shall use this final, most comprehensive calculation, summarized in Appendix Table A6.2, with the relative scores displayed in Figures 6.15a (*c.*2000) and b (2013). Unfortunately we lose some countries in the process, where data are missing for some of the relevant variables. These scores give us a measure not of the strength of EPL provisions but of the employment protection that these provisions offer on average to the workforce as a whole.

The revised data for *c.*2000 no longer show Portugal as having the highest level of protection. This is a position held by Slovakia, followed by three NWE countries (Netherlands, Austria and Germany). Also high are the Czech Republic, France and Denmark. It is now two SWE countries (Spain and Greece), which are seen to offer the lowest level of overall protection, despite the high level of their initial EPL score, followed by Poland, Ireland, Italy, Hungary and the UK. There are signs here of the trade-off asserted in much economics literature: in at least some countries, strong EPL exists for some workers at the expense of others. It

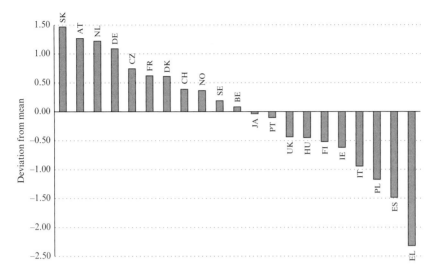

Figure 6.15a   Overall protection offered by EPL (permanent workers) to whole workforce c.2000 (country scores in relation to standard deviation around mean)

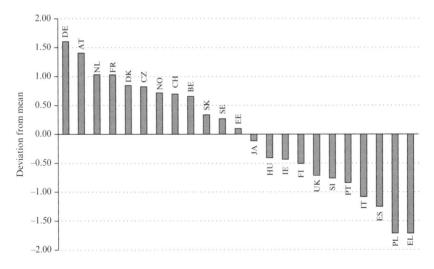

Figure 6.15b   Overall protection offered by EPL (permanent workers) to whole workforce c.2013 (country scores in relation to standard deviation around mean)

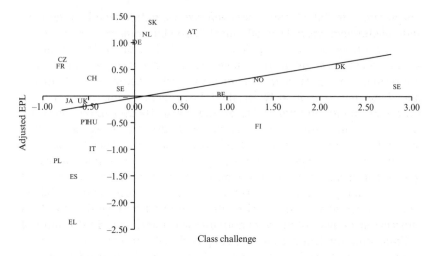

Figure 6.16a   Adjusted EPL by class challenge, c.2000 (country scores in relation to standard deviations around means)

must be noted that the reduction in the strength of EPL that takes place in certain countries when we exclude various categories of worker does not invalidate economists' criticisms that in these countries strict labour laws reduce flexibility, since the critics are pointing explicitly to the exclusionary nature of EPL.

The correlation with the class challenge indicator (Figure 6.16a) is very weak ($r^2 = 0.1020$); trade union strength was not related to EPL in the way that it was to ALMP. It is however also the case that the only country with strong class challenge to have a low relative level of EPL was Finland.

By 2010–13 data are available for a slightly larger number of countries. There have been various fluctuations in individual countries' scores, but no overall trend except for a major decline in Slovakia. The resulting revised relative scores are shown in Figure 6.15b. The overall correlation with class challenge (Figure 6.16b) remains very weak and is virtually the same ($r^2 = 0.0984$).

INCLUSIVE OR EXCLUSIVE?

Discussion of the position of temporary workers brings us to an appropriate point for considering to what extent the policies that tend to integrate consumption stability and labour income in general, and not just EPL as such, do so at the expense of certain outsider groups within society. Several

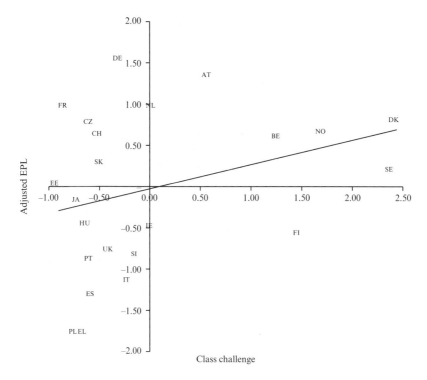

Figure 6.16b   Adjusted EPL by class challenge, c.2010 (country scores in relation to standard deviations around means)

points of evidence relative to answering this question have appeared in the course of the above discussion.

A first estimate of exclusion from the benefits of security that can be afforded by labour markets must be of all persons in the age range 20–64 years who are not in work of some kind. Appendix Table A6.2 provides statistics on our usual basis for this basic datum, and for the final adjusted figure. The basic number will be an exaggeration, as it will include the very small number of people who live on inherited wealth or investment earnings and the rather large group of mothers who work in the household only and not in the labour market. These latter might feel secure if they have a partner who can reliably provide for them, but that proportion is unknown and is always at risk. Particularly when we are looking at comparative data and seeking exceptional or extreme cases it seems reasonable to assume that the number in these categories will not vary much among countries. We rely on Eurostat statistics for further adjustments, which unfortunately leads us to exclude Croatia, Switzerland and our non-European comparators. We deduct from the total figure for those in work all those in temporary or short-term employment, as they lack expectations of security. Similar arguments apply to the self-employed. A minority of the self-employed are professional and business people who cannot be considered as insecure, but their numbers are small, and possibly evenly distributed. In countries where there are large numbers of self-employed, the great majority of them are likely to be in precarious positions, with little or no protection from the market. We therefore include among those who do not benefit from normal working status the number of self-employed. It has to be assumed that those working in the shadow economy have already been included among those stated to be not in work, though we cannot be sure that this will always be the case when people respond to labour-market survey questions. No further account is therefore taken here of the shadow economy.

When we add in the specified groups, the proportion of the potential workforce that is excluded from whatever protections come from 'normal' labour-market status (not just EPL) is high. The European mean for the excluded on this definition was 48.62 per cent, rising slightly to 49.34 per cent by 2012. In SWE, Hungary and Poland the figure was above 50 per cent in 2000. By 2012 this also applied to Ireland, Romania and Slovenia.

Details of relative positions on these basic exclusions are shown in Figures 6.17a and b for *c*.2000 and *c*.2010–12 respectively. It is notable that the four countries with the highest levels of exclusion around 2000 are the four SWE countries. Poland and Bulgaria also had relatively high levels. Those with least exclusion included the Nordic and Baltic countries, the UK, Austria and the Netherlands. By 2010–12 there had been little change. The SWE cases continue to have high exclusion levels, and the level of exclusion in Poland rose further, but that in Bulgaria declined considerably. The lowest levels cover similar countries as before.

There is considerable debate over whether part-time work counts as 'normal' employment, as there is evidence that many people, particularly women, positively seek this employment form. In several countries its growing availability has helped increase female labour-force participation and to reconcile that participation with the maintenance of family life. It does not make sense to include such workers as automatically among the excluded. However, for some EU countries we do have data, though only for 2010, for the numbers of part-time workers who would prefer to have been able to find full-time work – the so-called 'reluctant part-timers'. Statistics are given in Appendix Table A6.2. We can reasonably conclude that these workers are excluded from a form of labour-market

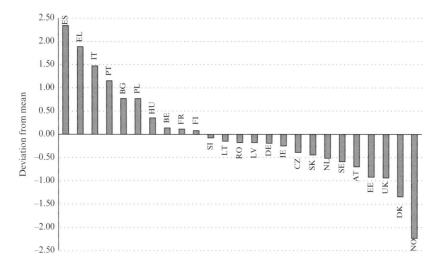

Figure 6.17a   Exclusion from core labour market, 2000 (country scores in relation to standard deviation around mean)

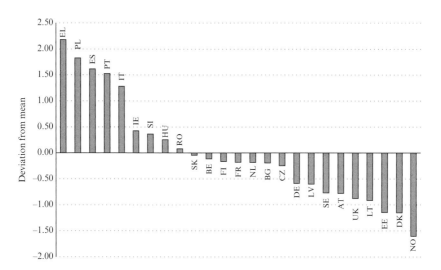

Figure 6.17b   Exclusion from core labour market, 2010–12 (country scores in relation to standard deviation around mean)

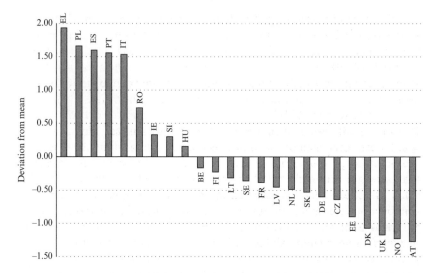

Figure 6.18   Exclusion from core labour market (including reluctant part-time), 2010–12 (country scores in relation to standard deviation around mean)

participation that they would prefer to have. If we add the proportion of the total number of employed persons who are reluctantly working only part time to the aggregate for the excluded for the years around 2010, we arrive at the data shown in Figure 6.18. This shows even more clearly the extremely high levels of exclusion in Poland and SWE, with Austria, Norway, the UK and Denmark having particularly low levels. By the time we have taken account of all these exclusions, the European average for the proportion of the population of workforce age not part of the core system of formal employment has risen to 65.74 per cent, ranging from 51.63 per cent in Austria to 87.25 per cent in Greece.

Given the lack of availability of data on reluctant part-timers for the years around 2000, we shall restrict further analysis to those that do not take account of this aspect, that is to those considered in Figures 6.17a and b. In 2000 there was a modest negative relationship between class challenge and exclusion from the core labour market (Figure 6.19a), with $r^2 = 0.2236$. No countries combined strong class challenge with high exclusion of more than marginally above the mean, while only the Czech Republic, Estonia and the UK combined weak challenge with more than marginally low exclusion.

By 2010 the correlation declines to $r^2 = 0.1688$ (Figure 6.19b). Again, no country combines strong challenge with high exclusion; as a result of

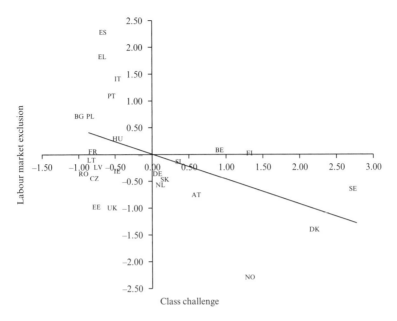

Figure 6.19a   *Exclusion from core labour market by class challenge,*
c.2000 (country scores in relation to standard deviations
around means)

the decline in its class challenge score, Germany and the two other Baltics
join Estonia and the UK as the only countries with minus scores of more
than marginal weight on both variables. The SWE group (with Poland)
again has the highest levels, with the rest of CEE being scattered around
the graph.

By comparing EPL scores with estimates of labour market exclusion,
we can consider whether formal employment protection is associated with
high levels of exclusion. There is considerable debate in the economics
literature over whether EPL causes labour-market exclusion, whether
by reducing overall employment rates, or by encouraging the use of
temporary contracts or the shadow economy. Some of this literature will
be reviewed in the next chapter. Our immediate concern is more modest
than this, as we are not seeking straightforward causal relations. Whether
strong EPL directly 'causes' exclusion is secondary to, and probably
included within, the wider question of the extent to which there is a positive association between the two variables. The causal relationship might
be less straightforward. It is possible, for example, that governments and
employers are more willing to accept high levels of labour protection when
they are aware that it will apply to only a small part of the workforce.

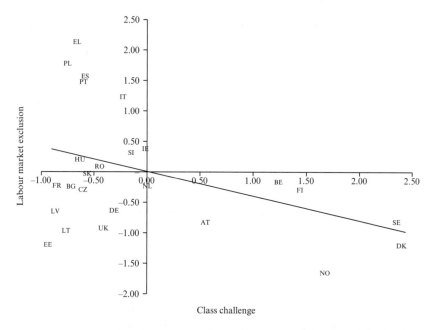

Figure 6.19b　　*Exclusion from core labour market by class challenge,
c.2010–12 (country scores in relation to standard deviations
around means)*

The appropriate measure of EPL here is the original unadjusted OECD scores for the strength of EPL for permanent employees, as the employment factors we used to deflate this now appear in the second variable. In Figures 6.20a (*c.*2000) and 6.20b (*c.*2010) we plot these against the exclusion figure reached in the previous discussion, counting as those excluded from labour market security all temporary workers and the self-employed.

Around 2000 there was a low but positive association between protection and exclusion ($r^2 = 0.1825$), consistent with the neoliberal hypothesis, but the spread of countries across the graph shows greater complexity. Consistent with the expectation that high protection will be associated with a high level of exclusion is the experience of the four SWE countries. The opposing quadrant (low protection, low exclusion) is populated, as one might expect if this is a neoliberal hypothesis, by Ireland and the UK, but also (if at only marginally low levels of EPL) by the Scandinavian countries and Austria. Only two countries (Hungary and Poland) occupy the least secure quadrant (low protection, high exclusion). Most of the remaining cases seem to be able to combine moderately high EPL with moderately low to low levels of exclusion: the Netherlands, Slovakia, and

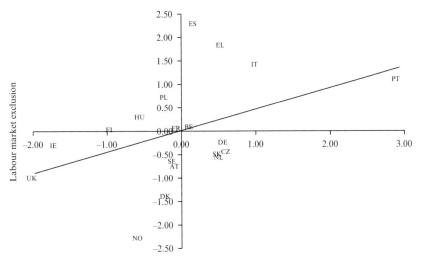

Figure 6.20a   *EPL by general labour market exclusion, c.2000 (country scores in relation to standard deviations around means)*

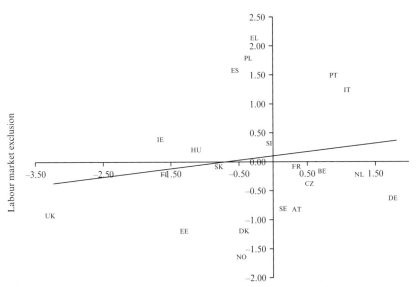

Figure 6.20b   *EPL by general labour market exclusion, c.2010 (country scores in relation to standard deviations around means)*

(marginally) the Czech Republic and Germany. This leaves Belgium and France with profiles too indistinct to classify.

Reductions took place in EPL in several countries by 2010, in response partly to the economic crisis, and partly to the recommendations of neo-liberal economists, and the countries included expand slightly to take in Estonia and Slovenia, though this has no effect on the overall distribution. The statistical correlation is now very weak ($r^2 = 0.0254$). The 'exclusion-ary protective' quadrant is occupied by just two cases, Italy and Portugal. Only Estonia and the UK adhere closely to the neoliberal hypothesis, though some Nordic countries are marginal members of this quadrant. The 'worst-of-all-worlds' quadrant (low EPL, high exclusion) includes a mix of CEE and SWE countries, while all remaining countries manage to occupy the 'best of all worlds'.

CONCLUSIONS

Organizing countries into paths through the variables under considera-tion in this chapter is easier than in the previous two chapters, as we have just two forms of governance: the state and associational governance via coordinated collective bargaining. Our data on relative inclusion and exclusion are then added, as in Chapter 5. The only complex variable is the set of state actions. The most important of these will be government revenue, as it is clearly the largest of the three components measured in terms of percentage of GDP, and also of more general reach than EPL. Special attention will therefore be paid to cases where the ranking on this variable diverges strongly from those on the other three state variables. Unfortunately we have been unable to collect enough data on Russia to be able to include it in this summary. Table 6.1 summarizes the positions of countries on the key relevant variables for the years around 2000 consid-ered in the chapter.

We can cluster countries on the following basis:

- X (use of state means): Countries with above-mean scores for government.
- Y (use of associational means): Countries with above-mean scores for coordinated collective bargaining.
- Z (neither): Countries with below-mean scores on both X and Y.
- Sub-clusters (i) and (ii) indicate degree of inclusion following the account in Table 5.4 (see Chapter 5, p. 150). In each cluster coun-tries are listed under (i) and counted as having strong inclusion if they score relatively highly on proportion of the population

Table 6.1 Summary table, approaches to labour market security, c.2000

	State actions				Bargaining encompassment	Inclusion
	Government revenue	Public employment	ALMP	EPL (adjusted)		
Extremely high	SE	HR			AT	
Very high	DK FI NO HR	RU NO DK	DK	SK AT NL DE	NL SE	NO AT UK DK
High	AT FR BE	LT LV SE SK BG	SE	CZ FR DK	SI DK BE NO	NL SK EE IE
Moderately high	NL DE IT	PL EE	NL DE FR BE FI NO	CH NO SE	FI DE ES	DE SE CZ FR LV
Indifferent	HU EL	FR FI	PT IE ES	BE JA	IE SK IT PT	FI
Moderately low	SI SK PL	RO SI	BG IT AT PL HU SI LT EL CZ RO SK LV UK EE	PT UK HU	FR EL	BE LT SI HU RO PL
Low	BG UK CZ ES EE PT IE LV	BE EL UK		FI IE IT	CH RO BG CZ EE PL HU LV JA UK LT US	PT BG IT EL ES
Very low	LT CH RO US JA	IE DE ES CH JA		PL ES EL		
Extremely low	RU	AT CZ HU IT NL PT US				
No data			HR JA RU CH US	BG HR EE HU LV LT RO RU SI US	HR RU	HR JA RU CH US

aged 20 to 64 years in non-precarious employment. They are listed under (ii) and counted as not having strong inclusion if they score below mean on this variable. Given the lack of data for several countries on this variable, we also need an intermediate 'unknown' category.

Proceeding on this basis enables us to identify the following *c*.2000:

- Cluster 6 (2000) X(i): strong role for state alone, high inclusion: France; possibly Croatia (inclusion and associational governance unknown).
- Cluster 6 (2000) X/Y(i): strong role for state and associational governance with high inclusion: Austria, Denmark, Germany, Netherlands, Norway, Sweden.
- Cluster 6 (2000) X/Y(ii): as X/Y(i) with low inclusion: Belgium; marginally Finland.
- Cluster 6 (2000) X/Y(ii): strong role for associational governance alone, low inclusion: Slovenia.
- Cluster 6 (2000) X/Z(i): low government revenue, but strong role for public employment; weak associational governance; high inclusion: Estonia, Latvia (partial exception: indeterminate level of collective bargaining: Slovakia).
- Cluster 6 (2000) X/Z(ii): as X/Z(i) but low inclusion: Bulgaria, Lithuania, Poland, possibly Russia (inclusion unknown).
- Cluster 6 (2000) Z(i): weak state and associational governance; high inclusion: Czech Republic (*note*: level of public employment unknown; could be X/Z(i)), UK (partial exception: indeterminate strength of collective bargaining: Ireland).
- Cluster 6 (2000) Z(ii): as Cluster 6 (2000) Z(i) with high levels of exclusion: Greece, Spain; Hungary and Romania (*note*: level of public employment unknown; could be X/Z(ii)) (partial exception: indeterminate collective bargaining: Portugal).
- Cluster 6 (2000) Z?: as Cluster 6 (2000) Z(i), but level of inclusion unknown: Japan, Switzerland, the USA.

Table 6.2 shows the distribution across these paths of countries ranked according to class challenge, and with inclusion indicated as in Chapter 5 (with high inclusion indicated in bold type; those with unknown or indifferent inclusion given in italics; and those with low inclusion shown in normal type). Class challenge emerges as a very strong predictor as to where countries will fall. Again the 11 countries with the strongest class challenge all have relatively strong state and/or associational governance,

Table 6.2   *Governance of labour market security by class challenge,*
            c.2000

		Clusters 6 (*c.*2000)		
X	X/Y	Y	X/Z	Z
	Sweden			
	Denmark			
	Norway			
	Finland			
	Belgium			
	Austria			
		Slovenia		
			(Slovakia)	
	Croatia			
	Netherlands			
	Germany			
				Hungary
				Switzerland
				Italy
				(Ireland)
				(Portugal)
				UK
			Russia	
				Spain
				Greece
				Japan
			Estonia	
				Czech Republic
France				
			Lithuania	
			Poland	
			Latvia	
				Romania
			Bulgaria	
				USA

Note:
Countries with high inclusion are indicated in bold type
Countries with unknown or indifferent inclusion are indicated in italic type
Countries with low inclusion are indicated in normal type

and the great majority of them have both. Only France stands out as a clear exception to this principle in having strong state governance alone and very weak class challenge. All countries with lower class challenge rankings have weak governance on these dimensions, irrespective of their geo-economic region or wealth. Some countries with weak challenge have low levels of exclusion, and these are a combination of the European Anglophone countries and certain cases in CEE. The X/Z group deserves special note: these are all CEE countries with generally weak state and associational governance, except for a high level of public employment. Apart from the problematic inclusion of Slovakia in this cluster, the countries where this particular form of protection applied were all those with the very weakest level of class challenge, except for France and the USA.

Table 6.3 shows the spread of countries across the key variables for the *c*.2010 data. This enables us to allocate them on the various paths as follows:

- Cluster 6 (2010) X(i): strong role for state alone, with high inclusion: France (possibly Croatia, inclusion and associational governance unknown).
- Cluster 6 (2010) X/Y(i): strong role for state and associational governance, high inclusion: Austria, Denmark, Finland, Germany, Netherlands, Norway, Sweden; also Belgium, with only marginally above-mean score for inclusion.
- Cluster 6 (2010) Y(ii): strong role for associational governance alone, with low inclusion: Spain, Slovenia (on margins of X/Y(ii), but state action indeterminate).
- Cluster 6 (2010) X/Z(i): strong role for public employment; otherwise weak governance; high inclusion: Latvia, Lithuania.
- Cluster 6 (2010) Z(i): weak state and associational governance; high inclusion: Estonia, Ireland, Slovakia, UK; possibly Czech Republic (*note*: level of public employment unknown; could be X/Z(i)).
- Cluster 6 (2010) Z(ii): as Z(i), but with low inclusion: Bulgaria, Greece; Poland, Portugal, Romania (partial exceptions: state action indifferent: Hungary, Italy).
- Cluster 6 (2010) Z?: as Z(i), but with inclusion unknown: Japan, Switzerland, the USA.

The picture is simpler than in 2000, with polarization around Clusters X/Y and Z. Changes in inclusion have the effect of raising the relative positions of Belgium, Finland and Lithuania; falls in state employment in CEE push several countries from Cluster X/Z to Z. General changes in collective bargaining, in particular the strong decline in CEE countries, move Spain to Y and Ireland firmly into Z.

Table 6.3   Summary table, approaches to labour market security, c.2010

	State actions				Bargaining encompassment	Inclusion
	Government revenue	Public employment	ALMP	EPL		
Extremely high						
Very high	NO DK FI SE HR	NO DK RU			AT NL SE	NO UK AT DK
High	FR BE AT HU	HR SE LV LT	DK		BE NO SI DK FI	EE DE SE
Moderately high	IT NL DE	FI FR	BE SE NL FI FR AT	DE AT NL FR DK CZ	DE ES	LT FR CZ LV NL SK FI
Indifferent	SI	EE SI	NO DE IE PT ES PL LV HU	CH BE SK SE EE JA HU IE FI UK SI		BE
Moderately low	PT EL UK	BE PL EL	SI IT CZ SK LT EL EE BG UK RO	PT IT ES PL EL	IT FR SK IE CH RO EL	IE HU BG
Low	CZ EE PL ES BG	SK UK			PT LV CZ HU BG PL EE JA LT UK	SI RO
Very low	IE LV LT CH RO SK JA	RO BG IE DE CH ES JA			US	IT PT ES PL
Extremely low	US					EL
No data	RU	AT CZ HU IT NL PT US	HR JA RU CH US	BG HR LV LT NO RO RU US	HR RU	HR JA RU CH US

Table 6.4   *Governance of labour market security by class challenge,*
              c.2010

		Clusters 6 (*c*.2010)		
X	X/Y	Y	X/Z	Z
	Denmark			
	Sweden			
	Norway			
	Finland			
	Belgium			
	Austria			
(*Croatia*)				
	Netherlands			
				Ireland
		Slovenia		
				Italy
	Germany			
				UK
				Romania
				Slovakia
				Switzerland
		Spain		
				Portugal
				Czech Republic
				Hungary
				Greece
				Bulgaria
				Japan
				Poland
			Lithuania	
France				
			Latvia	
				Estonia
				USA

Note:
Countries with high inclusion are indicated in bold type
Countries with unknown or indifferent inclusion are indicated in italic type
Countries with low inclusion are indicated in normal type

Table 6.4 provides the matching against the class challenge index. Even more clearly than in 2000, strong class challenge is associated with Cluster X/Y, strong state action and encompassing collective bargaining, and in particular with the inclusive form of that path (i). Only France once again provides a strong exception to that principle, alone in pursuing path X. Slovenia, and possibly also the other ex-Yugoslav case, Croatia, have strong class challenge and low inclusion. Cluster X/Z, with strong public employment but no other strong state action on this chapter's variables, which had been occupied by a number of CEE states, is now the resort of only Latvia and Lithuania; the third Baltic state, Estonia, has an indifferent score on this variable. All three are relatively inclusive. The great majority of countries with weak class challenge occupy Cluster Z, again with the Anglophone countries, the Czech and Slovak Republics, and Estonia occupying the more inclusive variant; all others for which we have data are relatively exclusive.

7. Drawing the threads together

We now need to bring together the conclusions of the three preceding chapters, to see if we can identify patterns of institutions and practices relevant to issues of labour market insecurity, examine change over time, and then relate the analysis to the central hypothesis proposed in Chapter 3, that 'the more market governance is challenged by associational and state (government and law) governance, the more egalitarian a society will be, and the more widely distributed the chances of its members to enjoy some form or other of labour market security'. While some of the topics that we have been examining according to the scheme set out in Chapter 2 relate to more than one mode of governance, the following are concerned more or less unambiguously with only one, and are therefore suited to further analysis:

Market

- Private social spending, from Chapter 5. This, and in particular private pensions, provide the main sustainable means used by middle-income people in market economies to provide insurance against market risk.
- Outstanding consumer credit, also from Chapter 5, enables people to use the market to sustain consumption despite risky labour market conditions, but in a non-sustainable way.

State

- Spending on social protection, from Chapter 5.
- Public debt, from Chapter 4, as the non-sustainable equivalent of outstanding consumer credit.
- Unemployment replacement pay (URR), from Chapter 5, as a means whereby workers' security is supported during times of economic instability and adjustment, in principle strengthening their willingness to accept labour market risk.
- The public share of health spending, also from Chapter 5, a means whereby a potentially worrying form of expenditure risk is removed from workers' security considerations.

- Public spending on education, also from Chapter 5, achieving a similar goal as public health spending while also potentially improving the quality of the future workforce.
- The share of GDP taken by the state in taxes and other revenue, from Chapter 6, representing the capacity of the state to manage demand.
- The proportion of the workforce in public employment, from Chapter 6, indicating a part of the labour force partly protected from market risks, with possible wider stabilizing effects.
- Spending on active labour-market policy, from Chapter 6, as a small but important means whereby workers can be helped to cope with risk and flexibility.
- The strength of employment protection law, deflated for the proportion of the workforce it protects from risk, from Chapter 6.

Association

- Associational governance produces only one key variable, from Chapter 6, the degree of encompassment of collective bargaining. If effective, this smoothes labour-market risk by adjusting pay and conditions to market realities.

Community

- A high level of shadow economy, although a form of exclusion and in itself exposed to risk, can provide a parallel economy countering instability in the formal economy (Chapter 4). It can function effectively only with community protection and support, and may serve as a good indicator of the strength of resistant local community and family governance. It is not sustainable in the long run.
- Remittances from workers abroad, from Chapter 5, stabilizing family incomes in the face of instability in the national economy.
- The average age at which adult sons leave the family home, from Chapter 5, indicating a role for the family in protecting its members' consumption in the context of employment uncertainty.

There is a further important step we can take in analysing market governance. Up to this point we have regarded private social policy and consumer credit as indicators for such governance. But that is not the main case made for the role of the market, which is, rather, that the fewer impediments to the free flow of market forces, the better will workers' positions be in the long run. According to neoliberal theory, it is the attempt by state policy and trade unions to try to make labour secure by damming up market forces that in the end destroys competitiveness and therefore employment. The appropriate indicators for this are an absence of state policies that intervene in the market and of collective bargaining, especially of the coordinated kind: in other words, low scores on most of our state items and on associational governance. We can therefore distinguish between what we shall call 'positive' forms of market governance (private social policy and outstanding consumer credit) and 'negative' forms of market governance (low state and associational governance).

The community mechanisms we have been considering create fewer problems for market forces, with the exception of the shadow economy. At one level the shadow economy has pure labour markets, in that the state and collective bargaining do not interfere with the free flow of market forces. However, Friedrich Schneider, to whom we owe most of the comparative knowledge we have on the shadow economy (Schneider 2005; Schneider and Buehn 2012), considers that government regulation and associated possibilities for incompetence and corruption are major causes of businesses operating outside the law, and that the shadow economy will be smallest in countries with free-market economies. This argument is slightly puzzling, as one of the lowest levels of shadow economy according to Schneider's measures is in his own country, Austria, which has a strong level of state governance. However, it is certainly likely (almost true *per definitionem*) that evasion of regulation will be lowest in countries where the level of regulation is lowest: there is no need to move into the shadow economy in order to employ child labour if there is no law against child labour. The relationship between the shadow economy and market governance is therefore complex, and we shall pay special attention to it.

The next step is to consider the profiles of each country on these governance forms at the two points of time we have been considering, the start of the present century and the most recent post-crisis years for which we have data. We shall continue to use the relative assessments of whether performances are strong or weak, high or low, on a given dimension by expressing them in terms of means and standard deviations. However, up to now it has been possible to do this using the comparable data provided by whichever countries for the variable concerned, as we have mainly been considering variables in isolation. Now that we are comparing indicators it is necessary to have a common basis of comparison, which means restricting the range of countries whose scores we use to calculate means and standard deviations to those for which we have all data. To facilitate comparison across time, we also need to use the same lists at both points in time, even though comparable data are often available for a wider range of countries at the later date. This means recalculating all means and standard deviations using only those EU countries for which both Eurostat and the

OECD were collecting data around 2000. There continue to be one or two gaps for individual countries in the scores we use, but these have a minor effect on the overall means. Other countries' scores, where available, can still be expressed in relation to these revised European OECD means. The main purpose for making the calculations is to have a reasonable range of countries at different economic levels and from different parts of Europe to provide a frame for making relative assessments.

The next task is to determine to what extent the characteristics of different countries across the selected variables can be grouped together in a small number of standard profiles. We have no wish to impose a rigid typology to which the reality of individual cases does not really correspond, and shall therefore distinguish between profiles and zones. A profile will be used in two senses: to identify an ideal typical category that has some logical coherence and empirical plausibility as a means of bracketing together a number of cases; and for the position of an individual country across the variables. A zone is then a looser grouping of cases around a profile but not corresponding to it in every respect. Cases may have affinities with a second zone apart from their principal one.

On this basis, we can start by identifying the two antagonistic ideal-typical profiles that implicitly have been at the heart of all preceding discussion. First is what we might call the social-democratic profile, in which, hypothetically in a situation of strong class challenge, state and associational governance act to manage labour-market risk and balance it against needs for strong consumption and labour flexibility. This gives a profile (Profile I) of strong state and associational governance, a weak market (both positive and negative) and weak community governance.

Confronting the social-democratic profile is Profile II, the neoliberal profile, in which the market alone is relied upon to reconcile consumption, labour flexibility and risk management. Here both positive and negative market governance are strong; state, associational and community governance are all weak.

It is also necessary to provide a third potential profile, Profile III, based on community governance. Both social democracy and neoliberalism represent 'modern' forms of governance, and under both the role of community is weak. However, in many societies these modern institutions are not strong. They then either have no labour-market governance at all (a possibility for which our frame of analysis provides) or they might have recourse to traditional institutions of family and community.

The implications of the differences among these governance profiles will be discussed further below. First, it is necessary to see how effectively the ideal types can be used to form groupings among the countries being studied.

GOVERNANCE PROFILES, *c*.2000

Table 7.1 presents the raw data on relative scores across the selected variables for the years around 2000, and Figure 7.1 shows the resulting profiles and their zones. Where countries scored above mean on a majority of items within a given governance mode, or had particularly strong scores in relation to the mean, they are considered to possess that mode within their repertoire of governance of social risks. (In the case of negative market, the score is strong if state and associational scores are predominantly *below* mean.) Scores between −0.09 and +0.09 are ignored as being too close to the mean to signify strength (or weakness). Where scores within a particular governance mode are ambiguous, the case needs further consideration. Because we are trying to take account both of a combination of numbers of items within a governance mode, these items not being commensurable, and of the relative strength of scores, we have to proceed by discussion of individual cases rather than by using a simple additive technique. Finally, arrows are used to indicate where countries occupy their profile solely because of a high score on an unsustainable item (public debt, consumer credit, shadow economy); the arrow points to the profile that the country would occupy if it were not for this unsustainable item.

Profile I

Profile I (social democratic: strong state, association; weak market, community). Only three countries, all Nordic, conformed fully to the ideal-typical social-democratic profile:

- *Finland* had above-mean scores on nearly all state governance variables, apart from state debt and URR, and an above-mean score for associational governance. It was below mean on both indicators of positive market, and had an overall low score for community governance (only remittances being slightly above mean).
- *Norway* had above-mean scores on nearly all state governance variables (some very high), apart from state debt, and an above-mean score for associational governance. It was below mean on private social policy, though we lack data on consumer debt. There was an overall low score for community governance, though data are missing for age of sons leaving home.
- *Sweden* had above-mean scores on all state governance variables (some very high), and a strong above-mean score for associational governance. It was above mean on private social policy, but very

low for consumer debt. We should therefore rate positive market governance as low, but only for the non-sustainable item. There was an overall low score for community governance.

Mainly in the same zone as Profile I, but with some strength of community governance and therefore coming partly within the zone of Profile III were two cases, Belgium and Slovenia. They cannot be fully bracketed together as they occupied different positions across the two profiles:

- *Belgium* had above-mean scores on all state governance variables (especially state debt) except for public employment, and a strong above-mean score for associational governance. It was below mean on both elements of positive market. The community scores were complex. Shadow economy and especially remittances were higher than for any other wealthy country, though average age of sons leaving home was low. It therefore belongs between the zones of Profiles I and III, though primarily in I.
- *Slovenia* had mixed positive market (low private social spending but above-mean consumer credit), and a mix of strong and weak state scores that enables us to regard it as ambiguously strong for both negative market and state. Uniquely outside NWE the country had a strong associational governance score, and very strong community governance. It therefore belongs between the zones of Profiles I and III.

Profile I/II (strong state, association; strong positive market; weak negative market, community). Four countries diverged from the ideal typical social-democratic profile as we have defined it mainly by having strong scores on both items of positive market. These cases belonged mainly to Profile I, as they had strong state (and therefore weak negative market) governance and strong associational governance, but they also come partly within the zone of Profile II.

- *Austria* had strong scores on both elements of positive market, but also on almost all items of state governance, and exceptionally strong associational governance. Community governance was weak.
- *Denmark* had very high consumer debt, though indifferent private social policy, overall justifying an attribution as strong positive market until the unsustainable item is discounted, when the country would fit better to Profile I itself. Nearly all state scores were very strong, as was associational governance. Community governance was unambiguously weak.

Table 7.1   *Summary account of governance variable scores against OECD European means, c.2000*

	Positive market		State				
	1	2	3	4	5	6	7
Austria	0.90	1.56	0.35	1.06	0.05	1.11	0.17
Belgium	−0.25	−0.12	2.14	0.40	−0.05	0.11	0.42
Bulgaria	n.a.	0.60	0.69	n.a.	n.a.	−1.74	−1.68
Croatia	n.a.	n.a.	n.a.	n.a.	n.a.	1.12	−1.34
Czech Republic	−0.84	−1.12	−1.51	−1.02	0.21	0.61	−1.17
Denmark	0.05	1.15	0.19	1.20	1.14	1.41	2.44
Estonia	−0.97	−1.30	−1.82	−2.17	n.a.	−1.01	0.00
Finland	−0.46	−0.71	−0.26	0.31	0.67	−0.64	0.59
France	0.13	0.52	0.09	1.07	0.00	1.61	0.09
Germany	0.30	1.15	0.14	1.27	0.21	1.81	−0.75
Greece	−0.08	−0.56	1.55	0.17	−1.66	−1.32	−1.59
Hungary	−0.97	−1.07	0.12	−0.81	−0.83	−0.67	−0.16
Ireland	−0.42	0.85	−0.40	−1.88	0.36	−0.80	−1.00
Italy	−0.04	−0.69	2.13	0.21	−2.96	−0.17	−0.75
Latvia	n.a.	−1.17	−1.59	−1.83	n.a.	−2.17	0.17
Lithuania	n.a.	−1.38	−1.18	−1.84	n.a.	−1.06	0.26
Netherlands	2.13	−0.41	0.31	0.42	0.36	−1.04	0.59
Norway	−0.12	n.a.	−0.86	0.45	0.93	1.06	1.77
Poland	−0.97	0.39	−0.58	−0.51	−0.21	−1.39	−0.08
Portugal	−0.33	0.13	−0.20	−0.78	−0.26	−0.23	−0.16
Romania	n.a.	−0.02	−0.97	−2.23	n.a.	−1.30	−1.68
Slovakia	−0.63	−1.02	−0.53	−0.96	1.40	−0.03	−1.00
Slovenia	−0.97	0.29	−1.26	0.20	n.a.	0.08	0.26
Spain	−0.84	0.46	0.28	−0.77	−0.73	−0.57	−1.09
Sweden	0.13	−1.43	0.38	1.48	0.57	1.20	1.60
Switzerland	2.55	n.a.	0.13	0.01	0.93	−1.13	0.09
United Kingdom	1.70	1.95	−0.39	0.66	−0.16	0.00	−0.25
Japan	0.73	n.a.	2.28	n.a.	0.36	0.43	−1.59
Russia	n.a.	n.a.	0.84	n.a.	n.a.	−2.07	−1.42
USA	3.52	n.a.	0.27	n.a.	−1.76	−1.58	0.09

Notes: 1. Private social policy; 2. Outstanding consumer credit; 3. Public debt; 4. Social protection; 5. URR; 6. Health; 7. Education; 8. Public revenue; 9. Public employment; 10. ALMP; 11. EPL; 12. Coordinated collective bargaining; 13. Shadow economy; 14. Remittances; 15. Age of sons leaving home. (*Note:* these are 2007 data)

(minus scores = negative market)				Associational governance	Community		
8	9	10	11	12	13	14	15
0.85	n.a.	−0.38	1.28	3.34	−1.70	0.14	−0.07
0.56	−0.47	0.30	0.09	0.50	0.44	1.21	−0.57
−0.91	0.87	−0.33	n.a.	−0.95	2.96	9.95	2.87
1.07	2.58	n.a.	n.a.	n.a.	2.36	2.79	n.a.
−0.93	n.a.	−0.78	0.75	−0.88	−0.10	−0.96	0.41
1.59	1.40	2.83	0.62	0.64	−0.29	−0.19	−1.70
−1.00	0.52	−0.93	n.a.	−0.95	1.02	0.29	−0.37
1.45	0.25	0.29	−0.52	0.24	−0.27	0.13	−1.46
0.76	0.37	0.52	0.62	−0.49	−0.77	0.30	−0.84
0.16	−1.09	0.58	1.07	0.17	−0.63	−0.40	−0.39
−0.15	−0.62	−0.74	−2.33	−0.68	1.55	0.66	1.62
−0.05	n.a.	−0.62	−0.44	−1.01	0.94	0.14	0.38
−1.07	−1.07	0.03	−0.62	−0.09	−0.65	−0.55	0.05
0.11	n.a.	−0.38	−0.95	−0.29	1.28	−0.32	1.12
−1.14	1.31	−0.89	n.a.	−1.08	0.68	1.45	0.41
−1.25	1.34	−0.72	n.a.	−1.28	1.28	0.32	0.26
0.19	n.a.	0.87	1.23	1.16	−1.13	−0.65	−0.66
1.34	1.69	0.17	0.37	0.37	−0.10	−0.65	n.a.
−0.53	0.65	−0.48	−1.17	−1.01	1.37	0.81	0.82
−1.00	n.a.	0.04	−0.11	−0.29	0.52	1.54	0.82
−1.81	0.16	−0.82	n.a.	−0.88	2.53	0.10	0.79
−0.50	0.88	−0.89	1.45	−0.16	−0.13	1.38	1.18
−0.32	0.15	−0.63	n.a.	0.50	1.28	0.57	1.33
−0.99	−1.41	−0.19	−1.48	−0.16	0.52	0.06	0.64
1.98	0.94	2.33	0.19	0.90	−0.08	−0.15	−1.61
−1.57	−1.47	−0.91	0.39	−0.62	−1.90	−3.35	n.a.
−0.91	−0.71	−1.01	−0.44	−1.21	−1.20	0.00	−0.69
−2.25	−2.53	n.a.	−0.04	−1.15	−1.45	−0.16	n.a.
n.a.	1.80	n.a.	n.a.	n.a.	4.55	−0.39	n.a.
−1.86	n.a.	n.a.	n.a.	−1.28	−1.88	−0.45	n.a.

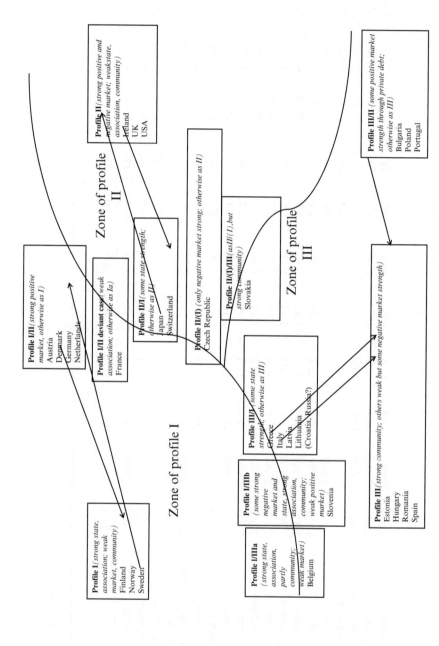

Profile I/II (*strong positive and negative market; weakstate, association, community*)
Ireland
UK
USA

Zone of profile II

Profile I/III (*strong positive market, otherwise as I*)
Austria
Denmark
Germany
Netherlands

Profile I/II deviant case (*weak association; otherwise as Ia*)
France

Profile II/I (*some state strength; otherwise as I*)
Japan
Switzerland

Profile II/(I) (*only negative market strong; otherwise as II*)
Czech Republic

Profile II/(I)/III (*as II/(I), but strong community*)
Slovakia

Profile III/II (*some positive market strength through private debt; otherwise as III*)
Bulgaria
Poland
Portugal

Zone of profile III

Zone of profile I

Profile III/I (*some state strength, otherwise as III*)
Greece
Italy
Latvia
Lithuania
(Croatia, Russia?)

Profile I/IIIb (*some strong negative market and state, strong association, community; weak positive market*)
Slovenia

Profile I/IIIa (*strong state, association, partly community; weak market*)
Belgium

Profile III (*strong community; others weak but some negative market strength*)
Estonia
Hungary
Romania
Spain

Profile I (*strong state, association; weak market, community*)
Finland
Norway
Sweden

Figure 7.1 Governance profiles and zones, c.2000

- *Germany* had unambiguously high scores for positive market. Its state profile was strong overall, but there were two below-mean scores indicating some role for negative market: education spending and public employment. Associational governance was above mean and community governance weak.
- *The Netherlands* also counts as having had strong positive market governance, as although consumer credit was low its private social spending was very high. Its state scores were above mean, except for public health spending, which was very low. Associational governance was very strong, and community governance very weak.

In the same basic zone as this profile but closer still to Profile II came:

- *France*, which had strong positive market and state governance, weak associational and community governance (except for an above-mean score for remittances).

Profile II

Profile II (neoliberal: strong positive and negative market; weak state, association, community). The three Anglophone countries, as often claimed in the literature, conformed to this profile, though with ambiguities.

- *Ireland* had below-mean private social policy, but stronger above-mean outstanding consumer credit, so on balance can be seen as having strong positive market governance until the unsustainable item is discounted, when it belongs to a hybrid Profile II/I. Its state scores are nearly all below mean, the only exception being a marginally above-mean score for ALMP. Associational governance was not strong (though only marginally weak). Negative market governance can therefore be rated strong. Community governance was weak.
- *The UK* had exceptionally strong positive market governance including the highest of all scores for outstanding consumer credit. Its state scores were predominantly weak, though the one exception, social protection spending, is an important variable. Associational and community governance were very weak. Negative market can be rated strong.
- *The USA* had very high private social spending; we do not have its comparable consumer debt statistic, though this is known to have been high. We do not have data on social protection spending, but this is known to have been low, as were all other items of state

governance for which we have data – except for public debt, which was above mean. Associational and community governance were both very low. Negative market governance was therefore high.

Profile II/I (some stronger state governance). In the same zone as Profile II, but with slightly stronger evidence of some state governance and therefore an element of Profile I (though not enough to displace an overall judgement of strong negative market), were Japan and Switzerland.

- *Japan* had missing consumer credit data, but private social policy spending was high. State debt was extremely high indeed, and there were also above-mean scores for URR and state health spending. We do not have data on social protection spending or ALMP, but on all other state items scores were sufficiently low to see evidence of strong negative market governance. Associational and community governance were very weak. If the strong state score was discounted as depending on the unsustainable item of very high public debt, the country would conform to Profile II itself.
- *Switzerland* also lacked data on consumer credit, but private social spending was exceptionally high. State debt, URR and EPL were above mean, while social protection spending and state education spending were indifferent. Other state scores were below mean, some strongly so, allowing an overall attribution of strong negative market. Associational governance was low, shadow economy and remittances very low.

In the same zone as this Profile, but with no positive market governance came:

- *The Czech Republic*, which had very low positive market, and overall weak state (and therefore strong negative market) scores. Associational and community governance were weak. However, URR, public health spending and EPL scores were above mean, giving minor evidence of some state governance.

Differing again, and the only case including aspects of all three profiles, was:

- *Slovakia*, which resembled the Czech Republic with a complex mix of state and negative market scores, low associational and positive market scores, and (uniquely among CEE countries) small shadow economies. However, Slovakia had very high scores on the other two elements of community governance. It therefore belonged between Profile III and the Czech exceptional case in the zone of Profile II, overlapping slightly into I.

Profile III

Profile III (strong community; all others weak). There were no cases of the pure community governance profile, with the possible exception of Croatia – though this may be because of the lack of data on that country. More generally, most countries with strong community profiles also had strong elements of negative (but never positive) market governance, except for the fact that the community profile included large shadow economies. The core of empirical as opposed to theoretical Profile III is therefore an ambiguous combination of strong community and compromised negative market governance. A number of countries, all in CEE or SWE, conformed to this pattern.

- *Estonia* had low or very low scores for both elements of positive market, all elements of state governance for which we have data on the country, and associational bargaining. Community governance was strong, except that the average age of sons leaving home was below mean.
- *Hungary* was very similar, except that it had above-mean public debt and no ambiguity in its strong community governance.
- *Romania* lacked data on private social spending, though it is almost certain that this was low. Private consumer credit was not strong; therefore there was low positive market governance. State governance was low apart from an above-mean score for public employment; associational governance was weak and community governance strong.
- *Spain* had above-mean consumer credit, but low private social policy; it was therefore on the cusp of this version of the profile and that where private governance is slightly stronger (discussed below). Apart from above-mean state debt, its state scores were all low or very low. Associational governance was weak, but community governance was strong.

Sub-profile III/I (some elements of state governance). A number of countries followed the basic Profile III of strong community and negative market governance (with shadow economy), but had some important points of state labour-market governance that brought them a little closer to the zone of Profile I.

- *Greece* conformed very strongly to Profile III except that it had very high state debt and also above-mean social protection spending. Without the public debt, state governance would not have been strong, and the country would have conformed to Profile III itself.
- *Italy* scored very highly for public debt, and above mean for social protection spending, also for public revenue. Otherwise it conforms to Profile III, where it would be located if state debt were discounted.
- *Latvia* and *Lithuania* resembled these cases, except that their strong elements of state governance were completely different: above-mean scores for education and very strong for public employment, but very low state debt and social protection spending.

Also probably belonging to this sub-profile, but difficult to determine because so many data are missing, are the following:

- *Croatia* lacked data on positive market, associational governance and five of the nine items of state governance. For the remaining items of state governance there were three very strong items and one very weak item. Community governance (or shadow economy, as that is all we have) was exceptionally strong.
- *Russia* also lacked data on private market, associational governance and six items of state governance. Of those remaining, state debt and state employment were high, while public health and education spending had very low scores. Community was strong, especially the shadow economy, which was the strongest of all the countries studied.

Sub-profile III/II (some elements of positive market governance). A small number of countries that otherwise fit absolutely into Profile III had high levels of outstanding consumer credit (though not of private social spending), giving them an element of positive market governance and therefore moving them slightly towards the zone of Profile II. If the high consumer debt is discounted, the sub-profile ceases to exist and becomes merged with Profile III itself.

- *Bulgaria* had an above-mean level of consumer credit; we do not know the private social spending figure, but it was probably low. There was high public debt, but all other state indicators for which we have data were weak, as was associational governance. Community governance was exceptionally high, the highest of all the countries being studied.

- *Poland* had a similar profile, except that we know its private social spending was low, its only item of state governance strength was for public employment, and its community governance was slightly less strong than Bulgaria's.
- *Portugal* was similar, though it had no points of state governance strength.

Testing the Class Challenge Hypothesis

One aim of this study is to test the hypothesis that the stronger the class challenge within a capitalist economy, the more important will be state and associational forms of governance – that is, the more likely countries are to share Profile I. Figure 7.2 displays the summary accounts of profiles in Figure 7.1, ranked by strength of class challenge. To simplify the presentation, deviant cases have been placed with their main profile among the three. We shall comment on any issues relevant to sub-profiles and exceptions. With a small number of exceptions the hypothesis is confirmed. Profile I and its variants had stronger class challenge than any other countries, except that France (in any case a deviant member of the profile) had a far lower score than the others, while Slovakia, and perhaps Croatia, had a stronger class challenge score than Germany and the Netherlands. However, the data do not discriminate between Profile I and either of its sub-profiles I/II and I/III. The hypothesis does not distinguish between

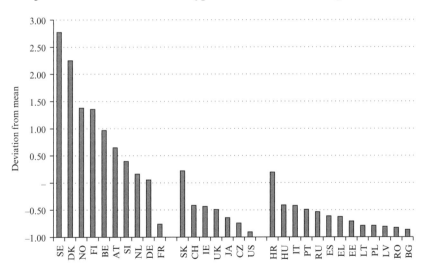

Figure 7.2   Governance profiles and class challenge, c.2000 (country scores in relation to standard deviation around mean)

Profiles II and the various parts of III, and this is also corroborated by the evidence. In other words, strength of class challenge helps distinguish a broadly social-democratic profile from both a neoliberal and a traditional one, but does not distinguish between neoliberalism and traditionalism. One might have expected stronger class challenge to be associated with Profile III/I, but this is not clear.

GOVERNANCE PROFILES, *c.*2010

We will now consider the years around 2010. Table 7.2 displays the basic data, as was done for 2000, and Figure 7.3 attempts an allocation by profiles. Again, arrows indicate reassignments of profile if unsustainable forms are ignored. The major forces for change in the years running up to and during the crisis have been deterioration in the private and/or public debt situation of some countries, and relative improvement in that of others. One implication of these changes is to obscure the difference between Profiles I and I/II, based on whether or not these countries with the basic social-democratic profile included positive market governance or not. The presence of Austria, the Netherlands and Sweden as ambiguous between these two groups is largely a result of their having relatively high private social spending but low outstanding consumer credit. If their low credit scores are discounted, they are unambiguously part of Profile I/II. Meanwhile, France's relatively high position on positive market governance has gone, making that country dependent on state governance alone for managing labour risk. As a result, France appears as a deviant case of Profile I, not of I/II.

The main changes affecting Profile II concern different relative roles of state governance. State social policy has risen in importance in the UK, moving it from a straight Profile II to the hybrid II/I (a similar finding is reported by Rubery et al. (2009) for a slightly earlier period). This leaves Ireland and the USA as the sole examples of neoliberal governance, but with both cases making strong use of the unsustainable state governance form of high public debt. State measures have declined considerably in importance in the Czech and Slovak Republics, making them now deviant cases of Profile II and not of II/I. They differ from each other in that community governance (though not shadow economy) is strong in the latter but not the former, which relies on negative market incentives alone to manage labour-market risk. As at the start of the century, the element of strong state governance in Japan was due only to its very high public debt. This makes it similar to Ireland and the UK, but with a far higher level of debt.

Declines in relative state governance also affect Profile III, moving Latvia, Lithuania and, so far as we can tell, Russia, away from Profile III/I to the main profile. This leaves only Italy, and possibly Croatia, as countries with a traditional approach to labour security but above mean for some state measures. It is notable that most countries (i.e., those from CEE) in straight Profile III have as their only important form of state labour policy the maintenance of high levels of public employment. Finally, while the statist hybrid Profile III/I has declined in importance, the market form of it (III/II) has grown in size, though solely because consumer credit increased in relative size in Greece and Romania. (Portugal moved in the other direction, from III/II to III.) With the exception of some points of strength in Italian state governance, this means that only debt of various kinds exists alongside community governance to support labour security throughout eastern and southern Europe, with the diverse exceptions of the Czech and Slovak Republics and Slovenia.

We now relate these profiles to the state of class challenge for the years around 2010. This is shown in Figure 7.4. There are only a few changes in the overall picture. The collapse of class challenge in Slovakia is mirrored in the change in its profile, and the country no longer appears exiguous. The only problems for our central hypothesis are: Ireland in Profile II and Italy in Profile III have stronger class challenge than Germany and the exceptional case of France in Profile I; and Croatia again might have stronger challenge than the Netherlands and Slovenia as well as Germany and France. The main hypothesis still stands, though overall the contrast between Profile I and its sub-profiles is not as strong as at the start of the century.

Finally, with the enhanced data available for recent years only, we can consider the different patterns of inclusion and exclusion presented by the various countries and relate these to profiles. Several authors have pointed to the growing role of exclusion or dualization as authorities, corporations and unions come to terms with the challenges confronting labour security (Emmenegger et al. 2012). Chapter 4 contained data on the general exclusion of the poor through particularly low incomes, the exclusion of immigrants, women and young people, and the size of the shadow economy (which can be included as a variable on this side of the equation if when we consider sustainable governance we exclude it as a governance form). From Chapter 5 we can take data on fiscal redistribution; the more the net effect of taxes and transfers redistributes income in a way that reduces inequality, the more inclusive is the fiscal system, and therefore the less redistribution the greater is the level of exclusion. Chapter 6 gave us data on exclusion from the core labour force through

Table 7.2 Summary account of governance variable scores against OECD European means, c.2010

	Positive market		State				
	1	2	3	4	5	6	7
Austria	0.46	−0.16	0.15	0.76	0.82	0.45	0.26
Belgium	−0.04	−0.83	0.98	0.51	0.53	0.47	0.80
Bulgaria	n.a.	2.50	−1.62	n.a.	n.a.	−2.16	−1.47
Croatia	n.a.	n.a.	−0.77	n.a.	n.a.	0.14	−1.29
Czech Republic	−0.75	−0.85	−0.94	−1.49	0.08	−0.14	−1.38
Denmark	0.36	0.32	−0.75	1.41	1.05	1.84	2.71
Estonia	−1.10	−0.79	−1.87	−1.84	n.a.	−1.14	−0.02
Finland	−0.50	−0.33	−0.66	0.81	0.82	−0.31	0.98
France	−0.70	−0.33	0.51	1.33	0.19	0.98	0.17
Germany	0.51	0.01	0.38	0.74	0.25	0.67	−0.56
Greece	−0.19	1.31	2.55	0.46	−2.31	−0.91	−1.47
Hungary	−1.00	1.91	0.43	−0.80	−0.95	−1.46	−0.74
Ireland	0.01	0.99	0.63	0.49	−0.43	−0.50	0.71
Italy	0.06	−0.62	1.71	0.55	−2.60	0.17	−1.11
Latvia	n.a.	−1.21	−0.95	−1.91	n.a.	−2.23	−0.65
Lithuania	n.a.	−1.46	−1.10	−1.75	n.a.	−1.38	−0.29
Netherlands	2.27	−0.96	−0.06	0.91	1.05	2.28	0.26
Norway	−0.09	n.a.	−0.70	−0.22	0.88	0.88	1.08
Poland	−1.10	0.91	−0.42	−1.68	−0.38	−1.34	−0.47
Portugal	−0.14	−0.03	0.98	−0.14	0.25	−0.78	0.07
Romania	n.a.	1.91	−1.24	−1.96	−1.69	−1.10	−1.38
Slovakia	−0.65	−1.63	−0.84	−1.81	−0.83	−1.27	−1.38
Slovenia	−0.50	−0.16	−0.87	−0.41	n.a.	−0.39	−0.02
Spain	−0.85	−0.10	−0.13	−0.21	−0.43	−0.16	−0.65
Sweden	0.51	−0.83	−0.86	0.85	0.59	0.52	1.17
Switzerland	2.92	n.a.	−0.51	−0.43	0.99	−0.50	−0.29
United Kingdom	0.51	2.18	0.31	0.23	0.42	0.67	−0.11
Japan	n.a.	n.a.	4.79	n.a.	1.16	0.36	−1.75
Russia	n.a.	n.a.	−1.81	n.a.	n.a.	−2.16	−1.47
USA	0.41	n.a.	0.94	n.a.	−1.06	−1.10	−0.11

Notes: 1. Private social policy; 2. Outstanding consumer credit; 3. Public debt; 4. Social protection; 5. URR; 6. Health; 7. Education; 8. Public revenue; 9. Public employment; 10. ALMP; 11. EPL; 12. Coordinated collective bargaining; 13. Shadow economy; 14. Remittances; 15. Age of sons leaving home. (*Note:* these are 2007 data)

(minus scores = negative market)				Associational governance	Community		
8	9	10	11	12	13	14	15
0.58	n.a.	0.41	1.41	3.36	−1.52	−0.09	−0.07
0.64	0.00	1.30	0.66	0.67	0.48	1.11	−0.57
−1.01	−0.80	−1.28	n.a.	−0.96	2.68	2.88	2.87
0.88	1.12	n.a.	n.a.	n.a.	3.32	2.07	n.a.
−0.68	n.a.	−0.93	0.83	−0.83	−0.55	−0.74	0.41
1.59	−3.95	2.65	0.86	0.48	−0.41	−0.76	−1.70
−0.73	1.62	−1.18	n.a.	−0.96	0.83	1.14	−0.37
1.32	0.17	0.80	−0.52	0.41	−0.29	0.08	−1.46
0.81	0.57	0.44	1.03	−0.31	−0.73	0.30	−0.84
0.00	0.50	0.10	1.61	0.15	−0.63	−0.19	−0.39
−0.52	−1.37	−1.05	−1.73	−0.64	1.34	0.00	1.62
0.47	n.a.	−0.54	−0.41	−0.96	0.95	0.64	0.38
−1.30	−0.86	0.01	−0.43	−0.38	−0.35	−0.75	0.05
0.28	n.a.	−0.84	−1.10	−0.31	1.66	−0.51	1.12
−1.32	0.95	−0.44	n.a.	−0.70	0.63	1.73	0.41
−1.41	0.90	−1.01	n.a.	−1.03	1.40	1.28	0.26
0.26	n.a.	0.92	1.03	1.00	−0.92	−0.57	−0.66
1.88	1.94	0.31	0.72	0.54	−0.02	−0.88	n.a.
−0.80	−0.01	−0.27	−1.73	−0.96	1.09	1.58	0.82
−0.36	n.a.	−0.08	−0.84	−0.70	0.77	0.83	0.82
−1.51	−0.79	−1.42	n.a.	−0.57	2.49	2.49	0.79
−1.62	−0.37	−1.01	0.34	−0.38	−0.49	1.59	1.18
−0.13	0.12	−0.67	n.a.	0.54	1.07	0.12	1.33
−0.99	−1.44	−0.21	−1.27	0.02	1.03	0.12	0.64
1.30	1.03	1.22	0.26	0.93	−0.04	−0.06	−1.61
−1.44	−1.37	n.a.	0.69	−0.57	−2.03	−3.02	n.a.
−0.55	−0.44	−1.38	−0.72	−1.10	−1.24	0.07	−0.69
−1.93	−2.75	n.a.	−0.12	−1.03	−1.44	−0.09	n.a.
n.a.	1.26	n.a.	n.a.	n.a.	5.54	−1.06	n.a.
−2.29	n.a.	n.a.	n.a.	−1.16	−1.81	−0.34	n.a.

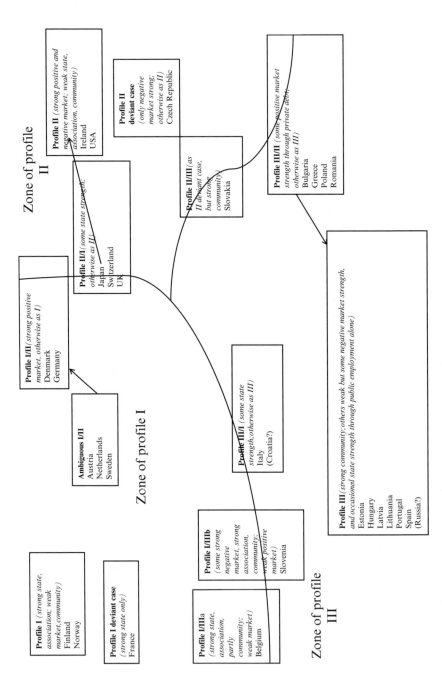

Zone of profile II

Profile II (*strong positive and negative market; weak state, association, community*)
Ireland
USA

Profile II deviant case
(*only negative market strong; otherwise as II*)
Czech Republic

Profile II/III (*as II deviant case, but strong community*)
Slovakia

Profile III/II (*some positive market strength through private action; otherwise as III*)
Bulgaria
Greece
Poland
Romania

Profile II/I (*some state strength; otherwise as II*)
Japan
Switzerland
UK

Profile I/II (*strong positive market, otherwise as I*)
Denmark
Germany

Ambiguous I/II
Austria
Netherlands
Sweden

Zone of profile I

Profile I (*strong state, association; weak market, community*)
Finland
Norway

Profile I deviant case
(*strong state only*)
France

Profile I/IIIa (*strong state, association, partly community; weak market*)
Belgium

Profile I/IIIb (*some strong negative market, strong association, community; weak positive market*)
Slovenia

Profile III/I (*some state strength; otherwise as III*)
Italy
(Croatia?)

Profile III (*strong community; others weak but some negative market strength, and occasional state strength through public employment alone*)
Estonia
Hungary
Latvia
Lithuania
Portugal
Spain
(Russia?)

Zone of profile III

Figure 7.3   Governance profiles and zones, c.2010

222

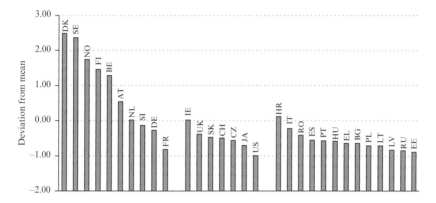

Figure 7.4   Governance profiles and class challenge, c.2010 (country scores in relation to standard deviation around mean)

people working in various forms of precarious employment. Table 7.3 maps the exclusion profiles of countries, summarizing the relevant data from those three chapters, on to the governance profiles developed above. Countries have been assigned to profiles that do not take account of non-sustainable governance forms.

Countries in Profiles I and I/II, including France, tend to make use of large numbers of immigrants and/or women in relatively subordinate or excluded positions. So does Belgium in the exceptional profile I/III. Only Austria and Germany do this for both groups, and we do not have enough data from Norway to assess its position. Apart from the relatively low level of fiscal redistribution in the Netherlands and Sweden, these are the only forms of exclusion where these countries rank relatively high. The other case of exceptional Profile I/III, Slovenia, has a pattern of its own, with wider exclusion than in Profile I and its hybrid, but considerably less exclusion than most members of III and its hybrid. There is some coherence in the high level of immigrant exclusion, as these countries score highly on what we might call citizenship characteristics: state and associational governance both imply membership of a 'community of fate' defined in national terms. Female exclusion is mainly a consequence of the large numbers of women in the labour force in these countries; but exclusion is less explicable unless women are regarded as not having achieved full socio-economic citizenship.

Against that, the market neither requires nor rewards citizenship membership; it is therefore also not surprising that countries with important elements of positive market governance (Profiles II and II/I) should

Table 7.3 Exclusion patterns by governance profiles, c.2010

Governance profiles	Forms of exclusion					
	Immigrants	Women	Young	Low income	From core labour market	Shadow economy
I	[FR] *(no data: NO)*	FI				
I/II	AT DE SE	AT DK DE NL		NL SE *(both fiscal only)*		
I/III	BE					SI
II/I		CH UK	UK	CH *(no fiscal data)* UK	SI	
II	*(no data: JA, US)*	[CZ] *(no data: JA, US)*	IE US	IE *(not fiscal)* JA US	IE	
II/III		SK	SK	SK *(fiscal only)*		
III/I	IT *(no data: HR)*	*(no data: HR)*	IT *(no data: HR)*	IT *(no data: HR)*	IT	HR IT
III	EE EL LV ES *(no data: RU)*	EE EL HU *(no data: RU)*	BG EL ES RO LV HU *(no data: RU)*	EE EL PL PT ES *(no data: BG, LV, LT, RO, RU)*	EL HU PL PT ES	BG EE EL HU LV LT PL PT RO RU ES

Notes:
'Low-income' exclusion means general income exclusion of poor plus weak fiscal redistribution
[ ] signifies exceptional cases within the profile

224

exclude the poor through both low incomes and low fiscal redistribution, but not exclude immigrants as such. Most of these countries also have high levels of NEETs (i.e., youth exclusion), something that was absent from Profile I. This may partly reflect the role of education in social citizenship in Profile I countries. The Czech Republic, the only CEE country to conform largely to Profile II, albeit with exceptional characteristics, was the only case here not to follow any elements of this profile, but to restrict any exclusion to women. Only Switzerland also scored relatively highly on this element. Ireland, like all other countries involved in the Euro crisis, also had a high level of exclusion from the core labour market.

The countries in the various parts of Profile III all practised multiple forms of exclusion. This is not surprising, as traditional community governance is based on local and often face-to-face relations, which implies a high level of exclusion.

CONCLUSIONS

As already suggested, governance Profile I clearly corresponds to what is often described in the literature as 'social democracy', the political stance primarily associated with parties rooted in trade union movements within capitalist economies. In such cases strong, institutionalized class challenge stimulates action by states and associations to amend the outcomes of pure market capitalism, hence the strength of state and associational governance. But social democracy is not socialism; it is not associated with the suppression of capitalism or free markets, but with their regulation and amendment. Hence market governance also appears in most countries in Profile I (i.e., Profile I/II). Further, we have defined associational governance not in terms of the pure strength or extent of collective bargaining but as the strength of encompassment in bargaining, which is not only a measure of organized labour's ability to wield power, but also of the discipline of its exercise in the interests of the efficient functioning of a market economy. Community governance is relatively weak in social democracy, because the latter is a force associated with modernization, with emergence from and often struggle against the rules of traditional society. In ideal typical social democracy, therefore, labour security is underwritten by a strong market economy, amended in workers' interests by state social policy and extensive, encompassing collective bargaining, with little or no support from traditional institutions.

Social democracy depends for its strength on concepts of membership of a society; for the state to be an instrument acting on behalf of a particular interest or group of interests, these must be in some sense members of that state, able to make claims on its support. While many non-citizens may be able to make some such claims (for example, it is not normally considered to be in states' interests to offend foreign investors, and such investors may well be able to make stronger claims on a state's help than its citizens), for ordinary working people unable to wield the power of capital the main means for making claims is through citizenship: to be accepted members of the society, in particular through having voting rights. Second, to benefit fully from the protection of associational governance, workers need to be members of trade unions.

Social-democratic parties and movements usually present themselves as being 'universalist', seeking to promote the rights of all without discrimination. However, this universalism implies sharing an identity that supports a membership claim, usually a national one, and is rarely able to address itself to humankind as a whole as 'universal' literally implies. In Chapter 2 we recognized the limitation of the means by which workers might access the various forms of security governance through their membership of certain 'communities of fate' limited in space and time. It is therefore not surprising that we found evidence in some cases of the exclusion of immigrants from full membership of the universalism of social democracy, though the relative exclusion of women was more surprising. It must be remembered that our measure of both immigrant and female exclusion was inflated by the size of immigrant populations and the number of women in paid work; it is not therefore a measure of exclusion per se, but a combined measure of exclusion and the size of the group concerned, in order to assess the dependence of an economy on immigrant and female labour. It may well be that societies with very small immigrant populations or female workforces discriminate more heavily against them than those with large ones, as was shown to some extent in Chapter 4. Nevertheless, the tendency, whether deliberate and conscious or not, to make use of immigrant and female labour to protect the security of a native and male 'breadwinner' population may become part of the social-democratic ideal type, as immigrant and female workers grow in number. This might be offset by the tendency for women to form the majority of union members in a growing number of countries, largely as a result of the growing importance for union membership of public employment, in many parts of which women predominate among middle and lower ranks of the hierarchy (Crouch 2012b). This will be an important area for future research.

The only region of the world where political parties representing labour movements dominated government for large parts of the second half of the twentieth century was the Nordic lands, which, not coincidentally, are the countries where class challenge has been strongest. This is why Esping-Andersen (1990) and others have seen the welfare regime of this part of the world as distinctive and have labelled it exclusively as social democratic. The data analysed in the foregoing chapters support this analysis, but also find other countries in NWE to have similar characteristics, albeit in a slightly weaker form: Austria, Belgium (with some complications), and, weaker still, Germany and the Netherlands. A study of recent developments in the so-called Bismarckian systems of Austria, Germany and the Netherlands concludes that there has been considerable change following a convergence of changes in the traditional Christian Democratic strategies that shaped them following World War II and the social-democratic challenge to these (Seeleib-Kaiser et al. 2008: 153).

As we have noted, Profile II corresponds closely to the ideal type of a neoliberal social regime, that is the form taken by a market economy when class challenge is weak, reflected in a weak role for states and associations. Here market forces alone are strong. Labour interests have been – or have become – unable to launch a strong class challenge, so state and, in particular, associational governance intervene less than in the social-democratic cases. The rise of markets has also seen the defeat of the institutions of traditional society and therefore of community governance; this was historically one of the first consequences of the rise of market capitalism (Polanyi 1944). Workers depend for their labour market security on their ability to benefit from the efficient functioning of markets. Neoliberalism and social democracy resemble each other in that both are 'modernizing' forces associated with strong market economies and weak traditionalism. They differ in that under neoliberalism only the market is strong. Most analyses of social regimes identify neoliberalism or economic liberalism with the Anglophone nations. This is partly borne out by our analysis, but the UK has at times encompassed elements of social democracy, including in recent years as it coped with the crisis. In addition, Ireland and the USA are making use of high state debt, which is not in the long term compatible with neoliberalism. The crisis has weakened neoliberalism in practice, although its policies are urged by many public authorities in Europe, Japan and the USA as the main route out of it. Outside the Anglophone group, Japan and Switzerland share major neoliberal characteristics, but Japan has exceptionally high state debt, while Switzerland has some social-democratic social policy. Had we been able to distinguish between market and corporation governance, we might well have found further differences here, as large Japanese corporations have historically provided forms of welfare and labour market security for their core employees, though this pattern is today in some decline.

In theory, a neoliberal economy produces no social exclusion. To benefit from the market it is not necessary to be a citizen, especially in the global economy. Provided one has a capacity to work and earn money, one can benefit from whatever opportunities and protections the market makes available. On the other hand, to the extent that the market produces inequalities in capacity to work and earn from work, it can exclude those at the bottom of the income ladder. Ideal-typical neoliberal countries should therefore have low levels of exclusions of identifiable social categories, but high levels of exclusion of the poor in general. There should also be a low level of fiscal redistribution from rich to poor, as this constitutes interference in the free market. This is what we have found in this study, the further exclusion of the young in several Profile II or II/I countries being attributable mainly to a relative lack of education and training opportunities, normally borne by non-market institutions.

All remaining countries, the majority of those being considered and more or less all of CEE and SWE, are primarily dependent on the traditional governance form of community for any claims to relative strength in the provision of labour-market security. This has been supplemented by variants of two forms of market and state governance. The first has been the use of various combinations of private and public debt, intensifying in usage as a response to the economic crisis in many of these countries. The second has been a particular form of market governance, comprising the negative form only, usually inconsistently combined with a strong shadow economy. Perhaps the most surprising result of this part of the study is the lack of any clear difference between south-west Europe and the countries emerging from state socialism after 1990. It may seem particularly strange that community appears as a form of governance in the latter, as state socialism was pledged to eliminate community and tradition. However, state socialist regimes in central Europe built on the Bismarckian systems established by pre-1918 Hapsburg social policy (Cerami 2010). Perhaps more important, it is well known that, within the state socialist system, the only access people had to institutional supports outside the party-controlled state were family, local community, and in Poland the church. Trade unions were part of the party-state apparatus, though some of them became involved in the final agitation against the regimes that led to their collapse. Exceptionally, in Poland the autonomous union movement, Solidarność, led the anti-communist uprising. But Solidarność is a largely Catholic organization, and therefore not at all hostile to traditional institutions in the manner common to social-democratic union movements. Similarities between CEE and SWE are therefore less surprising than might first appear.

Traditionalism, familism or conservatism appear in many characterizations of welfare regimes. Several authors include these ideas within their concept of Bismarckian welfare states because of their reliance on the male breadwinner. But this is a different, rationalized and modernized, sense of familism compared with the kinds of variables we have considered here: remittances from family members who have gone abroad; adult sons staying in the household; workers depending on whatever community support protects them from the vulnerability of the shadow economy. When we interpret familism and community in this way, acting apart from the modern state, the northern Bismarckian countries appear closer to the Nordics, and SWE and CEE appear as the real familists and traditionalists. A major characteristic of traditionalism is that security is provided on the basis of specific identities. As we have seen, societies with various forms of Profile III are characterized by multiple forms of social exclusion. The two CEE cases that made no use of community governance, the Czech and Slovak Republics, were also countries with little evidence of social exclusion – apart from female exclusion in both cases and youth and fiscal exclusion in Slovakia. These are once again the two most advanced Visegrád countries, which have therefore shared, before and during the Soviet period, in the 'modernization' similar to that of the advanced western economies.

Most European societies that went through a period of democratization at some point in the twentieth century saw the emergence of the three broad political forces that have proved to lie behind our analysis of contemporary approaches to the problem of labour insecurity. Two of these had been locked in struggle for much longer, sometimes – particularly in the case of France – dating back to the late eighteenth century: traditional conservatism, representing initially the elites of pre-capitalist society, but gradually joined by those of industrial capitalism as they grew in wealth and power; and the challenge of liberalism, based on the twin ideas of civil liberties and equalities and of market freedom. The third arrival on the scene was the organized working class, increasingly allied to some form of social democracy, socialism or communism. The political position of these forces has changed over the decades. The rise of the working class and the threat of socialism led many liberal interests to ally themselves with conservatism, and liberalism split along the divide between civil and economic liberties. Working-class parties gradually adopted reformist social democracy rather than attempting to replace the capitalist economy with a socialist one. In CEE countries where an anti-capitalist socialist economy was implemented, new elites emerged that in the end restricted civil rights and popular movements, including autonomous trade unions, more effectively than in most of those economies that remained capitalist.

It is remarkable therefore that the division between some form of traditionalism, economic liberalism and social democracy remains relevant for organizing major differences in means of coping with problems of labour security. For all its innovative capacity in so many ways, the late twentieth and early twenty-first century epoch has so far failed to add anything distinctly new to this ensemble of forces.

8. Governance, class challenge, inequality, innovation and capacity for solidaristic collectivity

The previous chapters have established the existence of a number of governance profiles. This follows the analysis in Chapter 2 of the components of an enlarged view of labour-market security, based on means of resolving the tension between labour-market flexibility and stable mass consumption. But the relationship of this discussion to the security of actual working lives is not clear. First, there is the problem of what constitutes labour-market security. It cannot be equated to labour-market *stability*; that is, a tendency for workers to remain in the same job for many years; this can simply imply labour-market stagnation, which will probably end in economic decline and a collapse of security itself. This was the situation in the state socialist countries of Russia, eastern Europe and elsewhere. Nor should we equate security with the strength of laws making it difficult for workers to lose their jobs, as by itself and not accompanied by a wider range of labour policies this may well lead to the growth of precarious employment outside a protected core, as seems to be the case in much of SWE today. We also cannot equate it with the existence of open-ended rather than time-limited contracts, as in countries where employment protection laws are very weak (such as the USA) an open-ended contract might actually give less assurance of future employment than a time-limited one.

At the level of global national statistics with which we are working, the first approximation to labour-market security is a simple measure of the level of employment, as this gives the best rough indication of the chances of finding and having a job, and of finding another if the first one is lost. This is what is known in the literature as employment security rather than job security. It does not enable us to discriminate between qualities of job contracts; for example, we cannot distinguish 'zero-hours' contracts of the kind that are highly popular among UK employers. These do not necessarily offer either work or wages, but may indeed prevent a person from taking up actual work by requiring them to be available at short notice to take on tasks should they appear. While this is the dream form of employment for neoliberals it is highly inefficient for everyone involved apart from the employer (or non-employer, as it might better be termed). However, in general, the more people who are in work and therefore the tighter the relationship between supply and demand, the better, on average, the quality of working conditions that employers need to offer to attract staff. The second requirement of employment security is that, in the event of a job being lost, there will be reasonable protection of living standards while a new one is being sought.

This dual definition is best operationalized in terms of: the overall level of employment expressed as the percentage of those of working age in employment; and the level of unemployment support, or what we have here called the URR. Statistics on these will be found in Appendix Tables A4.1 and A5.1 respectively. Unfortunately, complete data are available only for those countries in OECD membership at that time, so we lose Bulgaria, Croatia, the Baltic states, Romania, Slovenia and Russia. Figure 8.1a ranks the remaining countries on the two variables at the start of the present century, following the procedure for calculating means and distributions around the standard deviation followed in previous chapters. There is a modestly positive correlation between the two (r^2 = 0.3004). Concentrating first on those scoring at least +0.5 SD or −0.5 SD on both dimensions gives us the following allocations according to the profiles established in Chapter 7. (Note that weaker cases, countries scoring at least +0.5 SD or −0.5 SD on one variable and at least +0.1 SD or −0.10 SD on the other are indicated in brackets.)

First, the following countries provided high levels of both employment and unemployment compensation in the years around 2000:

- Profiles I and I/II: Denmark, Norway, Sweden (Finland, Netherlands) (but not Austria, Germany, or deviant case France)
- Profiles II and II/I: Switzerland (Japan) (but not Ireland, UK, USA, or deviant cases Czech and Slovak Republics)
- Profile III: none

Providing the worst combination of low employment and low URR were:

- Profiles I, II and hybrids: none
- Profile III (various kinds): Greece, Hungary, Italy, Spain (Poland)

Providing high employment but low URR were:

- Profile II: the USA (the UK)
- Profile III: (Portugal)

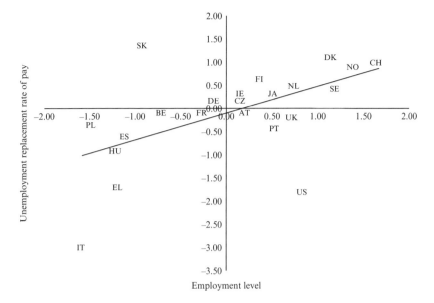

Figure 8.1a   Unemployment pay replacement rate by total employment, 2001 (country scores in relation to standard deviations around means)

Providing high URR but low employment:

- Profile II/III: Slovakia

We can conclude from this that Profile I countries were at that time more likely to provide optimal labour security as we have defined it, but that membership of that profile was neither necessary nor sufficient for this. Profile II countries had a mixed experience, with high employment for all its members except Ireland, but with a division between Japan and Switzerland providing optimal conditions, and the UK and the USA providing low unemployment support. Workers in hybrid Slovakia did receive excellent unemployment support but at a low level of overall employment. Profile III countries had a generally poor experience.

By 2012, data are available for all countries of interest to us except Croatia and Russia. Details are given in Figure 8.1b. The correlation between the two variables has risen considerably to $r^2 = 0.6605$, if only the 2001 range of countries is taken into account – the figure that compares directly with 2001. The correlation for all countries now being considered was slightly lower at $r^2 = 0.6220$.

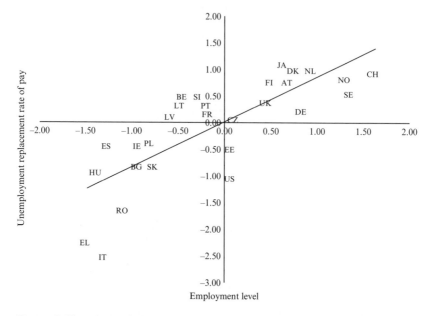

Figure 8.1b   Unemployment pay replacement rate by total employment,
2011–12 (country scores in relation to standard deviations
around means)

Undertaking the same analysis as before gives us the following list of countries providing the optimal combination:

- Profiles I and I/II: Austria, Denmark, Netherlands, Norway, Sweden (Finland, Germany) (but not deviant case France)
- Profile II: Japan, Switzerland (the UK) (but not Ireland or USA)
- Profile III: none

Providing the worst combination of low employment and low URR were:

- Profile II: (Ireland)
- Profile II/III: Slovakia
- Profile III: Bulgaria, Greece, Hungary, Italy, Romania (Poland, Spain) (but not the Baltic states)

Providing high employment but low URR:

- Profile III: (Latvia, Lithuania)

Providing high URR but low employment were:

- Profile I: (France)
- Profile I/III: (Belgium, Slovenia)
- Profile III: Portugal

That leaves three countries with insufficiently strong profiles to be able to be classified: the Czech Republic, Estonia and the USA.

With the exception of France, a deviant case, the countries of Profiles I and I/II demonstrated considerable resilience during the economic crisis, providing overall the optimal conditions for protecting labour security. Profiles II and II/I became fragmented as countries dealt with the crisis, with the UK acquiring a larger role for state governance and joining Japan and Switzerland in II/I. All three countries had good performances. Ireland became a poor performer, while the USA and the Czech Republic had indistinct profiles. Profile III continued to be associated with the poorest combinations of employment and URR in all cases.

A viable conclusion from the above analysis is that while neither the 'social democratic' nor the 'neoliberal' profile is uniquely associated with success in providing optimal labour market conditions for workers, the former has, with the exception of France and the two I/III hybrids (Belgium and Slovenia), the overall strongest record of providing both employment and protection during unemployment; and this relative superiority strengthened following the crisis.

INNOVATIVE CAPACITY

It is sometimes argued that countries that lack neoliberal labour market regimes can maintain employment only at the expense of sacrificing economic innovation, hoarding labour in firms and sectors that perform inadequately and avoiding change. One way to assess a country's innovative capacity is to examine its records in patent activity. The OECD publishes data on the so-called 'patent triad families'. These plot the number of patents attributed to residents in a particular country and deposited in the three main patent offices: the EU, the US government and the government of Japan. These are then expressed as a ratio per million inhabitants of the country concerned. Data are available only for OECD member states, and full data are available only for recent years. (See Appendix Table A8.1) One would expect this kind of innovative capacity to vary according to the wealth of an economy, so Figure 8.2 plots countries against per capita national income. A log scale is used to clarify display of the data,

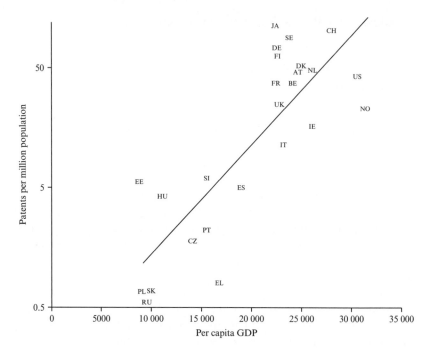

Figure 8.2   Patent ratios (log scale) by per capita GDP, 2010

because there is so much variation among countries. The straight line of best fit observed in the log scale implies a curvilinear relationship between the variables, the relationship between wealth and innovation increasing sharply as countries rise in wealth. If the hypothesis that strong welfare states achieve their strong employment performance at the expense of innovation were correct, then countries from Profiles I and I/II should all be found below the trend line, but in fact Norway is the only case to which this might apply. The Profile I/III hybrids, Belgium and Slovenia, also come slightly above the trend line. The neoliberal cases (Profiles II and II/I), which according to this hypothesis should all have exceptional patent performances, are a more mixed group: Japan and Switzerland, and very marginally the UK, conform to the hypothesis, but the Czech Republic, Slovakia, Ireland and the USA fall below it. The hypothesis does not have anything to say about Profile III, but for the record all cases for which we have data come below the line, except for Hungary. We also again find here a lack of difference between most of CEE and SWE. In a related study of technical skills, Tåhlin (2013b) found that several CEE countries were better equipped than those in SWE.

Overall, these data do not support the neoliberal hypothesis about innovation, but rather that developed by Kristensen and Lilja (2011), who argued that the Nordic welfare states have acquired an economic as well as a social capacity for innovation based on their negotiated approach and strongly participative work organizations – neither centralized bureaucracy nor market. The confrontation between neoliberalism and social democracy within these small, open economies, they suggest, has stimulated this commitment to innovation by providing a diversity of institutional forms that would be lacking in countries dominated by neoliberalism alone (see also Crouch 2013; Zeitlin and Trubeck 2003). In particular, we can see here the practical meaning of the idea of the 'social investment welfare state', referred to in Chapters 1 and 2, where strong public social policy of the kind found in Profiles I and I/II is associated not only with compensating the victims of economic change but with facilitating that change itself.

AN ALTERNATIVE APPROACH TO LABOUR-MARKET SECURITY

With the macro-level data we have been using here to compare national performances across a wide range of variables it is difficult to probe any closer into the dynamics of labour market behaviour. Other studies, which aggregate individual data, can take us further. Considerable progress has been made by Ute Klammer, Ruud Muffels, Ton Wilthagen and their colleagues in a number of studies associated with the flexicurity approach (Klammer 2004; Muffels 2013a and b; Muffels and Luijkx 2008a, 2008b; Muffels et al. 2008; Muffels et al. 2014; Muffels et al. 2002), and with the associated study of labour-market transitions pioneered by Günther Schmid (Schmid 2006, 2008; Schmid and Gazier 2002). These authors use extensive individual data from comparable national labour-market surveys.

Muffels et al. (2010) proposed four dynamic outcome indicators to measure the performance of countries on the flexibility-security balance instead of relying on static-institutional indicators and measurements of employment levels alone, as is done in most studies including the present one. The aim was to study the kinds of transitions between different positions on the labour market made by people in different countries. The authors defined indicators for the degree of voluntary and involuntary job-to-job mobility, calculated as the percentage of people moving from one job into another annually. Other indicators were defined for numerical flexibility, such as the number of workers moving between fixed-term and permanent contracts (contract mobility). This enabled the authors to measure to what extent non-standard contracts act as 'stepping stones' into standard jobs or as an 'employment trap' from which it is hard to escape. For employment security an indicator was defined for the percentage of people moving into a more secure employment status in the following year, and for income security an indicator was defined for the percentage of people improving their income security, measured by the likelihood of staying out of poverty or of moving out of it the year after. The two indicators on job and contract mobility were combined into a 'voluntary job and contractual mobility' measure and the two indicators on income and employment security were combined into an 'income and employment transition security' measure. Countries' positions on these indicators indicate how social risk is being managed, and how transition flexibility and security is managed within them. In subsequent work, Muffels et al. (2013a and b, 2014) found a very weak positive relationship between transition flexibility and transition security ($r^2 = 0.06$), suggesting that there is no necessary trade-off between flexibility and security. Second, they found countries falling into the following four quadrants when transitions were measured in terms of flexibility and security (though it must be remembered that the data used here were collected before the crash of 2008):

- high flexibility, high security (i.e., flexicurity): the Nordic countries plus the UK
- low flexibility, high security: Austria, France, Germany
- low flexibility, low security: southern Europe
- high flexibility, low security: CEE

The authors thus found that individual transition data are consistent with much macro-analysis (though less so our present study) in distinguishing the Nordic countries from the rest of NWE, or 'Continental' Europe. As in the current work, they also found that countries in SWE and CEE overlapped, not forming separate groups; and that there was no 'Anglo' group, Ireland and the UK being far apart from each other. There was also variation within regimes. Within CEE, two of the Baltic countries (Estonia and Latvia) were doing better than predicted on voluntary job mobility, whereas among Continental countries the Netherlands performed worse in that respect due to a low level of job mobility and, especially, upward contractual mobility (from a temporary to an open-ended contract).

The authors interpret their results in terms of 'mutual risk management'. Most Continental countries (France, Austria and Germany) were in a trade-off quadrant with a low transition flexibility and high transition security, whereas SWE and CEE countries appeared in either the inflexi-curity (low flexibility and low security) quadrant or another, liberal unregulated, trade-off quadrant with high flexibility but low security. In all three cases mutual risk management had not yet materialized or risk management was skewed, as some risks – for companies or workers – were left relatively unmanaged. There was, however, a difference in that most CEE countries showed higher levels of mobility and flexibility than SWE countries, but showed similarly low transition income and employment security levels. Muffels et al. (ibid.) interpret this to indicate skewed risk management practices, especially for young and low-skilled workers.

These same researchers have also used their individual datasets to examine the complex implications of EPL, suggesting that it is not uniformly negative as claimed in much orthodox economics literature (Muffels et al. 2014; for similar findings see also Auer 2008; Avdagic and Salardi 2013). They suggest that the reason might be that employment protection can encourage employers to invest more in training if they cannot easily dismiss staff, raising productivity and therefore employ-ment. The positive effect of EPL becomes greater when account is taken of the variation in business cycle or macroeconomic conditions (GDP per capita growth over the previous five years) and demographic conditions (Muffels et al. 2014). Similar findings are reported by Belot et al. (2007) and Cazes et al. (2012), who showed that employment increased with pro-tection up to some optimal point after which it decreased. In a statistical study of a number of leading advanced industrial economies, De Beer and Schils (2009a) also found complex interactions between unemployment pay levels, EPL and ALMP. These recent findings tend to vindicate the evidence presented by Schömann et al. (2013) that deregulation has had hardly any effect on European employment patterns, and the earlier con-clusions of Esping-Andersen and Regini (2000a) that deregulation is no certain route to improving employment performance, while coordinated or encompassing collective bargaining and strong skills policies may well be important.

Muffels et al. (2014) go on to suggest that the effect of EPL may be positive in some welfare regimes and negative in others, reinforcing the position being taken here that variables operate differently in different regime contexts. For example, they argue that before the economic crisis employment growth in the dual labour markets of SWE consisted mainly of a growth in non-standard jobs, even though the formal regulations for temporary employment were rather strict. For the same reason, the growth in unemployment during the crisis was strongest in these countries, because temporary workers were the first to be laid off.

Single-country studies of Danish employment (Bredgaard et al. 2008;

Madsen 2009) suggest that it is not flexicurity alone that accounts for Danish workers' confident acceptance of flexibility, but a whole ensemble of economic, social and collective bargaining practices. In Denmark, and in Austria (Hermann and Flecker 2009) and Sweden (Anxo and Niklasson 2009), there is evidence of adaptation of the existing system of associational governance to keep pace with economic change. Ebbinghaus and Eichhorst (2009) suggest that the absence of such coordination, and in particular the lack of a role for cross-sectoral tripartite political exchange, accounts for the weakness of flexicurity arrangements in Germany. Similarly, Davidsson and Emmenegger (2012) present data from a number of countries to demonstrate that unions will contribute to the reform of job security arrangements provided they are operating in a helpful institutional context.

Muffels et al. (2013a and b, 2014) found that high average URR over a five-year period (as discussed here in Chapter 5 and used further above) had a small positive effect on employment, even after taking account of the business cycle and demographic controls. They speculate that this might be associated with the positive effect of unemployment insurance on improving job match and on stabilizing consumption, supporting claims made on behalf of flexicurity theory for secure and enabling benefits. However, the authors also point to the positive association between URR and involuntary job mobility (dismissals), suggesting that in countries with strong income protection employers tend to shift the costs of economic adjustment to the government, knowing that employees are well covered. These may well be an example of what we have argued in this book to be one of the ways in which measures like URR can both support workers' security and sustain labour-market flexibility.

Finally, Muffels et al. (2013a and b) found that both ALMP spending and the level of encompassment of collective bargaining had a positive effect on employment. This has also been found in research on the crisis by the OECD (2013a), and is consistent with the findings of our present study. However, in Muffels et al. (2014) the positive effect of ALMP seemed to be restricted to western Europe; it turned strongly negative when applied to CEE countries – though ALMP is in general far weaker in CEE than in the west. The effect of ALMP on employment seemed strongly dependent on the content and design of ALMP in the various countries. Training and working-time arrangements appeared particularly successful to curtail unemployment in the recent crisis, but particularly in countries with a strong tradition in these policies. In other countries, such as France, Italy and the Netherlands, during the crisis reform proposals were launched aimed at increasing flexibility through reducing the protection of insiders while improving security through improving the protection of outsiders. Overall, the authors conclude from these findings that welfare state regimes or social models seemed to matter in terms of the way in which institutions influence employment performance, but that each regime seeks its own way in which to reform its policies in response to a crisis.

Like many other studies, this research on labour market transitions finds that success – here defined as workers' ability to make transitions that optimize flexibility and security – can be found in more than one kind of economic arrangement. They share the frequent finding that the most successful forms were advanced welfare states of the Nordic type, and their ostensible nemesis – the so-called neoliberal regimes of the Anglophone world. The 'Continental' regimes of the rest of NWE came next, followed by SWE and CEE countries, with a gap between the latter two becoming ever less perceptible. Our results in the current study share this view of the Nordic group, though we have found less of a gap between the Nordic countries and the rest of NWE, apart from the important points that both stronger forms of class challenge and stronger employment performances are associated with the former. However, if there are exceptions within the Continental north-west as a whole these are, for different reasons, Belgium and France. We have found the idea of a neoliberal, 'Anglophone' group elusive, partly because the geo-cultural definition of such a group is weakened by the closeness of Japan and Switzerland to it; partly because since the crisis the UK has behaved more like a hybrid of the social democratic and neoliberal profiles; and partly because of the internal heterogeneity of this small group of countries, with its ostensible leading case, the USA, being more of an outlier than a paradigm. Like the labour-market transitions research, we have also found a diminishing gap between SWE and CEE, with these two regions possibly becoming a periphery to a north-western core, with only community institutions supporting workers' security in the great majority of cases.

As has been emphasized at several points, our methodology does not enable us to find causal relationships, although in formal statistical terms Chapter 3 contained independent variables and Chapters 4–6 contained dependent variables. While one can make a plausible case that, for example, the more balanced power relations found in Chapter 3 for Austria or the Nordic countries produced the labour-friendly outcomes described in Chapter 6, the causal flow could also run the other way: the labour-friendly policies of Chapter 6 help sustain the power balance described in Chapter 3. Alternatively again, certain characteristics of societies determine both the level of class challenge likely to develop in them and their dominant modes of governance. However, we can do a little better than this. As we know from evolutionary biology, the egg came before the chicken, because non-birds (e.g., reptiles) laid eggs, while no birds emerged from non-eggs. Policy outcomes must emerge from a political context, and pro-labour policy outcomes would not emerge from a political context hostile to labour. In the beginning, therefore, power relations must come before the policy outcomes. However, once the process gets going, the influences can become reciprocal and self-reinforcing; or a kind of path dependency might sustain a set of policy outcomes even after the power balance has changed. Strong labour movements developed in the Nordic countries well before the development of modern social policy.

Our research overall, like that of the labour market transitions school discussed above, as well as other studies (e.g., Amable 2003), has effectively refuted the dominant claim of policy makers, business spokespersons and orthodox economists that strong welfare states and collective bargaining arrangements are incompatible with long-term employment stability and economic success. It is possible that further research could show that consistent strong but institutionalized challenge by organized employee interests to the dominance of markets and corporate hierarchies actually has a positive effect on performance. Unchallenged dominance can produce complacency; challenge stimulates innovation. This raises further aspects of differences in performance of the social democratic and neoliberal profiles that require some exploration before we conclude.

TWO KINDS OF UNIVERSALISM

Although social democracy and neoliberalism (or Profiles I and II and their hybrids) appear as the central antagonists in the struggle over the labour market, the countries with the strongest contrast with Profile I are those in Profile III. Profile I has strong state and associational governance, sometimes with strong positive market, and weak community and negative market; Profile III is the exact opposite. In this sense, and rather curiously, neoliberalism appears almost as a hybrid between social democracy and traditionalism, sharing strong positive market and weak community with the former but strong negative market, weak state and associational governance with III. This requires further analysis.

Behind the contemporarily prominent confrontation between social democracy and neoliberalism stands an older and better-known, often taken-for-granted, confrontation between modernity and tradition. This has been a theme of conflict within societies for centuries – many of the contours of its current form having been established during the Enlightenment period of the eighteenth century. It has also been a theme of contrasts between societies, as when in the twentieth century inter-war years both North America and Scandinavia came to stand for forms of cultural modernity and willingness to break with past traditions that were not shared in the UK or in much of continental Europe. It was also in those two parts of the western world and at that same time that the first experiments in innovative economic policy of what became known as Keynesian demand management were attempted. These were also the world regions where women's rights, especially in the economy, developed fastest; and where a secular approach to many public issues took hold most strongly. In the second-half of the twentieth century the shared agenda became split, as Scandinavia became the place where labour movements and therefore social democracy took strongest root, while the USA became the country in which both the political power of capital and a resurgence of religious conservatism become more dominant than elsewhere in the west. Today the confrontation between a declining Nordic social democracy and a vigorous US neoliberalism strikes us as the leading socio-economic political confrontation, but the shared legacy of those two forces in earlier conflicts with tradition still leaves its traces.

An important part of the shared Enlightenment legacy is that both neoliberalism and social democracy lay claim to forms of universalism and equality rights. For neoliberalism this relates to the formal equality of all participants in a market that is gender-, age-, ethnicity- and nationality-blind. In the market no one has any social characteristics that might have invidious consequences; we are just rationally maximizing units of economic action. For social democracy there is a less formally elegant aspiration towards a substantive equality of citizenship rights making use of redistributive public policies and a strong representation of employee rights. These are two aspects of modernity. Traditionalism, familism and community do not promise any form of equality, but by definition imply barriers erected by particularistic institutions that defend specific groups. This does not mean that social democratic and neoliberal societies lack such barriers. Family inheritance of highly unequally distributed wealth creates privileges in neoliberal economies very similar to some of those typical of traditionalism; and social democracy can involve the protection of categories defended by trade unions if union membership and power are unevenly distributed across the economy. But formally neoliberalism and social democracy differ from traditionalism in the centrality of their claims to universalism and an absence of discrimination. We saw some aspects of these differences in Chapter 7, where there was evidence of higher social exclusion of immigrants in the more social-democratic societies, more isolation of the poor in neoliberal societies, but more exclusion of multiple kinds than in either of those societies where traditionalism and familism were stronger.

We can explore further some aspects of these claims. It is clear that more universalist societies should have lower levels of material inequality than particularistic societies, as various forms of equality are implied by the idea of universalism. But should the formally equalizing tendencies of the operation of markets or the substantive attempts of redistributive social policy have greater effect? This can be operationalized to predict that countries characterized by Profiles I and II will have less unequal distributions of incomes than those in Profile III. We might then hypothesize that substantive attempts at redistribution in societies with strong class challenge will lead to lower levels of inequality than the operation of the market alongside weak class challenge.

Figure 8.3a ranks countries within their grouped governance profiles according to their income inequality scores for the years around 2000. (Details of the Gini scores used here will be those found in Appendix A4.1.) There is clearly support for the hypothesis that at that time social-democratic systems provided a high level of egalitarian universalism. The countries in Profiles I, I/II and I/III all had Gini coefficients below 30, a characteristic shared only by Switzerland in II/I, the Czech and Slovak Republics in the deviant form of II/I, Croatia in III/I and Bulgaria, Italy and Hungary in III.

However, there is little support for the hypothesis that the second, neoliberal form of universalism produces a lower level of inequality than

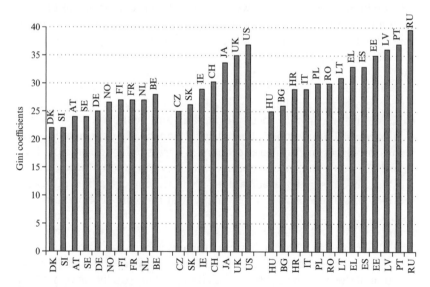

Figure 8.3a   Income inequality by governance profiles, c.2000 (Gini coefficients)

societies that embody considerable elements of traditionalism. Countries with Gini scorcs of over 35 come from Profile II (the UK and the USA) and both CEE (Estonia, Latvia) and SWE (Portugal) forms of Profile III and its hybrids. All four SWE countries had high levels of inequality. The remainder of Profile III and also II and II/I were more mixed. It is notable that the three more 'modernized' Visegrád countries (the Czech Republic, Hungary and Slovakia) had low levels of inequality, close to the social-democratic group, as did the ex-Yugoslav countries Croatia and Slovenia, while all others had high or very high levels. This corroborates the argument of Bohle and Greskovits (2006) that the Visegrád countries (with, in my view, some doubt over Poland) are developing economies somewhat more dependent on worker cooperation and skill than the Baltics, Bulgaria and Romania.

Figure 8.3b shows the situation around 2010, at which time some countries change their positions. Inequality in Bulgaria, France, Ireland and Italy rises to slightly above 30. Overall, however, the patterns remain the same. With the exceptions of Hungary and the Czech and Slovak Republics, the most egalitarian countries are those in the various forms of Profiles I. And, again, nothing systematically distinguishes the various forms of Profile II from those of Profile III.

The social-democratic hypothesis would also predict that, separately from the governance profiles, the stronger the class challenge the lower

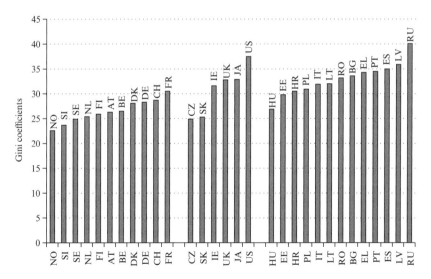

Figure 8.3b   Income inequality by governance profiles, c.2010 (Gini coefficients)

inequality should be, and that is indeed the case. Figure 8.4a displays the relationship ($r^2 = 0.3266$) found in the years around 2000, as usual converting numbers into distributions around the mean. There are no cases at all of countries having strong class challenge but a high level of inequality, and only four that have low inequality despite weak class challenge: the Czech Republic, France, Hungary and Switzerland.

By *c*.2010 the relationship has strengthened slightly to $r^2 = 0.3447$. Again no country with strong class challenge has a low level of inequality. There has been some change in the combination of weak class challenge and low inequality, with this quadrant now occupied by the three most industrialized Visegrád countries and (marginally) Germany and Switzerland. Bulgaria and France have both shifted to one of the two 'predicted' combinations: weak challenge and high inequality, which contains all remaining countries except the Nordics, Austria and Belgium, which occupy the other 'predicted' quadrant.

It is possible that forces of the following kind are at work. Overall, as countries move into post-industrialism the more the contrasting sociopolitical variables of social democracy and neoliberalism begin to be

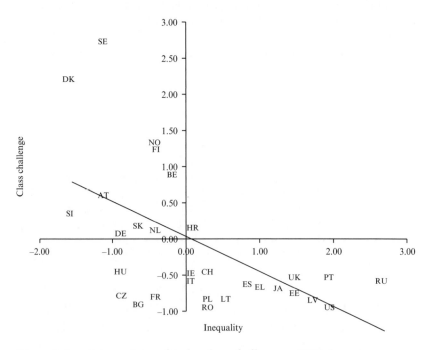

Figure 8.4a   Income inequality by class challenge, c.2000 (country scores in relation to standard deviations around means)

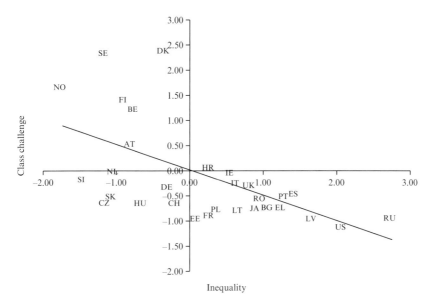

Figure 8.4b   *Income inequality by class challenge, c.2010 (country scores in relation to standard deviations around means)*

associated with new, sometimes stark differences. Neoliberalism is inconsistent with strong class challenge; some authors have also presented data suggesting that the UK and the USA achieve high levels of employment only through high levels of inequality (Blossfeld et al. 2012). Therefore the societies in which neoliberalism is dominant stand alongside those in SWE in which traditional, ultimately pre-industrial, power structures have remained strong. These are being joined by those societies in CEE in which decades of state socialism discredited both labour movements and welfare states. While very different from each other in several respects, societies dominated by post-industrial neoliberalism, traditionalism and post-communism are alike in having dominant elites that reject the egalitarian NWE welfare state. It is notable that Hungary and the Czech and Slovak Republics comprise the most consistent exceptions to our generalizations about governance, class challenge and inequality. With Slovenia, these are the most industrialized countries in CEE, with the smallest agricultural sectors in that region, but with lower levels of post-industrial employment than in most western economies. Does this mean that they have retained features of dependence on an industrial working class, even if the class challenge presented by that class has weakened? The early post-communist years saw a politically strong social democracy and temporarily strong trade union in those countries, characteristics that survive in Slovenia and survived in Slovakia until after the turn of the century. Are we seeing a continuing legacy of that period in the egalitarian profiles of these countries? There have been particularly strong policy fluctuations during the post-communist years in these countries and in Poland, making it difficult to define stable models (Cerami 2010; Keune 2006; Spieser 2007). The Hungarian case in particular suggests that the initial post-1989 pattern had been erected on an unsustainable base, coming increasingly to depend on both state and consumer debt, and later on the shadow economy, to rebuild employment after the post-2008 shock (Neumann and Tóth 2009; Tóth et al. 2012).

CONCLUSIONS

Certain countries in NWE, those in membership of our Profiles I and I/ II, have developed a capacity to act as solidaristic collectivities via both state and (with the exception of France) association that is unrivalled elsewhere. Particularly in the Nordic countries Kettunen (2011: 26) has argued that:

> Influential social liberal and social democratic policies were oriented towards recognizing asymmetrical social relations and regulating them in a way that empowered the weaker party to take care of his or her own needs and interests and constrained the stronger party from presenting his or her particular interests as the common interest. Symmetry should be brought into asymmetrical social relations – most notably those associated with employment and working life – and individual autonomy thus increased. This would happen through regulation by law, and especially by collective agreements based on collective action and organization.

The only major form of governance where these and other NWE countries are weak is community, which is not a successful form. This capacity is inextricably linked to their egalitarian character (Wilkinson and Pickett 2009) and both are then related to the relative strength of institutionalized class challenge. In recent years, all – again with the partial exception of France – have shown success in maintaining strong levels of employment and innovative capacity alongside reasonable levels of equality. In a study of a number of countries across Europe, Tåhlin (2013a: 49) has shown that the more egalitarian countries were less affected by the 'boom and bust' of the 2008 crisis. Also sharing some of these characteristics, but not all, have been Belgium and Slovenia.

As we have noted, the cause–effect relationship among these variables is difficult to disentangle. However, in all cases the class challenge characteristic was developed before the present pattern of equality, labour-market governance and employment security patterns. On the basis of the strength of class challenge there is a distinction between the Nordic countries and the remainder of NWE. This follows the distinction made in most of the relevant literature between countries with universalist welfare states and Bismarckian countries, but the evidence in this study, based on a wider range of variables than the design of social insurance systems on which these other classifications are based, suggests that the more fundamental split is between north-western and south-western Bismarckian countries, and that the division between Nordic countries and the rest of NWE (less France) is a matter of sub-types. In the Nordic countries, as is still clear from their exceptional levels of union strength, there was an early and powerful development of trade union strength during the 1930s in small, export-dependent economies where an attempt to achieve labour security through a rejection of market forces could have had disastrous consequences for competitiveness. The history was established nearly 40 years ago by Walter Korpi (1978). Representatives of capital and labour, as well as political forces, were under strong pressure to develop productive compromises. The result was a continuing series of inventive initiatives in governance forms and social policies that continues today, as we have seen.

The situation in the other members of Profiles I and I/II was different. In the wake of World War II these economies faced a major challenge of reconstruction, and also had to cope with legacies of class mistrust that had developed as employers had collaborated with Nazism. Majorities of the labour movements rejected outright opposition to capitalism and were available for class compromise, which employers and governments felt constrained to offer. There was therefore a major institutionalization of the role of unions within economy and polity, but not on the basis of the kind of sheer strength that the Nordic unions had developed. As seen in Chapter 3, in these former countries the strength of class challenge remains based more on institutional integration than on union strength. This continues to mark their approaches to managing labour security today, as their membership strength ebbs away while, so far, their institutional position remains.

Among the western European countries emerging from the war France and Italy stood outside this pattern of compromise. Their labour movements were dominated by communist groups who rejected the capitalist economy, and by 1948 employers and governments had turned aggressively against compromise strategies. There is however a strong difference between the two countries, in that France had long developed a strong, modernizing state that carried its own vision of solidaristic collectivity, of a kind that elsewhere had to await the arrival of strongly organized and integrated trade union movements. This helps to explain why today France continues to cut a different profile from the rest of NWE, achieving several similar outcomes but with major differences (Berrebi-Hoffmann et al. 2009). However, it is also likely that our measure of class challenge underestimates the French situation, where unions have an implanted role within many public institutions (especially the pension system) that belies their numerical weakness (Palier 2010a).

Italy was a far less developed economy in 1945, with extreme class antagonisms, and a poorly functioning political system. Over the years there have been many attempts at constructing class compromise arrangements similar to those of Germany or elsewhere in NWE, but they have had only short-term success. Divisions between political factions, ideological currents among unions, and major disparities between economic sectors as well as regions of the country have brought these attempts to failure (Jessoula and Alti 2010; Simonazzi et al. 2009). Today the country's performance on the issues of interest to this study have drawn it closer not only to the less advanced economies in SWE, but also to those in the centre and east.

Italy resembles Greece, Portugal and Spain in having an approach to labour issues on the part of state elites that has sustained particularistic traditional policies. There is however a difference in that in the three other countries fascist dictatorships remained in power until the 1970s, excluding labour far more effectively from participation in public life than the exclusion of communist movements alone in France and Italy. In all these countries, and also France, states long pursued protectionist trade strategies, protecting 'national champion' firms, whose leaders were usually closely connected to political elites, from international competition. Eventually EU competition rules wore down these protections, but for many years labour security had been framed within this context. The easiest way in which governments could stem popular discontent at the uncertainty of working-class life was to provide employment protection for the key sectors. This could be achieved through employment protection law. It placed a burden on employers, who could not easily dismiss workers, but that was a kind of exchange for the privileged positions enjoyed by the national champion firms. Today, a major legacy of these arrangements is the creation of major barriers between labour-market 'insiders' and 'outsiders' (Berton et al. 2012; O'Higgins 2011), including also in France (Gautié 2011).

Although these countries all count as having Bismarckian welfare states, their trajectory over the past 70 years has been quite different from those in Austria, Belgium, Germany and the Netherlands, and this explains the state of their inherited labour market governance. We still see in SWE countries a reliance on employment protection legislation, protecting existing job holders, and a lower development of unemployment pay, ALMP, and sometimes general social protection expenditure. Despite heroic but unsuccessful attempts at change in Italy over the years, collective bargaining remains uncoordinated and cannot assist with governance. Governments are therefore inclined to press for increasingly neoliberal policies, which means primarily an attack on EPL, since the other arrangements for protecting labour are already weak. Since EPL is among the few protective mechanisms available, unions find themselves defending it. The neoliberal climate of debate is not conducive to unions proposing, say, an exchange of EPL for generous unemployment replacement pay that might make major improvements in the functioning of the labour market. As a result, unions are in danger of protecting a minority of workers while young people in particular are forced to work in precarious situations outside unions' reach.

There are extensive differences among the SWE countries. For example, there have been important attempts at ALMP and other constructive social policies in Spain, but very few in Greece. However, in the prevailing neoliberal climate, it has not been possible to take major policy strides in this direction. The pressure from employers, international organizations, ratings agencies and stock markets is always to press for more deregulation, not for constructive social policy. As in Italy, unions, unable to demand more constructive policies, end up fighting to save EPL. Neoliberalism does not bring the 'modernization' that might flow from a successful market economy; traditional governance, including the shadow economy, continues to be extensive. Neoliberal reforms only intensify the steep inequalities and weak social policies that already exist in the traditionalist context (Karamessini 2012). In particular, these countries lack the historical development of class compromise institutions that might have given them a capacity for solidaristic collectivity.

The countries of CEE have had completely different histories from those of western Europe since World War II, and there are considerable differences among them, but in the area of labour security and with some exceptions they are tending to develop certain similarities with each other and with the countries of SWE. Governance of all kinds except for community is weak, as is class challenge. In theory unions under communism would have scored extremely high on our class challenge index: membership was virtually compulsory, and unions were deeply integrated into the administration of social policy. But all this was carried out in a context of state control that reduced unions' capacity for a true representative function to almost nothing. For a few years after the fall of communism, the huge memberships inherited from the past were maintained, but during the 1990s and early 2000s they collapsed completely. In the early post-communist years, when governments were highly insecure and uncertain of their legitimacy, there were important attempts to incorporate union leaders, and to enact pro-labour social policies of various kinds. However, Avdagic (2004) has argued that, if anything, union links with political parties in CEE were used almost solely to ensure that unions did not raise awkward demands, weakening them further. Unions' roles were particularly important in the early years in the Visegrád countries, where there were in any case longer-term links with western social democracy and labour movements, as well as with Bismarckian social policy, through the Austro-Hungarian Empire and the brief inter-war democratic period (Cerami 2010; Keune 2006). The situation in the Baltic states was very different, as these countries had been part of Russia, which not only implied a different historical legacy but also provided a different basis for post-Soviet state legitimacy through the assertion of a long-suppressed anti-Russian national identity.

The legacy of these years remains in some of the differences that we have seen among countries, particularly the extreme differences in inequality that the region contains. However, across all these countries (with the exception of Slovenia, to be discussed below) the strength of class challenge was low, and became ever lower as the swollen post-communist membership collapsed. Internal neoliberal elites, who associated social democracy and the role of unions with communism, welcomed recommendations coming from the OECD, the IMF and the European Commission that there was an important need to deregulate labour markets and withdraw social protection. The trend in all countries has therefore been to dismantle the state governance of labour security, while there was very little in the way of coordination through corporatist collective bargaining. However, the market, as a source of employment stability, has also not been delivering. As in SWE, therefore, the main form of governance of labour security that exists is that from the traditional institutions that we have discussed. The region continues to display diversity in levels of inequality, some resembling the Nordics, others resembling SWE or the USA, but the overall tendency towards no other strong forms of governance remains. Collective capacity has been generally low, once the initial enthusiasm after the fall of communism wore off. The formal institutional legacy of communism was very weak, a fact which in itself strengthened traditional and community institutions, both during the communist period and since. But, as in SWE, local community and family solidarities do not build a capacity for wider solidaristic collectivity.

There is however considerably more diversity in employment success in CEE than is found in SWE; the Czech Republic and Estonia in particular having developed relatively high levels of employment – in the former case within a context of low levels of inequality, in the latter the opposite.

That Slovenia is an exception has been noted by many authors, and it has fitted awkwardly into almost all discussions in this study. At one level it is the only country in CEE to develop anything like institutions associated with the social-democratic ideal type. It has a strong, if declining, level of class challenge that has survived the fall of state socialism for two decades; it has strong associational governance; stronger state policies than most of the rest of CEE; and a low level of inequality. However, it also has strong community governance, including a large shadow economy. It stands part-way between the economies typical of CEE and SWE but with certain institutions that give it characteristics and policy outcomes similar to those of Austria and the rest of NWE. Institutionally as geographically, Slovenia lies between Austria and Hungary.

The country also had a different state socialist experience from the countries of the Soviet bloc or Romania. Yugoslav state socialism maintained a form of worker participation in management and also permitted more pluralism and open debate than in the countries under Russian influence. It is tempting to see echoes of that distinctive past in the country's present position. In determining how valid this might be, much hangs on the development of Croatia, another ex-Yugoslav successor state. For that reason I have tried to include Croatia in this study, but it has been difficult, as the country has been emerging from the consequences of the post-Yugoslav wars, and has only very recently joined the EU, which means that data sources on it are inadequate (but see Franičević 2011). All we can say on the basis of the country's inadequate presence in the evidence we have examined is that it possibly has some characteristics in common with Slovenia. However, there is also evidence that it might fall into the general central tendency of CEE institutional development.

Finally, we need to discuss the neoliberal group, Profile II. Neoliberalism forms the dominant social policy ideology of the present period, and virtually all countries, including all those in Profile I, are seeing some kind of convergence on its pattern. In particular, associational governance, and along with it the place of trade unions and class challenge, is weakening everywhere, while inequality is rising. State social policy is under considerable pressure, though paradoxically in the wake of the financial crisis it has grown in several countries. The USA continues to be an extreme case of neoliberal social policy. The other two Anglophone countries (Ireland and the UK) have more state policy and stronger class challenge than the ideal requires, though they share the US pattern of weak associational governance, a high level of inequality and general exclusion of those on low incomes while not discriminating specifically against immigrants. Switzerland is sometimes reckoned among the Bismarckian countries, and that remains the main logic of its social policy (Häusermann 2010: 209), but its overall profile increasingly fits a neoliberal frame rather than the social-democratic frame. However, the country has distinctive institutions of cohesion and participative democracy, which possibly also contribute independently to a capacity for solidaristic collectivity. Japan fits the neoliberal pattern better than it does any other, though, as noted above, this is partly because we have been unable to take account of the specific role of corporate as opposed to market measures.

Although movements towards neoliberalism are occurring almost everywhere, full convergence on the US pattern would require very extensive changes indeed in many societies. Meanwhile, the USA itself has become increasingly dependent on two unsustainable forms of support in public and private debt.

Final Reflections

There is a puzzle within some of the results of this research. Returning to the themes of Chapter 4, one might have expected that the stronger the class challenge experienced by a given national capitalism the more there would be evidence of escapes from confrontation through practices that avoid the need for internal solidarity. We do find this on two variables. First, all countries with strong class challenge, with the exception of Slovenia, are wealthy; and Slovenia is the wealthiest of the CEE cases. Second, there is a growing tendency for strong class challenge countries to be among those with high immigrant exclusion. But the account in Chapter 4 showed that for all other variables (dependence on state debt, levels of environmental unsustainability, the use of social exclusion other than immigration) the countries with strong class challenge are among the most dependent on internal solidarity. Also, during the period of the crisis the countries with the highest class challenges were (with the exception of Belgium) more likely to see a relatively reduced dependence on both state debt and consumer credit than most more neoliberal wealthy economies. The main difference among wealthy countries was in fact the opposite from what one might expect: those with the stronger class challenges were those that made least use of what we called solidarity-avoidance devices, while those with weaker class challenge were less sustainable. A different logic is at work.

If we assume a certain level of formal democracy and human rights, we should expect that the less inequality a society has the more interdependent is its population and therefore the more solidaristic it is, and the more use it can make of national institutions for risk-sharing. Highly unequal societies have less need for such institutions, as wealthier groups can more easily 'dump' risk-bearing on to poorer groups. This will be especially the case if the lower classes lack the means to challenge the distribution of risks. Unequal societies where the lower classes have little power to challenge would seem relatively immune from any need to develop solidaristic institutions, while egalitarian societies with weak class challenge capacity should be relatively uninventive in terms of solidaristic institutions.

Such an account must not be understood mechanistically. A society might have a 'need' for certain institutions but not be able to have them, in which case we might expect certain symptoms of stress, but not necessarily any change. There are also many institutional possibilities apart from solidaristic institutions through which these issues can be resolved. Overall, however, there is strong support in our data for the hypothesis that countries with strong institutionalized class challenge – the countries of NWE in general and the Nordic lands in particular – are also those that have managed to achieve a 'social universalism' going beyond the formal universalism of a market economy. The strongest evidence of this is that they, unlike the 'purer' market economies, have managed to combine economic success in terms of both employment and innovation with a low level of income inequality. They also tend (with some exceptions) to have better records of sustainability (in terms of state debt, environmental sustainability and high trust), stronger systems of collective protection of income levels in the face of labour-market risk on a number of scales, strong protection in the labour market (not from EPL alone but from strong unemployment support and ALMP), and coordinated collective bargaining. The most egalitarian of them present few indicators of social exclusion, though others show a tendency to exclude immigrants. In the case of Denmark, Pedersen (2006) has shown how habits of coordinated, neo-corporatist behaviour acquired initially within collective bargaining have gradually been extended to other areas of the polity.

Unravelling what is going on here leads us to a fuller understanding of the roots of the differences between different types of governance regime and forms of labour security. In particular, we return to the clash between the two forms of universalism discussed above. The idea of universalism entered European philosophical and political debate around the late seventeenth and the eighteenth centuries, alongside ideas about a free market economy. As we noted, the market is a universalistic mechanism in that its formal processes recognize no claims to privilege or obstructions to free competition. The early stage of the introduction of capitalist markets in a society is therefore usually associated with a reduction in inequalities – those inequalities based on inherited positions and pre-defined categories of people. The market creates its own inequalities, but in principle these are of achievement, not ascription, and they should in the long run be relatively limited in extent. According to the pure theory of market competition, high levels of inequality should be transitional. They arise because demand for the products of a particular set of skills or owned resources exceeds supply, leading to a rise in prices that increases the rewards of those engaged in the sector concerned and hence to increased inequalities. If markets are functioning perfectly, that rise serves as a signal to potential new entrants to the market concerned that there are high rewards available. More people will therefore acquire the skills needed to enter the sector, prices will eventually decline as supply increases, and inequalities will be reduced. This is a very sticky process; it can take years for such adjustments to take place, with inequalities remaining or rising in the meantime. Also, where the supply shortage lies in the ownership of a resource rather than possession of a skill (as, for example, in the energy sector), there may be little possibility of an increase in supply – other than the discovery of alternative products. This will be the case especially where property and wealth can be inherited, as this intensifies the accumulation of ownership rights.

The long-run tendency to reduced inequality in a pure market economy is also weakened by equally long-term tendencies towards a concentration of ownership that leads to quasi-monopolies able to restrict new entrants into a sector. The outcome of economic competition is usually the emergence of a number of successful firms and the disappearance of the unsuccessful. As Karl Marx noted long ago, over time competition destroys itself. Once a small number of large producers dominates a market it can be difficult for new firms to enter, weakening the tendency for high rewards to encourage newcomers to enter a market on which a capitalist economy depends for its long-term equalitarian trend – unless tough competition laws operate to prevent this from happening, and this is very difficult if market dominance has really been achieved through superior efficiency. Also, in some sectors – for example certain kinds of banking, energy supply, or the construction of large aircraft and certain kinds of military equipment – firms need to have a large amount of capital to operate at all, which further discourages new entrants and maintains high prices and therefore high profits.

Capital resources, which provide the base of the returns to capital, can usually be inherited (unless the law were to provide otherwise, which it normally does not do), so subsequent generations start off with a more unequal distribution of resource endowments than their predecessors. The distinction between capital resources and skill forms the basis of the argument in favour of meritocracy as an equalizing force: inherited material wealth may be unequally distributed, but if the most able of any generation are able to compete on equal terms irrespective of their parents' wealth they will be able to offset this effect, restoring the egalitarian trend. But this overlooks the fact that abilities and skills can be culturally inherited, as parents have very strong incentives to use their wealth, contacts and other resources to advance their children's chances. Inequality of wealth in one generation reproduces itself in the next as material capital translates itself into cultural capital (Bourdieu and Passeron 1990). Running against capitalism's long-term theoretical trend to reduced inequalities are therefore several strong counter tendencies, which at the present time are proving far more powerful than the former, as inequalities are increasing in virtually all market economies (OECD 2011a; Piketty 2013; Salverda et al. 2014).

The universalism of the straightforward market economy is therefore very limited, despite the claims made for liberal capitalism as being a universalist, non-discriminatory system. It might avoid maintaining people in social exclusion because they belong to ascribed categories, but when its tendencies to inequality outweigh the opposite tendencies, it can exclude through the fact of inequality itself, given that being on lower incomes than the majority of one's society leads to exclusion from access to many capabilities (Sen 2005; Sen and Nussbaum 1993) and social activities.

In democracies there is usually some political pressure to reassert an egalitarian universalism against the inegalitarian tendencies of the pure market economy. This happens when the interests that are held back by the inequalities of the free market organize themselves effectively to challenge the outcome of class distribution – the process that we have termed 'class challenge'. The list of demands to reduce inequalities made by the excluded classes of the twentieth century is well known: redistributive taxation; the provision of income transfers and important services on the basis of need rather than of market strength; the management of the economy so that there would always be a high demand for labour that will reduce inequalities of bargaining power in the labour market; and the existence of trade unions with the power and right to bargain on behalf of relatively less-well-paid employees. This array of approaches, broadly known as social democracy, has historically been the main opposing force to neoliberalism, the doctrine of the free market economy. As we have seen, like the latter, its universalist credentials have blemishes: it depends on an array of different social policy measures rather than capitalism's simple logic of the free market; these do not necessarily operate in universalist terms, as they might be used to support privileged groups within the workforce, much depending on their precise design. Trade unions and labour rights might operate in the same way, privileging rather small groups of organized workers against the rest. Also, to the extent that welfare states are national structures, their universalism is really limited to an individual nation state.

Both the social-democratic and the neoliberal model have been associated with some successes in coping with the calamity caused by the 2008 crisis. In the first instance it was a neoliberal crisis, as it originated in Ireland, the UK and the USA, countries where deregulated financial markets had become involved in highly irresponsible behaviour. States intervened to resolve the crisis on the grounds that the sector was too important to the general economy to be allowed to collapse. This was a triple defeat for the neoliberal model. First, its economic theory had argued that the failure of deregulated finance was impossible. Second, if firms can become so large that they cannot be permitted to fail, then the economy is not a true market one. Third, state intervention of the kind involved in the rescue contradicted the tenets of free market doctrine.

Of more direct relevance to our present concerns, the crisis revealed the relationship between the financial model and excessive use of consumer credit to finance consumption – one of the key themes of Chapter 5. Not surprisingly, some of the main neoliberal countries (Ireland, the UK and the USA) were deeply involved in that economic pattern; it was a classic neoliberal response to a need to protect consumption from the insecurities of the neoliberal labour market. However, some social-democratic countries (in particular Austria and Germany) acted similarly, and some others maintained extremely high levels of household debt, if not outstanding credit (Denmark and the Netherlands in particular). There is no clear-cut distinction here between neoliberal countries and social-democratic countries.

Because of the state rescue of the banks, the crisis became one of state debt in the years after 2008. In theory, neoliberal economies do not run high debts, but the involvement of several of them in the crisis meant that Ireland, the UK and the USA became among the major state debtors; Japan was already chronically in that condition. Meanwhile, most social-democratic countries achieved a major reduction in their public debt, contrary to the neoliberal stereotype of social democracy as vulnerable to large debts because of its public spending commitments. In fact, it was the most social-democratic countries, the Nordics, which most reduced their debt.

But the main debt crisis was concentrated on the SWE countries – though Spain's public debt remains lower than that of Germany. The reasons for this are too varied to concern us here, but the consequences are of considerable importance. First, what had originally been a crisis of private debt and bank irresponsibility was redefined as one of public debt and state irresponsibility, which was in turn redefined by the neoliberal authorities in the European Commission, the European Central Bank and the IMF as a crisis of welfare state irresponsibility and excessively protective labour laws. The policy response has therefore been for an indiscriminate demolition of virtually all forms of public policy to support employees against insecurity, including coordinated collective bargaining (Banyuls and Recio 2012). A crisis of the neoliberal model has been redefined as one of the social-democratic model. In particular there is a renewed attack on the so-called 'European social model', which is deemed to be at the heart of the problems of certain European economies.

The present study enables us to set some counter-arguments to this overwhelmingly dominant orthodoxy. First, as we have seen, the SWE countries are not examples of a social-democratic labour security regime. Their patterns of policies and practices form an extreme contrast with the social-democratic ideal type. Second, they do not feature coordinated collective bargaining as one of their forms of bargaining; their bargaining is highly fragmented and their unions weak. Third, against this, nearly all the economies that do feature social-democratic labour policies as well as coordinated collective bargaining and strong trade unions have emerged well from the crisis, maintaining high levels of employment and strong innovation performances. The only real exception to this is Belgium.

The social support systems of the crisis countries are indeed so remote from those of social democracy that it is not easy to argue that they could all solve their problems by becoming more like the Nordic countries (see also Barbier 2008b). It is however even less clear that the pursuit of neoliberal remedies would help them. That route involves exposing labour to an extreme level of insecurity, so that its consumption standards decline severely. Given that these are countries with weak export performances, it is difficult to see how this would enable them to recover, except by forcing wages so low that their goods start to compete with very low-cost producers in CEE, if not also in the Far East. This is essentially what is being imposed, on Greece in particular. It is one thing for already very poor workers in the Baltic states, Bulgaria or Romania to pursue such a strategy when starting on existing low incomes, with a prospect of gradually earning more. To imitate them, workers in SWE countries would first have to accept a very major decline in their living and social standards. It is not clear that populations can accept this without serious dislocation and social disorder.

As in the 1990s, the most influential voices in policy-making in Europe are insisting that there is only one way, and that is the American way, to achieve economic success. This happens despite the extreme outlier characteristic of many US social policy institutions, and the difficulty of other countries imitating the only nation that maintains a global currency and is therefore able to ease its economic problems by printing money. The 1990s arguments of this kind subsided during the early 2000s, when the success of the Nordic economies became impossible to ignore, and organizations like the EU and OECD began to revise their views and accept a variety of ways in which economies might find success, in particular by combining labour market flexibility with new ways of achieving security for workers' lives – flexicurity. This redirection of thinking might have been intensified when the US, UK and Irish economies became involved in the banking crisis, and the earlier success of the neoliberal economic approach could be seen as having been based in part on an unsustainable financial model. Many countries resorted to increases in social protection in order to ease the impact of the crisis on their populations, and there was often even a temporary return to the use of associational governance to combine reduced working hours and pay with the maintenance of employment (Carley and Marginson 2010; Marginson et al. 2014). While this was most prominent in western European countries, in particular Germany, where it received government support (Bosch 2011), it also extended to Bulgaria and some other CEE countries (Tzanov 2011). Further, some recent studies have suggested the superiority of countries in NWE in coping with various aspects of the crisis. Within Europe, Gash and Inanc (2013: 162–6) found that peripheral workers' relative security and pay worsened during the 2004–10 period in Ireland and the UK, as well as in SWE and some CEE countries, but improved in Nordic and other NWE countries. Russell et al. (2013: 246) found a greater decline in life satisfaction as a result of financial strain in two Profile II countries, Ireland and the UK, than anywhere else.

In addition to the redefinition of the financial crisis as one of the welfare state, the depth of the recession has enabled business interests to argue that, unless they are given full freedom to operate, they will be unable to deliver prosperity and employment will suffer. This is being used not only to oppose the role of unions and social policy but also to produce a reversal of EU policy on environmental damage and climate change. Policy makers in the EU and individual nation states have turned their backs on the concept of the social investment welfare state (Schmid 2014), despite its continuing success, as Hemerijck (2012b) has demonstrated.

Meanwhile, other major developments in societies and economies are undermining neoliberalism's social-democratic rival. As our data have shown, overall class challenge became weaker during the 2000s as trade union membership density declined from 23.63 per cent to 19.70 per cent in Europe, from 11.0 per cent to 9.6 per cent in the USA, and from 36.8 per cent to 27.2 per cent in Russia, though it was fairly stable in Japan (declining from 15.7 per cent to 15.0 per cent). (For a detailed discussion of the problems of unions in western Europe, see Gumbrell-McCormick and Hyman 2013.) The average Gini coefficient rose from 28.46 to 29.53 in Europe, from 35.7 to 37.8 in the USA, and from 39.6 to 40.1 in Russia, though in Japan it fell from 33.7 to 32.9. Most dramatically, as we saw in Chapter 5, the Swedish state has recently moved from being among the most fiscally redistributive states in the advanced world to being among the least redistributive, though the country's overall level of inequality remains low.

Consistent with the neoliberal shift, market governance has been expanding, but mainly through the unsustainable form of outstanding consumer credit supported by a high-risk financial sector. Several measures of state-provided security have also risen, though again the main one has been public debt. There is therefore an overall decline in sustainability. Some public measures (URR, ALMP and EPL) declined rather than expanded; in the case of the first two, this is certainly a retrograde step. Further, the evidence in this study suggests that state governance is most effective when accompanied by associational governance, but associational governance has declined in importance even more strongly, especially as governments reduce the role of associations in managing aspects of labour-market policy and transfer their work to profit-making corporations (Marginson 2014; Marginson and Welz 2014; for the Netherlands, see Schils 2009; for Sweden, see Wadensjö 2009).

In Germany, the major changes associated with unification after 1989 have sharply accelerated existing trends towards a declining role for associational governance, as well as produced a major increase in income inequality (Lehndorff et al. 2009; Streeck 2009a). The policy preferences of the EU are generally hostile to coordinated bargaining (Meardi 2011), and decisions of the European Court, single-mindedly pursuing a competition agenda, are making it difficult for the Nordic unions to maintain the coordination and encompassment that have been an important part of the successful labour-market institutions in that part of the world (Deakin and Rogowski 2011; Höpner 2008, 2014). The overall change has been for stronger market governance, a move from ALMP to workfare, slightly stronger state governance, and declining associational and community governance, associated with increased inequality, a deteriorating position for the poor, and a decline in the strength of employees' voices. One paradoxical consequence of this combined development is that, at a time when the capacity of societies for solidaristic collectivity might seem to be most needed, its supports are being systematically opposed and undermined by those most responsible for their governance.

Statistical appendix

Table A3.1

	A 2001	A 2011	B 2001	B 2011	C 2001	C 2011	D 2001	D 2011	E 2001	E 2011	F 2001	F 2011	G 2001	G 2011
Austria	35.7	27.8	13.1	13.8	31.0	24.0	9.8	10.6	28.4	21.9	0.8	0.9	22.7	19.7
Belgium	49.6	50.4	15.8	14.4	41.8	43.1	22.2	20.7	34.0	34.9	0.8	0.8	27.2	28.0
Bulgaria	28.1***	19.8**	(12.0)*	(11.8)	24.7	17.5	36.9	31.9	16.7	11.8	0.1	0.4	1.7	4.7
Croatia	(40.0)	(34.0)	(20.0)*	(18.0)	32.0	27.9	33.4	35.1	23.5	20.2	(0.7)	(0.7)	16.4	14.2
Czech Republic	23.6	17.3	15.2	17.8	20.0	14.2	19.1	15.5	16.8	12.0	0.2	0.5	3.3	6.0
Denmark	73.8	68.5	8.7	8.8	67.4	62.5	18.0	16.2	56.3	52.2	0.8	0.8	45.1	41.8
Estonia	13.7****	6.0**	9.1	8.3	12.5	5.5	25.6	22.5	9.6	4.2	0.4	0.5	3.8	2.1
Finland	74.5	69.0	13.7	13.5	64.3	59.7	18.1	16.8	54.3	50.3	0.6	0.6	32.6	30.2
France	7.9	7.9	8.0	9.1*	7.3	7.2	15.2	14.6	6.2	6.2	0.5	0.5	3.1	3.1
Germany	23.7	18.0	11.0	11.6	21.1	15.9	16.0	15.1	18.1	13.7	0.8	0.7	14.5	9.6
Greece	25.8	25.4	42.0	35.5	15.0	16.4	28.7	25.1	12.5	13.4	0.4	0.4	5.0	5.3
Hungary	20.0	16.8**	15.2	12.3	17.0	14.7	25.1	23.1	13.4	11.5	0.6	0.5	8.0	5.8
Ireland	36.2	36.1	18.8	17.4	29.4	29.8	15.9	16.5	25.6	25.9	0.3	0.5	7.7	13.0
Italy	34.2	35.2	28.5	25.5	24.5	26.2	27.1	26.7	19.7	20.9	0.4	0.5	7.9	10.5
Latvia	17.3	10.0	(9.0)*	(9.9)	15.7	9.0	23.6	21.5	12.4	7.9	0.2	0.4	2.5	2.8
Lithuania	20.5***	14.8**	(13.9)*	(9.1)	17.7	13.5	27.1	25.4	13.5	10.1	0.2	0.4	2.7	4.1
Netherlands	22.6	19.0	11.2	12.4*	20.1	16.6	13.1	13.6	17.7	14.7	0.9	0.9	16.0	13.3
Norway	53.9	54.6	7.4	7.7	49.9	50.4	19.1	18.2	41.1	41.5	0.8	0.8	32.9	33.2
Poland	15.5	14.1	27.4	22.8	11.3	10.9	27.6	23.8	9.0	8.6	0.3	0.5	2.7	4.3
Portugal	22.4	19.3	26.0	22.9	16.6	14.9	22.7	22.2	13.8	12.3	0.5	0.5	6.9	6.1
Romania	36.1****	32.8**	(19.0)*	(19.5)	29.2	26.4	34.4	30.9	21.9	19.8	0.1	0.4	2.2	7.9

Slovakia	30.5	16.7	8.0	16.0	28.1	14.0	18.9	15.8	24.0	12.2	0.7	0.6	16.8	7.3
Slovenia	40.8	24.4	16.1	17.3	34.2	20.2	27.1	23.7	27.4	16.2	0.7	0.7	19.2	11.4
Spain	15.9	15.6	20.2	16.9	12.7	13.0	22.7	23.5	10.3	10.4	0.5	0.6	5.2	6.3
Sweden	77.3	68.9	10.3	10.9	69.3	61.4	19.2	18.1	58.1	51.5	0.9	0.8	52.3	41.2
Switzerland	19.7	17.2	13.2	11.2*	17.1	15.3	8.6	8.0	15.9	14.2	0.5	0.5	8.0	7.1
UK	29.4	27.1	12.8	13.9	25.6	23.3	12.7	12.0	22.9	20.9	0.3	0.4	6.9	8.4
Japan	20.9	19.0	16.6	12.3	17.4	16.7	11.2	11.0	15.8	15.0	0.3	0.3	4.7	4.5
Russia	59.8	42.7**	10.1	6.9	53.8	39.8	46.1	46.4	31.3	22.6	0.2	0.1	6.3	2.3
USA	12.9	11.3	7.4	7.0	12.0	10.5	8.7	9.1	10.9	9.6	0.1	0.1	1.1	1.0

Notes:
Data are sometimes for one year earlier or later than column heading implies; where they diverge by more than one year, they are indicated as
follows: * = 2005; ** = 2008; *** = 2003; **** = 2002
( ) indicate use of sources other than those specified below
A = union density per workforce in dependent employment (source Visser 2013)
B = proportion of workforce in self-employment (from OECD 2013a; for bracketed cases, source is Eurostat websource)
C = adjusted union density taking into account self-employment
D = proportion of workforce in shadow economy (from Schneider and Buehn 2012)
E = final adjusted union density taking into account shadow economy
F = union incorporation in politico-economic decision-making (Source: own calculations based on Visser 2013)
G = combined class challenge index (E*F)

Table A4.1

	A		B		C		D		E		F
	2001	2012	2001	2012	2001	2012	2001	2012	2001	2012	2005
Austria	29648	41908	24.0	26.3	−0.7	1.9	14.87	54.08	71.5	75.2	
Belgium	27976	37459	28.0	26.5	4.0	−0.5	78.05	214.34	65.0	67.3	
Bulgaria	6908	14103	26.0	33.6	−5.5	−0.7	0.24	3.67	54.8	63.9	
Croatia	11664	17618	29.0	30.5	−3.0	−0.1	3.85	7.89	58.4	57.0	5.08
Czech Republic	16340	27000	25.0	24.9	−4.8	−2.7	1.76	7.74	71.2	70.9	
Denmark	29201	37324	22.0	28.1	1.6	5.3	48.77	73.56	78.3	75.7	
Estonia	10939	21714	35.0	29.8	−5.2	−1.2	7.08	26.52	67.8	70.4	2.82
Finland	25571	35771	27.0	25.9	8.1	−1.7	41.93	56.99	72.6	73.8	18.50
France	26976	35295	27.0	30.5	1.6	−2.4	59.54	57.33	68.5	69.2	11.82
Germany	27115	38666	25.0	28.3	−1.7	7.0	32.84	45.62	69.1	76.3	38.56
Greece	20088	24260	33.0	34.3	−7.8	−2.9	5.36	17.03	61.5	59.9	
Hungary	12800	14497	25.0	26.9	−8.4	1.7	2.95	27.40	61.3	60.7	
Ireland	31599	40716	29.0	31.6	−0.4	4.9	38.62	170.54	71.1	63.8	
Italy	26727	29812	29.0	31.9	−0.5	−0.5	14.96	28.07	58.5	61.2	
Latvia	8478	18058	36.1*	35.9	−7.7	−1.7	0.48	3.89	65.1	66.3	
Lithuania	9323	21383	31.0	32.0	−4.7	−0.9	0.39	5.98	64.2	67.0	
Netherlands	30829	41527	27.0	25.4	1.9	8.3	82.90	126.34	75.4	77.0	29.62
Norway	40676	54397	26.6***	22.6	15.0	14.2	21.92	43.50	80.1	79.6	16.15
Poland	10746	20562	30.0	30.9	−6.0	−3.6	0.61	11.80	59.4	64.8	3.76
Portugal	19021	23047	37.0	34.5	−10.2	−1.5	18.55	33.57	73.9	69.1	9.72

	A		B		C		D		E		F
Romania	6 640		30.0	33.2	−4.4	−3.8	0.29	0.81	68.3	62.8	
Slovakia	11 966	24 142	26.2*	25.3	−3.4	2.3	2.40	4.81	63.5	65.1	1.27
Slovenia	18 485	27 837	22.0	23.7	0.2	2.3	4.82	17.10	69.4	68.4	
Spain	23 481	30 058	33.0	35.0	−4.0	−1.1	23.57	46.43	62.1	61.6	20.01
Sweden	27 452	40 304	24.0	24.9	3.8	7.1	54.22	77.51	78.7	80.0	19.92
Switzerland	33 133	44 864	30.3****	28.7	12.2	13.4	97.96	176.91	81.9	81.8	
UK	27 782	36 569	35.0	32.8	−2.6	−3.5	59.14	74.34	74.4	73.6	24.53
Japan	26 320	35 855	(33.7)	(32.9**)	2.6	1.0	7.33	17.77	73.8	74.9	
Russia	8 249	17 518	(39.6)	(40.1*****)	11.1	4.0	14.44	20.89	63.8	67.4	
USA	37 253	51 704	(36.9)	(37.5**)	−4.3	−3.0	22.46	33.07	76.1	70.4	27.25

Notes:

Data are sometimes for one year earlier or later than column heading implies; where they diverge by more than one year, they are indicated as follows: * = 2005; ** = 2008; *** = 2003; **** = 2007; ***** = 2009

A = per capita gross domestic product expressed in purchasing power parities (PPP) in current international dollars (Source: IMF 2013)

B = Gini coefficient of equivalized household disposable incomes (Source: Eurostat websource; [except for Japan and USA, where source is OECD 2011b, and 2012 figures are for 2008; Russia, where source is World Bank (website a), and 2012 figures are for 2009]). The figures for the three non-European countries may be underestimates of inequality in 2012, as inequality was increasing over this period. Likewise, the Swiss data for 2001 probably exaggerate inequality, as the earliest available data were for 2007

C = balance on external trade as percentage of GDP (Source: World Trade Organization annual)

D = outward stocks of foreign direct investment as % GDP (Source: UNCTAD 2013)

E = employment as percentage of population aged 20–64 (Source: Eurostat websource)

F = research workers as a percentage of multinational enterprise employees (Source: OECD 2008)

Table A4.2

	A		B		C		D	E			F		G
	2000	2005	1996–2000	2008–2012	2001	2010	Late 2000s	(i)	(ii)	(iii)	(i)	(ii)	2011
Austria	543344	570654	65.94	70.22	8.2	8.0	1.8	11.1	−9	−0.999	46.74	23.7	6.9
Belgium	521329	562363	115.27	95.56	11.2	10.0	1.9	9.0	−12	−1.08	45.73	10.2	11.8
Bulgaria	46892	63993	75.29	16.29	5.8	5.9	1.7	0.1	−23	−0.023	47.57	13.0	22.6
Croatia	137597	166497		42.25	4.7	4.7							
Czech Republic	152942	180820	14.52	36.94	12.2	10.6	1.7	1.5	4	0.06	43.23	21.0	8.3
Denmark	687959	742954	61.36	42.66	9.2	8.1	1.7	5.1	−9	−0.459	47.61	16.4	6.3
Estonia			6.03	8.50	11.4	13.7	2.3	18.7	−5	−0.935	50.13	27.3	11.8
Finland	481870	570256	49.13	45.69	10.9	11.5	1.9	2.1	−11	−0.231	48.53	18.2	8.4
France	541594	586448	58.65	81.20	6.3	5.6	1.8	5.4	−15	−0.81	47.84	14.7	12.0
Germany	526329	547201	60.03	77.25	10.4	9.1	1.9	9.5	−14	−1.33	46.31	22.2	7.5
Greece	341860	392815	98.81	143.77	8.6	7.7	2.2	9.6	5	0.48	40.72	22.0	17.4
Hungary	134456	173007	59.54	79.00	5.6	5.1	1.8	0.9	7	0.063	46.39	18.0	13.3
Ireland	511867	599115	45.03	85.02	11.4	8.9	2.2	14.9	−1	−0.149	47.08	13.9	18.4
Italy	478252	498227	114.74	117.92	7.9	6.7	2.1	8.7	7	0.609	41.67	5.8	19.8
Latvia	75566	121274	12.26	36.62	2.9	3.4		16.4	−7	−1.148	51.03	13.6	15.7
Lithuania		132915	23.57	32.17	3.7	4.1		0.5	−12	−0.06	51.62	11.9	12.5
Netherlands	556176	593547	64.58	63.92	10.4	11.0	1.9	3.7	−13	−0.481	46.46	17.9	3.8
Norway	832478	861797	32.61	44.32	9.1	11.7	1.8				47.23	15.9	
Poland	113350	135941	40.31	52.88	7.9	8.3	2.4	0.1	2	0.002	44.65	4.5	11.6
Portugal	293743	305832	50.60	95.77	6.1	4.9	2.2	4.7	1	0.047	47.94	12.5	12.7

Romania	61 643	80 906	29.52	27.97	4.3	3.7	1.9	0.1			44.30	12.1	17.4
Slovakia	112 471	142 373	41.59	40.00	7.3	6.6	1.9	0.2	6	0.012	44.06	20.5	13.8
Slovenia			21.37	39.01	7.6	7.5	1.9	1.2	−13	−0.156	45.97	2.3	7.1
Spain	375 243	408 385	63.92	61.72	7.3	5.9	2.3	16.0	−3	−0.48	45.45	16.2	18.5
Sweden	563 351	627 950	66.55	39.41	5.7	5.6	1.7	5.1	−15	−0.765	47.64	15.8	7.5
Switzerland	715 610	736 795	59.77	50.13	5.9	5.0	1.9				45.90	17.9	
UK	575 979	662 664	45.48	75.09	9.3	7.9	2.2	8.2		−0.328		20.1	14.3
Japan	509 112	548 751	118.98	212.07	9.5	9.2	2.4						
Russia	52 207	73 166	79.42	10.49	10.7	12.2							
USA	667 626	734 195	63.67	94.38	19.7	17.6	2.7						

Notes:

A = per capita wealth in US dollars (Source: World Bank 2011a)

B = average public debt as a percentage of GDP (Source: Eurostat websource; for Japan, Switzerland and USA, the source is OECD 2013a; for Russia IMF 2011)

C = carbon dioxide emissions (metric tons per capita) (Source: World Bank annual)

D = ratio of lowest household income decile to median (Source: OECD 2013a)

E = data on immigrant workforce: (i) as a percentage of total workforce; (ii) difference in employment rate relative to that of the native workforce; (iii) exposure to risks of poverty or social exclusion, again as a proportion of that of the native population (Source: Eurostat 2011)

F = data on female workforce: (i) as a percentage of total workforce; (ii) percentage gap between average unadjusted male and female hourly pay (Source: Eurostat websource)

G = data on NEETs: people between the ages of 15 and 24 years not in employment, education or training (Source: Eurostat websource)

Table A5.1

	A		B		C		D		E	
	2003	2010	2000	2010	2001	2010	2001	2011	(i)	(ii)
Austria	0.29	−0.04	4.4	3.1	27.75	29.51	64	69	26.1	23.7
Belgium	1.37	1.28	1.7	2.1	24.71	28.40	62	64	24.4	23.3
Bulgaria	10.25	3.24				17.56		40	36.0	25.0
Croatia	2.98	2.34								
Czech Republic	−0.83	−0.76	0.3	0.7	18.09	19.49	67	56	27.7	25.1
Denmark	−0.05	−0.78	2.4	2.9	28.38	32.41	85	73	20.6	19.8
Estonia	0.44	1.32	0.0	0.0	12.79	17.89		46	25.1	23.0
Finland	0.27	0.15	1.2	1.2	24.25	29.74	76	69	21.4	23.0
France	0.45	0.39	2.6	0.8	27.81	32.04	63	58	23.5	22.1
Germany	−0.26	−0.15	3.0	3.2	28.70	29.44	67	59	25.0	22.3
Greece	0.81	0.06	2.1	1.8	23.61	28.16	31	14	31.8	27.4
Hungary	0.28	0.77	0.0	0.2	19.08	22.55	47	38	27.6	25.0
Ireland	−0.42	−0.77	1.3	2.2	14.11	28.33	70	47	26.5	24.1
Italy	−0.18	−0.50	2.2	2.3	23.82	28.57	6	9	30.1	28.0
Latvia	1.62	1.97			14.35	17.60		57	27.7	25.4
Lithuania	0.47	1.47			14.28	18.30		61	27.2	24.8
Netherlands	−0.52	−0.57	7.3	6.7	24.77	30.19	70	73	24.1	24.1
Norway	−0.52	−0.91	2.0	2.3	24.92	25.12	81	70		
Poland	0.97	1.80	0.0	0.0	20.49	18.63	59	48	29.1	26.3

Portugal	1.71	0.98	1.5	1.9	19.21	25.50	58	59	29.1	27.4
Romania	0.24	2.81			12.51	17.39		25	29.0	25.0
Slovakia	1.54	1.81	0.8	0.9	18.37	18.02	90	40	30.3	27.8
Slovenia	0.72	0.19	0.0	1.2	23.78	24.27		64	30.8	28.0
Spain	0.20	−0.19	0.3	0.5	19.24	25.19	49	47	28.5	27.0
Sweden	−0.01	−0.01	2.6	3.2	29.69	29.90	74	65	20.9	20.3
Switzerland	−3.26	−3.27	8.3	8.0	22.87	24.19	81	72		
UK	0.14	0.14	6.3	3.2	25.89	27.15	60	62	24.0	22.0
Japan	−0.02	−0.04	4.0			22.40	70	75		
Russia	−0.25	−1.11				15.00				
USA	−0.31	−0.32	10.6	3.0	19.90	19.90	29	36		

Notes:

A = net remittances from emigrants and earnings of migrant workers as a percentage of GDP (Source: World Bank 2011b)

B = private spending on social provision as a percentage of GDP (Source: OECD 2013a)

C = public spending on social protection (percentage of GDP) (Source: Eurostat websource)

D = unemployment pay replacement rate as a percentage of average pay, family with two children, after five years of unemployment (Source: OECD 2013a)

E = mean age of leaving parental home for (i) males, (ii) females (Source: Iacovou and Skew 2010, 2011)

Table A5.2

	A		B		C	D	
	2000	2010	2000	2009	2008	(i)	(ii)
Austria	73.8	91.4	18.2	12.6	9.9	12	−2
Belgium	65.2	85.9	8.0	9.1	5.6	13	−1
Bulgaria	19.0	51.8	12.4	26.5	9.0		
Croatia						24	−20
Czech Republic	20.0	60.5	1.9	9.0	6.1	2	0
Denmark	238.5	309.5	15.7	15.1	5.4	49	4
Estonia	20.2	102.0	0.8	9.3	2.2	78	−32
Finland	64.6	110.2	4.4	11.7	3.3	33	−5
France	66.0	93.6	11.9	11.7	6.6	20	−6
Germany	109.0	91.1	15.7	13.5	9.3	−9	−4
Greece	57.7	90.9	5.3	20.3	12.8	27	−12
Hungary	15.2	75.5	2.2	23.4	5.9	25	−47
Ireland	115.0	217.8	13.9	18.6	8.9	80	−22
Italy	52.8	85.9	4.5	10.2	6.9	17	−5
Latvia	5.8	68.5	1.6	7.1	4.0	57	−26
Lithuania	1.9	47.5	0.3	5.8	0.2	36	−21
Netherlands	163.7	277.3	6.2	8.4	5.8	59	−10
Norway	135.1	196.3				47	0
Poland	11.5	55.5	11.1	18.2	0.2	10	4
Portugal	106.4	142.9	9.5	13.3	1.7	24	−5
Romania	0.5	32.3	8.6	23.4	3.1	38	−27
Slovakia	20.1	75.9	2.5	4.9	7.4	24	5
Slovenia	30.4	53.7	10.5	12.6	6.9	13	−2
Spain	81.5	136.3	11.5	12.9	3.1	42	−13
Sweden	105.5	168.4	0.0	9.1	2.3	34	−5
Switzerland	173.9	190.5				14	0
UK	111.7	157.0	20.6	24.8	13.7	37	−12
Japan	130.4	121.3				−7	−7
Russia							
USA	100.5	122.5				24	−10

Notes:
A = household debt as a percentage of GDP (Source: OECD 2013a)
B = outstanding consumer credit as a percentage of GDP (Source: European Commission Social Situation Observatory 2010)
C = percentage of households below 60 per cent of median income with debts of more than 100 per cent of disposable income (Source: European Commission Social Situation Observatory 2010)
D = household debt and consumption: (i) household debt to income increase 2002–06; (ii) estimated consumption loss 2010 (Source: IMF 2012)

Table A5.3

	A		B		C		D	
	2000	2010	2000	2009	2004	2011	2004	2011
Austria	5.75	6.05	5.7	6.0	46.1	49.6	26.9	26.9
Belgium	4.55	6.07	6.0	6.6	50.3	48.3	28.7	26.4
Bulgaria	2.31	2.21	3.5	4.1				
Croatia	5.77	5.59	3.9	4.3				
Czech Republic	5.15	5.18	4.1	4.2	47.0	46.0	26.9	25.8
Denmark	6.12	8.09	8.4	8.7	41.6	43.1	23.2	25.6
Estonia	3.20	3.71	5.5	5.7	50.6	48.3	34.6	32.3
Finland	3.64	4.94	6.2	6.8	47.9	48.3	26.7	26.5
France	6.35	6.83	5.6	5.9	48.5	51.2	28.3	30.9
Germany	6.60	6.38	4.6	5.1	49.9	50.6	28.5	29.3
Greece	2.82	4.04	3.6	4.1	47.1	55.5	33.6	33.5
Hungary	3.61	3.24	5.3	4.9				
Ireland	3.45	4.65	4.3	6.5	51.1	56.8	32.3	30.2
Italy	4.21	5.64	4.6	4.5	51.2	50.2	33.1	32.1
Latvia	1.80	2.11	5.7	5.0				
Lithuania	3.14	3.35	5.8	5.4				
Netherlands	3.16	8.74	6.2	6.0	42.6	42.1	28.4	28.3
Norway	5.69	6.68	7.6	6.9	44.7	42.3	27.6	25.0
Poland	2.73	3.42	5.4	5.2	57.0	46.6	38.1	30.4
Portugal	4.13	4.23	5.3	5.8	50.4	53.7	38.2	34.1
Romania	2.84	3.77	3.5	4.2				
Slovakia	4.38	3.51	4.3	4.2	45.8	42.0	26.8	26.1
Slovenia	4.51	4.80	5.8	5.7	45.4	46.0	24.7	24.5
Spain	3.72	5.15	4.2	5.0	46.7	52.0	33.1	34.4
Sweden	5.86	6.15	7.4	7.0	43.2	43.5	23.4	27.3
Switzerland	3.05	4.64	5.6	5.4				
UK	4.41	6.37	5.2	5.6	50.0	52.5	33.1	34.4
Japan	4.93	5.92	3.6	3.8	44.3	48.8	32.1	33.6
Russia	1.92	2.21	3.8	4.1				
USA	2.51	3.76	5.6	5.6	48.6	50.8	36.0	38.9

Notes:
A = public spending on health as a percentage of GDP, deflated by proportion of all health spending not from public sources (Source: World Bank website a)
B = public spending on education as a percentage of GDP (World Bank website c)
C = Gini income coefficient pre-tax and -transfers, c.2000 and c.2010 (Source: OECD website)
D = Gini income coefficient post-tax and -transfers, c.2000 and c.2010 (Source: OECD website)

Table A6.1

	A		B		C		D		E		F		G	
	1996–2000	2007–2011	2000	2011	2001	2011	2001	2011	2000	2008	2001	2011	2000	2010
Austria	51.10	48.20	0.92	0.93	87.32	85.73	78.76	76.65	22.1	23.0	0	0	0.38	0.66
Belgium	49.04	48.62	0.45	0.46	81.79	81.79	63.63	64.86	31.2	18.3			0.96	1.27
Bulgaria	38.60	37.10	0.32	0.30	34.45	26.40	21.73	17.98	42.8	29.5			0.66	0.09
Croatia	52.70	50.30												
Czech Republic	38.44	39.44	0.27	0.25	37.06	35.36	29.98	29.88	34.8	32.4			0.15	0.23
Denmark	56.36	55.28	0.49	0.44	76.11	72.72	62.41	60.94	28.8	24.0	25.0	23.0	1.73	1.41
Estonia	37.96	39.08	0.32	0.35	26.69	17.08	19.86	13.24	27.0	26.3			0.07	0.14
Finland	55.40	53.36	0.39	0.40	78.30	77.58	64.13	64.55	27.8	25.9	18.0	15.0	0.75	0.86
France	50.50	49.82	0.21	0.21	80.46	81.63	68.23	69.71	17.9	15.0	10.0	10.0	1.01	0.83
Germany	46.20	44.14	0.48	0.48	59.67	54.81	50.12	46.53	21.1	22.4	30.6	39.5	1.03	0.56
Greece	44.02	40.54	0.34	0.33	44.20	41.93	31.51	31.40					0.24	0.22
Hungary	44.70	47.44	0.22	0.24	36.40	29.21	27.27	22.46			7.2	-3.5	0.33	0.52
Ireland	37.42	35.12	0.52	0.46	45.46	36.17	38.23	30.20	18.0	17.8	67.0	67.6	0.64	0.74
Italy	45.86	46.14	0.38	0.34	60.48	59.84	44.09	43.86					0.56	0.35
Latvia	36.98	34.94	0.44	0.51	16.24	22.48	12.41	17.64	34.2	28.5			0.10	0.51
Lithuania	36.18	34.32	0.26	0.36	10.60	13.43	7.73	10.02	34.4	28.2			0.21	0.23
Netherlands	46.42	45.96	0.58	0.57	76.80	71.19	66.74	61.51			18.2	18.5	0.97	0.78
Norway	54.62	57.30	0.50	0.51	66.71	68.01	53.97	55.63	36.8	34.3	37.0	41.0	0.49	0.51
Poland	41.30	38.60	0.19	0.19	32.83	29.37	23.77	22.38	29.7	22.9			0.47	0.60

Country	A	A	B	B	C	C	D	D	E	E	F	F	G	G
Portugal	37.96	41.68	0.34	0.34	65.34	34.29	50.51	26.68			13.0	15.0	0.58	0.58
Romania	32.20	33.62	0.21	0.28	55.69	55.65	36.53	38.45	26.4	18.4	25.0	24.0	0.14	0.03
Slovakia	41.50	32.86	0.50	0.50	47.04	33.72	38.15	28.39	31.3	20.8	0	10.0	0.11	0.23
Slovenia	42.82	43.30	0.33	0.32	89.73	82.34	65.42	62.83	26.3	23.7	20.1	35.9	0.25	0.34
Spain	38.04	37.24	0.34	0.38	73.44	70.14	56.77	53.65	15.7	14.6	10.0	13.0	0.66	0.67
Sweden	59.18	53.24	0.52	0.50	83.66	81.26	67.60	66.55	31.7	29.0			1.48	0.81
Switzerland	33.90	34.10	0.22	0.30	47.00	42.96	42.96	39.52	15.3	15.0				
UK	38.60	40.36	0.10	0.12	32.14	28.19	28.06	24.80	20.5	20.4	51.7	47.7	0.06	0.04
Japan	29.06	30.69	0.29	0.31	16.95	13.76	15.05	12.25	8.1	7.0				
Russia									37.5	30.3				
USA	31.81	28.23	0.15	0.18	13.78	12.05	12.58	10.96			32.0	32.3		0.04

Notes:

A = government total revenue as a percentage of GDP (Source: Eurostat websource and OECD 2013a)

B = index of collective bargaining coordination (Source: Visser 2013)

C = collective bargaining coverage as a proportion of employed population, including self-employed (Source: own calculations based on Visser 2013)

D = collective bargaining coverage as a proportion of employed population, including self-employed and shadow economy (Source: own calculations based on Visser 2013)

E = public employment as a percentage of all employment (Source: ILO annual)

F = bargaining coverage in public sector less coverage in private sector (Source: Visser 2013)

G = public spending on active labour market policy measures (ALMP) as percentage of GDP (Source: Eurostat websource)

Table A6.2

	A		B		C		D		E		F
	2000	2013	2000	2010	2000	2013	2000	2012	2000	2012	2010
Austria	2.621	2.621	7.9	9.3	1.82	1.74	28.6	24.4	42.09	41.56	11.4
Belgium	2.723	2.757	9.1	8.1	1.35	1.48	34.2	32.8	49.93	48.19	11.4
Bulgaria							44.7	37.0	55.86	47.40	54.4
Croatia											
Czech Republic	2.968	2.696	9.3	8.8	1.61	1.54	29.0	28.5	44.99	46.88	16.0
Denmark	2.561	2.392	10.2	8.5	1.56	1.55	22.0	24.6	36.04	37.80	18.7
Estonia	2.459	2.114		3.7		1.28	32.6	27.9	39.99	37.85	22.9
Finland	2.185	2.012	16.5	15.7	1.11	1.07	28.4	26.0	49.38	47.68	29.6
France	2.637	2.668	15.5	15.2	1.56	1.61	32.2	30.7	49.69	47.54	31.7
Germany	2.949	3.085	12.7	13.9	1.74	1.81	31.2	23.3	46.82	43.47	22.3
Greece	2.930	2.442	13.1	10.0	0.39	0.65	38.1	44.7	66.26	71.19	55.0
Hungary	2.396	2.170	7.1	9.4	1.14	1.11	38.8	37.9	51.93	51.87	35.2
Ireland	1.812	1.998	4.7	10.2	1.07	1.10	29.6	36.3	46.28	53.63	33.3
Italy	3.151	2.886	10.1	13.8	0.94	0.87	42.6	39.0	62.40	62.18	50.4
Latvia		2.990					36.5	31.8	46.96	43.33	43.6
Lithuania							34.4	31.3	47.24	40.16	39.3
Netherlands	2.918	2.926	14.0	19.5	1.80	1.61	25.7	22.8	43.83	47.50	6.3
Norway	2.381	2.381	9.3	8.4	1.46	1.50	19.7	20.1	27.69	33.28	18.8
Poland	2.557	2.414	5.8	26.9	0.85	0.65	39.0	35.3	55.86	67.65	22.9

Country											
Portugal	4.095	2.810	20.4	20.7	1.27	0.96	26.5	33.5	59.43	64.62	43.2
Romania							30.9	36.4	46.96	50.14	54.2
Slovakia	2.910	2.279	4.8	6.8	1.89	1.37	36.5	34.9	44.48	48.90	27.3
Slovenia	2.858	2.506		17.1		0.98	31.5	34.9	47.92	53.00	8.4
Spain	2.755	2.355	32.1	23.6	0.73	0.81	39.3	40.7	70.56	65.55	50.0
Sweden	2.611	2.577	15.2	17.5	1.39	1.34	22.3	20.6	43.12	41.64	27.7
Switzerland	2.175	2.175	11.5	12.9	1.47	1.49	19.1	18.0			
UK	1.677	1.487	6.8	6.3	1.14	1.00	26.0	24.8	39.84	40.57	16.4
Japan	2.145	1.906	12.5	13.7	1.30	1.21	26.0	24.8			5.0
Russia							38.2	36.6			
USA	1.005	1.005					23.1	29.1			1.0

Notes:

A = employment protection law (EPL) index for permanent workers (Source: OECD 2013a)

B = proportion of employees on temporary contracts (Source: OECD 2013a)

C = adjusted EPL index, deflated by proportions of workforce on temporary contracts, self-employment or shadow economy (Source: own calculations)

D = percentage of population aged 20–64 years not in paid employment (Source: Eurostat websource)

E = total 'excluded' from normal employment conditions as a percentage of the working-age population (age 20–64): sum of those not in employment, in temporary, and in self-employment

F = percentage of part-time workers declaring that they would prefer to be in full-time work (Source: Eurostat websource)

Table A8.1

| | A |
	2010
Austria	48.54
Belgium	39.14
Bulgaria	
Croatia	
Czech Republic	1.88
Denmark	54.74
Estonia	5.86
Finland	65.91
France	39.19
Germany	68.63
Greece	0.84
Hungary	4.43
Ireland	17.07
Italy	11.99
Latvia	
Lithuania	
Netherlands	50.31
Norway	24.06
Poland	0.71
Portugal	2.32
Romania	
Slovakia	0.72
Slovenia	6.29
Spain	5.25
Sweden	94.07
Switzerland	108.27
UK	26.05
Japan	118.47
Russia	0.51
USA	44.77

Note: A = patents per million inhabitants, 2010 (OECD 2013b)

References

Amable, B. (2003), *The Diversity of Modern Capitalism*. Oxford: Oxford University Press.

Anxo, D. and Niklasson, H. (2009), 'The Swedish model: revival after the turbulent 1990s?', in Bosch, Lehndorff and Rubery (eds) (2009b), q.v., pp. 81–104.

Attias-Donfut, C. and Ogg, J. (2009), 'Evolutions des transferts intergénérationnels: vers un modèle européen?', *Retraite et Société*, 5, 8: 11–29.

Auer, P. (2008), 'Labour market institutions and the European social model in a globalizing world', in Rogowski (ed.) (2008b), q.v., pp. 323–50.

Avdagic, S. (2004), 'Loyalty and power in union-party alliances', MPIfG Discussion Paper 04/7. Cologne: MPIfG.

Avdagic, S. and Salardi, P. (2013), 'Tenuous link: labour market institutions and unemployment in advanced and new market economies', *Socio-Economic Review*, 11, 4: 739–69.

Banyuls, J. and Recio, A. (2012), 'Spain: the nightmare of Mediterranean neoliberalism', in Lehndorff (ed.) (2012b), q.v., pp. 199–218.

Barbier, J.-C. (2008a), *La longue marche vers l'Europe sociale*. Paris: Presses Universitaires de France.

Barbier, J.-C. (2008b), 'Social Europe and the limits of soft law: the example of flexicurity', in Rogowski (ed.) (2008b), q.v., pp. 171–86.

Beccattini, G. (2000), *Il Distretto Industriale*. Turin: Rosenberg and Sellier.

Beck, U. (1986), *Risikogesellschaft*. Frankfurt am Main: Suhrkamp.

Bellofiore, R. and Halevi, J. (2009), 'Deconstructing labor. A Marxian-Kaleckian perspective on what is "new" in contemporary capitalism and economic policies', in Gnos, C. and Rochon, L.-P. (eds), *Employment, Growth and Development. A Post-Keynesian Approach*. Cheltenham, UK and Northampton, MA: Edward Elgar.

Belot, M., Boone, J. and Van Ours, J. (2007), 'Welfare-improving employment protection', *Economica*, 74, 295: 381–96.

Berrebi-Hoffmann, I., Jany-Catrice, F., Lallement, M. and Ribault, T. (2009), 'Capitalizing on variety: risks and opportunities in a new French social model', in Bosch, Lehndorff and Rubery (eds) (2009b), q.v., pp. 178–200.

Berton, F., Richiardi, M. and Sacchi, S. (2012), *The Political Economy of*

Work Security and Flexibility: Italy in Comparative Perspective. Bristol: Policy Press.

Blossfeld, H.-P., Buchholz, S., Hofäcker, D. and Bertolini, S. (2012), 'Selective flexibilization and deregulation of the labor market. The answer of Continental and Southern Europe', *Stato e Mercato*, 96: 363–90.

Bohle, D. and Greskovits, B. (2006), 'Capitalism without compromise: strong business and weak labor in Eastern Europe's new transnational industries', *Studies in Comparative International Development*, 41, 1: 3–25.

Bohle, D. and Greskovits, B. (2012), *Capitalist Diversity on Europe's Periphery*. Ithaca, NY: Cornell University Press.

Bonoli, G. (2007), 'Time matters', *Comparative Political Studies*, 40, 5: 495–520.

Bonoli, G. and Natali, D. (2012a), 'The politics of the "new welfare states"', in Bonoli and Natali (eds) (2012b), q.v., pp. 3–20.

Bonoli, G. and Natali, D. (eds) (2012b), *The Politics of the New Welfare States*. Oxford: Oxford University Press.

Bosch, G. (2011), 'The German labour market after the financial crisis: miracle or just a good policy mix?', in Vaughan-Whitehead (ed.) (2011), q.v., pp. 243–77.

Bosch, G., Lehndorff, S. and Rubery, J. (2009a), 'European employment models in flux: pressures for change and prospects for survival and revitalization', in Bosch, Lehndorff and Rubery (eds) (2009b), q.v., pp. 1–56.

Bosch, G., Lehndorff, S. and Rubery, J. (2009b), *European Employment Models in Flux: A Comparison of Institutional Change in Nine European Countries*. Basingstoke: Palgrave Macmillan.

Bourdieu, P. and Passeron, J.C. (1990), *Reproduction in Education, Society and Culture*. London: Sage.

Bouwen, P. (2002), 'Corporate lobbying in the European Union: the logic of access', *Journal of European Public Policy*, 9, 3: 365–90.

Bredgaard, T., Larsen, F. and Madsen, P.K. (2007), 'The challenges of identifying flexicurity in action – a case study on Denmark', in Jørgensen, H. and Madsen, P.K. (eds), *Flexicurity and Beyond: Finding a New Agenda for the European Social Model*. Copenhagen: DJOF Publishing, pp. 365–391.

Bredgaard, T., Larsen, F. and Madsen, P.K. (2008), 'Transitional labour markets and flexicurity arrangements in Denmark: what can Europe learn?', in Rogowski (ed.) (2008b), q.v., pp. 189–208.

Burroni, L. and Crouch, C. (2008), 'The territorial governance of the shadow economy', *Environment and Planning C*, 26, 2: 455–70.

Burroni, L. and Keune, M. (2009), 'Understanding the multiple sources of and relationships between flexibility and security: towards a governance approach', Working Paper, European Trade Union Institute, Brussels: ETUI.

Calmfors, L. and Driffill, D.J. (1988), 'Bargaining structure, corporatism and macro-economic performance', *Economic Policy*, 6: 14–61.

Canto, V.A., Jones, D.H. and Laffer, A.D. (1983), *Foundations of Supply-Side Economics: Theory and Evidence*. New York: Academic Press.

Carley, M. and Marginson, P. (2010), 'The crisis: social partner responses, European industrial relations survey 2010'. Luxembourg: Office for Official Publication of the European Communities, chapter 3.

Cazes, S., Khatiwada, S. and Malo, M. (2012), 'Employment protection and collective bargaining: beyond the deregulation agenda', ILO Employment Working Paper No. 133. Geneva: ILO.

Cerami, A. (2010), 'The politics of social security reforms in the Czech Republic, Hungary, Poland and Slovakia', in Palier (ed.) (2010c), q.v., pp. 233–54.

Chami, R., Fullenkamp, C. and Jahjah, S. (2005), 'Are immigrant remittance flows a source of capital for development?', IMF Staff Papers, 52, 1. Washington, DC: IMF.

Clasen, J. (2007), 'Distribution of responsibility for social security and labour market policy. Country report: United Kingdom', AIAS Working Paper 07–50. Amsterdam: Amsterdam Institute for Advanced Labour Studies.

Clasen, J. (2009), 'United Kingdom', in De Beer and Schils (eds) (2009b), q.v., pp. 70–95.

Coen, D. (1997), 'The evolution of the large firm as a political actor in the European Union', *Journal of European Public Policy*, 4, 1: 91–108.

Coen, D. (2007), 'Empirical and theoretical studies in EU lobbying', *Journal of European Public Policy*, 13, 3: 333–45.

Crompton, R. (1989), 'Class theory and gender', *British Journal of Sociology*, 40, 4: 565–87.

Crouch, C. (1993), *Industrial Relations and European State Traditions*. Oxford: Oxford University Press.

Crouch, C. (1996), 'Revised diversity: from the neo-liberal decade to beyond Maastricht', in Van Ruysseveldt, J.J. and Visser, J. (eds), *Industrial Relations in Europe. Traditions and Transitions*. London: Sage.

Crouch, C. (2005), *Capitalist Diversity and Change*. Oxford: Oxford University Press.

Crouch, C. (2009), 'Privatised Keynesianism: an unacknowledged policy regime', *British Journal of Politics and International Relations*, 11: 382–99.

Crouch, C. (2010), 'Flexibility and security on the labour market: an analysis of the governance of inequality', *Zeitschrift für Arbeitsmarkt Forschung*, 43: 17–38.

Crouch, C. (2011a), *The Strange Non-Death of Neoliberalism*. Cambridge: Polity.

Crouch, C. (2011b), 'Beyond the flexibility/security trade-off: reconciling confident consumers with insecure workers', *British Journal of Industrial Relations*, 50, 1: 1–22.

Crouch, C. (2012a), 'National varieties of labour market exposure', in Morgan, G. and Whitley, R. (eds) (2012), *Capitalisms and Capitalism in the 21st Century*. Oxford: Oxford University Press.

Crouch, C. (2012b), 'Il decline delle relazioni industriali nell'odierno capitalismo', *Stato e Mercato*, 1/2012: 55–76.

Crouch, C. (2013), *Making Capitalism Fit for Society*. Cambridge: Polity.

Crouch, C. and Keune, M. (2012), 'The governance of economic uncertainty: beyond the "new social risks" analysis', in Bonoli and Natali (eds) (2012b), q.v., pp. 45–67.

Davidsson, J.B. and Emmenegger, P. (2012), 'Insider-outsider dynamics and the reform of job security legislation', in Bonoli and Natali (eds) (2012b), q.v., pp. 206–29.

Davies, J.B., Sandström, S., Shorrocks, A. and Wolff, E.N. (2010), 'The level and distribution of household wealth', *Economic Journal*, 1, 21: 223–54.

Davies, P. and Freedland, M. (1993), *Labour Legislation and Public Policy*. Oxford: Clarendon Press.

Davies, P. and Freedland, M. (2007), *Towards a Flexible Labour Market: Labour Legislation and Regulation since the 1990s*. Oxford: Oxford University Press.

Deakin, S. and Rogowski, R. (2011), 'Reflexive labour law, capabilities and the future of social Europe', in Rogowski, Salais and Whiteside (eds) (2011), q.v., pp. 229–55.

De Beer, P. and Schils, T. (2009a), 'Introduction: achieving an optimal social policy mix', in De Beer and Schils (eds) (2009b), q.v., pp. 1–25.

De Beer, P. and Schils, T. (2009b), *The Labour Market Triangle. Employment Protection, Unemployment Compensation and Activation in Europe*. Cheltenham, UK and Northampton, MA: Edward Elgar.

Ebbinghaus, B. (2012), 'Europe's transformations towards a renewed pension system', in Bonoli and Natali (eds) (2012b), q.v., pp. 182–205.

Ebbinghaus, B. and Eichhorst, W. (2009), 'Germany', in De Beer and Schils (eds) (2009b), q.v., pp. 119–44.

Ebbinghaus, B. and Visser, J. (1997), 'Der Wandel der Arbeitsbeziehungen im westearopäischen Vergleich', in Hradil, S. and Immerfall, S. (eds), *Die westearopäischen Gesellschaften im Vergleich*. Opladen: Leske + Budrich.

EIRO (2012), *Croatia: Industrial Relations Profile*. Dublin: EIRO.

Emmenegger, P., Häusermann, S., Palier, B. and Seeleib-Kaiser, M. (eds) (2012), *The Age of Dualization*. Oxford: Oxford University Press.

Erne, R. (2008), *European Unions: Labor's Quest for a Transnational Democracy*. Ithaca, NY: Cornell University Press.

Esping-Andersen, G. (1990), *The Three Worlds of Welfare Capitalism*. Cambridge: Polity Press.

Esping-Andersen, G. (1999), *The Social Foundations of Post-Industrial Economies*. Oxford: Oxford University Press.

Esping-Andersen, G., with Gallie, D., Hemerijck, A. and Myles, J. (2003), *Why We Need a New Welfare State*. Oxford: Oxford University Press.

Esping-Andersen, G. and Regini, M. (2000a), 'Conclusions' in Esping-Andersen and Regini (eds) (2000b), q.v., pp. 336–41.

Esping-Andersen, G. and Regini, M. (eds) (2000b), *Why Deregulate Labour Markets?* Oxford: Oxford University Press.

European Commission (1993), *Growth, Competitiveness and Employment*. Luxembourg: Office for Official Publication of the European Communities.

European Commission (2001), *A Sustainable Development Strategy*. Luxembourg: Office for Official Publication of the European Communities.

European Commission (2005), *Working Together for Growth and Jobs. Integrated Guidelines for Growth and Jobs 2005–2008*. Luxembourg: Office for Official Publication of the European Communities.

European Commission (2006), *Green Book*. Luxembourg: Office for Official Publication of the European Communities.

European Commission (2007), *Employment in Europe 2007*. Luxembourg: Office for Official Publication of the European Communities.

European Commission (2009), *Industrial Relations in Europe*. Luxembourg: Office for Official Publication of the European Communities.

European Commission Social Situation Observatory (2010), 'Over-indebtedness: new evidence from the EU-SILC special module', Research Note 4/(2010). Luxembourg: Office for Official Publication of the European Communities.

Eurostat (2007), *Employment in Europe 2007*. Luxembourg: Office for Official Publication of the European Communities.

Eurostat (2011), *Indicators of Immigrant Integration. A Pilot Study. 2011 Edition*. Luxembourg: Office for Official Publication of the European Communities.

Eurostat (websource), *Statistics Database*. http://epp.eurostat.ec. europa. eu/portal/page/portalstatistics/search_database. 3 September 2014.

Fama, E.F. (1971), 'Risk, return and equilibrium', *Journal of Political Economy*, 79, 1: 30–55.

Fama, E.F. (1991), 'Efficient capital markets II', *Journal of Finance*, XVVI, 5: 1575–1617.

Ferrera, M. (1996), 'The "southern model" of social Europe', *Journal of European Social Policy*, 6, 1: 17–37.

Ferrera, M. (2012), 'The new spatial politics of welfare in the EU', in Bonoli and Natali (eds) (2012b), q.v., pp. 256–83.

Franičević, V. (2011), 'Croatia: prolonged crisis with an uncertain ending', in Vaughan-Whitehead (ed.) (2011), q.v., pp. 143–97.

Freedland, M. (2006), 'From contract of employment to the personal work nexus', *Industrial Law Journal*, 35, 1: 1–29.

Gallie, D. (ed.) (2013), *Economic Crisis, Quality of Work, and Social Integration*. Oxford: Oxford University Press.

Gash, V. and Inanc, H. (2013), 'Insecurity and the peripheral workforce', in Gallie (ed.) (2013), q.v., pp. 142–68.

Gautié, J. (2011), 'France: protecting the insiders in the crisis and forgetting the outsiders?', in Vaughan-Whitehead (ed.) (2011), q.v., pp. 198–242.

Giddens, A. (1973), *The Class Structure of the Advanced Societies*. London: Hutchinson.

Giddens, A. (1994), *Beyond Left and Right. The Future of Radical Politics*. Cambridge: Polity Press.

Giddens, A. (1998), *The Third Way: The Renewal of Social Democracy*. Cambridge: Polity Press.

Giordano, R., Depalo, D., Pereira, M.C., Eugène, B., Papapetrou, E., Perez, J.J., Reiss, L. and Roter, M. (2011), 'The public sector wage gap in a selection of Euro area countries', Working Paper 1406, Frankfurt: European Central Bank.

Glassner, V., Keune, M. and Marginson, P. (2011), 'Collective bargaining in a time of crisis', *Transfer*, 17: 303–21.

Goldthorpe, J.H. (1983), 'Women and class analysis', *Sociology*, 17, 4: 465–88.

Government of Greece (2012), *Memorandum of Understanding on Specific Economic Policy Conditionality, 9 February 2012*. Athens: Government of Greece.

Gumbrell-McCormick, R. and Hyman, R. (2013), *Trade Unions in Western Europe: Hard Times, Hard Choices*. Oxford: Oxford University Press.

Hall, P.A. and Soskice, D. (eds) (2001), *Varieties of Capitalism*. Oxford: Oxford University Press.

Häusermann, S. (2010), 'Reform opportunities in a Bismarckian late-comer: restructuring the Swiss welfare state', in Palier (ed.) (2010c), q.v., pp. 207–32.

Häusermann, S. (2012), 'The politics of old and new social policies', in Bonoli and Natali (eds) (2012b), q.v., pp. 111–34.

Hay, C., Riiheläinen, J.M., Smith, N.J. and Watson, M. (2008), 'Ireland: the outside inside', in Dyson, K. (ed.) (2008), *The Euro at 10*. Oxford: Oxford University Press.

Hayward, J. (ed.) (1995), *Industrial Enterprise and European Integration: From National to International Champions*. Oxford: Oxford University Press.

Hemerijck, A. (2012a), *Changing Welfare States*. Oxford: Oxford University Press.

Hemerijck, A. (2012b), 'Stress-testing the new welfare state', in Bonoli and Natali (eds) (2012b), q.v., pp. 68–90.

Hemerijck, A. and Marx, I. (2010), 'Continental welfare at a cross-roads: the choice between activation and minimum income protection in Belgium and the Netherlands', in Palier (ed.) (2010c), q.v., pp. 139–56.

Héritier, A. and Lehmkuhl, D. (2008), 'The shadow of hierarchy and new modes of governance', *Journal of Public Policy*, 28, 1: 1–17.

Hermann, C. and Flecker, J. (2009), 'Is institutional continuity masking a creeping paradigm shift in the Austrian social model?', in Bosch, Lehndorff and Rubery (eds) (2009b), q.v., pp. 131–54.

Hermann, C. and Flecker, J. (2012), 'The Austrian model and the financial and economic crisis', in Lehndorff (ed.) (2012b), q.v., pp. 121–36.

Hinrichs, K. (2010), 'A social insurance state withers away. Welfare state reforms in Germany', in Palier (ed.) (2010c), q.v., pp. 45–72.

Hollingsworth, J.R. and Boyer, R. (eds) (1997), *Contemporary Capitalism: The Embeddedness of Institutions*. Cambridge: Cambridge University Press.

Höpner, M. (2008), 'Usurpation statt Delegation: Wie der EuGH die Binnenmarktintegration radikalisiert und warum er politischer Kontrolle bedarf', MPIfG Discussion paper 08/12. Cologne: MPIfG.

Höpner, M. (2014), 'Wie der Europäische Gerichtshof und die Kommission Liberalisierung durchsetzen', MPIfG Discussion paper 14/8. Cologne: MPIfG.

Iacovou, M. and Skew, A. (2010), 'Age at which 50% of young people are living away from parental home, 2007, Household Structure in the EU', ISER Working Paper series 2010–10. Colchester: University of Essex Institute of Social and Economic Research.

Iacovou, M. and Skew, A. (2011), 'Household composition across the new Europe: Where do the new member states fit in?', *Demographic Research*, 25, 14: 465–90.

ILO (annual) http://www.ilo.org/ilostat/faces/home/statistical, data 3 September 2014.

IMF (2011), *World Economic Outlook*. Washington, DC: IMF.

IMF (2012), 'Dealing with household debt', *IMF World Economic Outlook*, April: chapter 3. Washington, DC: IMF.

IMF (2013), *World Economic Outlook Database*. Washington, DC: IMF.

Index Mundi (annual), at http://www.indexmundi.com, 3 September 2014.

Jessoula, M. and Alti, T. (2010), 'Italy: an uncompleted departure from Bismarck', in Palier (ed.) (2010c), q.v., pp. 157–82.

Jørgensen, H. and Madsen, P.K. (eds) (2007), *Flexicurity and Beyond: Finding a New Agenda for the European Social Model*. Copenhagen: DJOF Publishing.

Jurado Guerrero, T. (1999), 'Why do Spanish young people stay longer at home than the French? The role of employment, housing and social policies', unpublished PhD thesis. Florence: European University Institute.

Jurado Guerrero, T. and Naldini, M. (1996), 'Is the south so different? Italian and Spanish families in a comparative perspective', *South European Society and Politics*, 1, 3: 42–66.

Kahancová, M. (2011), 'Embedding multinationals in postsocialist host countries', MPIfG Discussion Paper 08/11. Cologne: MPIfG.

Karamessini, M. (2012), 'Sovereign debt crisis: an opportunity to complete the neoliberal project and dismantle the Greek employment model', in Lehndorff (ed.) (2012b), q.v., pp. 155–82.

Kenney, M. (2000), *Understanding Silicon Valley: The Anatomy of an Entrepreneurial Region*. Stanford, CA: Stanford University Press.

Kettunen, P. (2011), 'The transnational construction of national challenges: the ambiguous Nordic model of welfare and competitiveness', in Kettunen and Petersen (eds) (2011), q.v., pp. 16–40.

Kettunen, P. and Petersen, K. (eds) (2011), *Beyond Welfare State Models: Transnational Historical Perspectives on Social Policy*. Cheltenham, UK and Northampton, MA: Edward Elgar.

Keune, M. (2006), 'Creating capitalist labour markets: a comparative-institutionalist analysis of labour market reform in the Czech Republic and Hungary, 1989–2002', unpublished PhD thesis. Florence: European University Institute.

Klammer, U. (2004), 'Flexicurity in a life-course perspective', *Transfer*, 10, 2: 282–99.

Klammer, U. (2013), 'Gleichstellungspolitik als Baustein von Demografiepolitik und Teil-Antwort auf den Fachkräftemangel', in Hüther, M. and Naegele, G. (eds) (2013), *Demografiepolitik: Herausforderungen und Arbeitsfelder*. Wiesbaden: Springer, pp. 299–314.

Klammer, U. and Tillmann, K. (2002), *Flexicurity – Soziale Sicherung und Flexibilisierung der Arbeits- und Lebensverhältnisse*. Düsseldorf: Ministerium für Arbeit und Soziales, Qualifikation und Technologie des Landes NRW.

Knegt, R. (ed.) (2008), *The Employment Contract as an Exclusionary Device. An Analysis on the Basis of 25 Years of Developments in The Netherlands*. Antwerp: Intersentia.

Knight, F.H. (1921), *Risk, Uncertainty and Profit*. Boston, MA and New York: Houghton Mifflin.

Kocka, J. (1981), *Die Angestellten in der deutschen Geschichte 1850–1980: Vom Privatbeamten zum angestellten Arbeitnehmer*. Göttingen: Vandenhoeck & Ruprecht.

Kohl, H. and Platzner, H.-W. (2007), 'The role of the state in central and east European industrial relations: the case of minimum wages', *Industrial Relations Journal*, 386: 614–35.

Kohli, M. (1999), 'Private and public transfers between generations: linking the family and the state', *European Societies*, 1, 1: 81–104.

Kohli, M., Albertini, M. and Künemund, H. (2010), 'Linkage among adult family generations: evidence from comparative survey research', in Heady, P. and Kohli, M. (eds) (2010), *Family, Kinship and State in Contemporary Europe: Volume 3: Perspectives on Theory and Policy*. Frankfurt am Main: Campus.

Köllő, J. (2011), 'Hungary: Crisis coupled with a fiscal squeeze – effects on inequality', in Vaughan-Whitehead (ed.) (2011), q.v., pp. 278–314.

Kooiman, J. (1993), 'Socio-political governance', in Kooiman (ed.) (1993), *Modern Governance: New Government-Society Interactions*. London: Sage.

Korpi, W. (1978), *The Working Class in Welfare Capitalism: Workers, Unions and Politics in Sweden*. London: RKP.

Kristensen, P.H. and Lilja, K. (eds) (2011), *Nordic Capitalisms and Globalization. New Forms of Economic Organization and Welfare Institutions*. Oxford: Oxford University Press.

Lehndorff, S. (2012a), 'German capitalism and the European crisis: part of the solution or part of the problem?', in Lehndorff (ed.) (2012b), q.v., pp. 79–102.

Lehndorff, S. (ed.) (2012b), *A Triumph of Failed Ideas: European Models of Capitalism in the Crisis*. Brussels: ETUI.

Lehndorff, S., Bosch, G., Haipeter, T. and Latniak, E. (2009), 'From the "sick man" to the "overhauled engine" of Europe? Upheaval in the

German model', in Bosch, Lehndorff and Rubery (eds) (2009b), q.v., pp. 105–30.

Léonard, E. (2001), 'Industrial relations and the regulation of employment in Europe', *European Journal of Industrial Relations*, 7, 1: 27–47.

Loveridge, R. and Mok, A.L. (1979), *Theories of Labour Market Segmentation: A Critique*. The Hague: Nijhoff.

Luhmann, N. (1991), *Soziologie des Risikos*. Berlin: De Gruyter.

McGinitty, F. and Russell, H. (2013), 'Work-family conflict and economic change', in Gallie (ed.) (2013), q.v., pp. 169–94.

Macovicky, N. (2014), *Economies of Favour after Socialism*. Oxford: Oxford University Press.

Madsen, P.K. (2009), 'Denmark', in De Beer and Schils (eds) (2009b), q.v., pp. 44–69.

Mansoor, A. and Quillin, B. (eds) (2006), *Migration and Remittances*. Washington, DC: World Bank.

Marginson, P. (2014), 'Coordinated bargaining in Europe: From incremental corrosion to frontal assault?', *European Journal of Industrial Relations*, published online 15 April 2014.

Marginson, P., Edwards, P. and Ferner, A. (2013), 'Multinational corporations in cross-national perspective', special issue of *Industrial and Labor Relations Review*.

Marginson, P., Keune, M. and Bohle, D. (2014), 'Negotiating the effects of uncertainty? The governance capacity of collective bargaining under pressure', *Transfer*, 20: 37–51.

Marginson, P. and Welz, C. (2014), 'Changes to wage setting mechanisms in the context of the crisis and the EU's new economic governance regime', EIRONLINE, 2014–09–09. http://www.eurofound.europa.eu/eiro/studies/tn1402049s/tn1402049s.htm, 9 September 2014.

Masso, J. and Krillo, K. (2011), 'Mixed adjustment forms and inequality effects in Estonia, Latvia and Lithuania', in Vaughan-Whitehead (ed.) (2011), q.v., pp. 38–102.

Meardi, G. (2011), 'Flexicurity meets state traditions', *International Journal of Comparative Labour Law and Industrial Relations*, 27, 3: 255–70.

Meardi, G. (2012), *Social Failures of EU Enlargement: A Case of Workers Voting with Their Feet*. London: Routledge.

Miller, D. (2009), 'Wage determination in outsourced multi-buyer apparel supply chains', *International Journal of Labour Research*, 1, 2: 183–200.

Mirowski, P. (2013), *Never Let a Serious Crisis Go to Waste: How Neoliberalism Survived the Financial Meltdown*. London: Verso.

Morel, N., Palier, B. and Palme, J. (2012), *Towards a Social Investment Welfare State?* Bristol: Policy Press.

Muffels, R.J.A. (2013a), 'Governance of sustainable security: the impact of institutions and values on labour market transitions using ESS and SILC data', unpublished GUSTO paper. Tilburg: University of Tilburg.

Muffels, R.J.A. (2013b), 'Young workers, job insecurity and employment uncertainty in times of crisis: exploring the impact of governance, economic resources and trust in Central-Eastern and Western Europe', unpublished GUSTO paper. Tilburg: University of Tilburg.

Muffels, R.J.A., Chung, H., Fouarge, D., Klammer, U., Luijkx, R., Manzoni, A., Thiel, A. and Wilthagen, T. (2008), *Flexibility and Security over the Life Course*. Dublin: European Foundation for the Improvement of Working and Living Conditions.

Muffels, R.J.A., Crouch, C. and Wilthagen, T. (2014), 'Flexibility and security: national social models in transitional labour markets', *Transfer*, 20, 1: 99–114.

Muffels, R.J.A. and Luijkx, R. (2008a), 'The relationship between labour market mobility and employment security: "trade-off" or "double bind"', *Work Employment and Society*, 22, 2: 221–42.

Muffels, R.J.A. and Luijkx, R. (eds) (2008b), *Flexibility and Employment Security in Europe: Labour Markets in Transition*. Cheltenham, UK and Northampton, MA: Edward Elgar.

Muffels, R.J.A. and Tros, F. (2004), 'The concept of "flexicurity": a new approach to regulating employment and labour markets', *Transfer*, 10, 2: 166–86.

Muffels, R.J.A., Wilthagen, T. and Chung, H. (2010), 'The state of affairs in flexicurity: a dynamic perspective', unpublished paper delivered to DG Employment of the European Commission.

Muffels, R.J.A., Wilthagen, T. and van den Heuvel, N. (2002), 'Labour market transitions and employment regimes: evidence on the flexicurity-security nexus in transitional labour markets', WZB Discussion paper FS I 02–204. Berlin: Wissenschaftszentrum.

Mulligan, C.B. (2008), 'A depressing scenario: mortgage debt becomes unemployment insurance', NBER Working Paper W14514. Cambridge, MA: US National Bureau of Economic Research.

Naldini, M. (2003), *The Family in the Mediterranean Welfare States*. London: Frank Cass.

Neumann, L. and Tóth, A. (2009), 'Crisis of the post-transition Hungarian model', in Bosch, Lehndorff and Rubery (eds) (2009b), q.v., pp. 155–77.

OECD (1994), *The Jobs Study*. Paris: OECD.

OECD (2006), *Boosting Jobs and Incomes. Policy Lessons from Reassessing the OECD Jobs Study*. Paris: OECD.

OECD (2008), *The Impact of Foreign Direct Investment on Wages and Working Conditions*. Paris: OECD.

OECD (2011a), *Divided We Stand: Why Inequality Keeps Rising*. Paris: OECD.

OECD (2011b), *OECD Factbook 2011*. Paris: OECD.

OECD (2012), *OECD Factbook 2012*. Paris: OECD.

OECD (2013a), *OECD Factbook 2013*. Paris: OECD.

OECD (2013b), iLibrary http://www.oecd-ilibrary.org/science-and-tech nology/data/oecd-patent-statistics_patent-data-en, 3 September 2014.

OECD (2014), *OECD Economic Statistics 2014*. Paris: OECD.

O'Higgins, N. (2011), 'Italy: limited policy responses and industrial relations in flux, leading to aggravated inequalities', in Vaughan-Whitehead (ed.) (2011), q.v., pp. 314–49.

Olson, M. (1966), *The Theory of Collective Action*. Cambridge, MA: Harvard University Press.

Olson, M. (1982), *The Rise and Decline of Nations*. New Haven, CT: Yale University Press.

Ost, D. (2000), 'Illusory corporatism: tripartism in the service of neoliberalism', *Politics and Society*, 28, 4: 503–30.

Palier, B. (2010a), 'The dualizations of the French welfare system', in Palier (ed.) (2010c), q.v., pp. 73–100.

Palier, B. (2010b), 'The long conservative corporatist road to welfare reforms', in Palier, B. (ed.) (2010c), q.v., pp. 333–88.

Palier, B. (ed.) (2010c), *A Long Goodbye to Bismarck? The Politics of Welfare Reform in Continental Europe*. Amsterdam: Amsterdam University Press.

Pascual, A.S. and Magnusson, L. (eds) (2007), *Reshaping Welfare States and Activation Regimes in Europe*. Frankfurt am Main: Peter Lang.

Pedersen, O.K. (2006), 'Corporatism and beyond: the negotiated economy', in Campbell, J.L., Hall, J.A. and Pedersen, O.K. (eds) (2006), *National Identity and the Varieties of Capitalism*. Copenhagen: DJOF Publishing, pp. 365–91.

Piketty, T. (2013), *Le capital au XXI siècle*. Paris: Seuil.

Polanyi, K. (1944), *The Great Transformation: The Political and Economic Origins of Our Time*. Boston, MA: Beacon Press.

Reeskens, T. and Hooghe, M. (2008), 'Cross-cultural measurement equivalence of generalized trust. Evidence from the European Social Survey 2002 and 2004', *Social Indicators Research*, 85: 515–32.

Reich, R. (1991), *The Work of Nations*. New York: Knopf.

Roberts, P.C. (1984), *The Supply Side Revolution*. Cambridge, MA: Harvard University Press.

Rogowski, R. (2008a), 'The European social model and the law and policy of transitional labour markets in the European Union', in Rogowski, R. (ed.) (2008b), q.v., pp. 9–28.

Rogowski, R. (ed.) (2008b), *The European Social Model and Transitional Labour Markets: Law and Policy*. Aldershot: Ashgate.

Rogowski, R., Salais, R. and Whiteside, N. (eds) (2011), *Transforming European Employment Policy. Labour Market Transitions and the Promotion of Capability*. Cheltenham, UK and Northampton, MA: Edward Elgar.

Ronit, K. and Schneider, V. (2000), *Private Organizations, Governance and Global Politics*. London: Routledge.

Rostow, W.W. (1965), *The Stages of Economic Growth*. Cambridge: Cambridge University Press.

Round, J. (2013), *The Role of Informal Economies in the Post-Soviet World*. London: Routledge.

Rubery, J., Grimshaw, D., Donnelly, R. and Urwin, P. (2009), 'Revisiting the UK model: from basket case to success story and back again?', in Bosch, Lehndorff and Rubery (eds) (2009b), q.v., pp. 57–80.

Rueda, D. (2005), 'Insider-outsider politics in industrialized democracies: the challenge to social democratic parties', *American Political Science Review*, 99, 1: 61–74.

Rueda, D. (2007), *Social Democracy Inside Out: Partisanship and Labour Market Policy*. Oxford: Oxford University Press.

Russell, H., Watson, D. and McGinnity, F. (2013), 'Unemployment and subjective well-being', in Gallie (ed.) (2013), q.v., pp. 229–55.

Salverda, W., Nolan, B., Checchi, D., Marx, I., McKnight, A., Tóth, I.G., Van de Werfhorst, H. (eds) (2014), *Changing Inequalities in Rich Countries*. Oxford: Oxford University Press.

Schils, T. (2009), 'The Netherlands', in De Beer and Schils (eds) (2009b), q.v., pp. 96–118.

Schmid, G. (2006), 'Social risk management through transitional labour markets', Socio-Economic Review, 4, 1: 1–32.

Schmid, G. (2008), 'Sharing risks: on social risk management and the governance of labour market transitions', in Rogowski, R. (ed.) (2008b), q.v., pp. 29–60.

Schmid, G. (2014), 'Inclusive Growth: What Future for the European Social Model?', *IZA Policy Paper No 82*. Bonn: Forschungsinstitut zur Zukunft der Arbeit.

Schmid, G. and Gazier, B. (eds) (2002), *The Dynamics of Full Employment: Social Integration through Transitional Labour Markets*. Cheltenham, UK and Northampton, MA: Edward Elgar.

Schmidt, V.A. (2002), *The Futures of European Capitalism*. Oxford: Oxford University Press.

Schmidt, V.A. (2006), *Democracy in Europe*. Oxford: Oxford University Press.

Schneider, F. (2005), 'Shadow economies around the world: what do we really know?', *European Journal of Political Economy*, 21, 3: 598–642.

Schneider, F. and Buehn, A. (2012), 'Shadow economies in highly developed OECD countries: what are the driving forces?', IZA Discussion paper 6891. Bonn: IZA.

Schneider, F., Buehn, A. and Montenegro, C.E. (2010), 'Shadow economies all over the world', Policy Research Working Paper 5356, World Bank Developing Economics Group. Washington, DC: World Bank.

Schömann, R., Rogowski, R. and Kruppe, T. (2013), *Labour Market Efficiency in the European Union*. London: Routledge.

Seeleib-Kaiser, M., Van Dyk, S. and Roggenkamp, M. (2008), *Party Politics and Social Welfare: Comparing Christian and Social Democracy in Austria, Germany and the Netherlands*. Cheltenham, UK and Northampton, MA: Edward Elgar.

Sen, A. (2005), 'Human rights and capabilities', *Journal of Human Development*, 6, 2: 151–66.

Sen, A. and Nussbaum, M. (eds) (1993), *The Quality of Life*. Oxford: Oxford University Press.

Shalev, M. (ed.) (1996), *The Privatization of Social Policy? Occupational Welfare and the Welfare State in America, Scandinavia and Japan*. Basingstoke: Macmillan.

Simonazzi, A., Villa, P., Lucidi, F. and Naticchioni, P. (2009), 'Continuity and change in the Italian model', in Bosch, Lehndorff and Rubery (eds) (2009b), q.v., pp. 201–22.

Sinzheimer, H. (1921), *Grundzüge des Arbeitsrechts*. Berlin: Fischer.

Spieser, C. (2007), 'Labour market policies in post-communist Poland: explaining the peaceful institutionalisation of unemployment', *Politique européenne*, 2007/1, 21: 97–132.

Standing, G. (1999), *Global Labour Flexibility*. London: Macmillan.

Standing, G. (2011), *The Precariat: The New Dangerous Class*. London: Bloomsbury.

Stinchcombe, A.L. (1965), 'Social structure and organizations', in March, J.G. (ed.), *Handbook of Organization*. Chicago, IL: Rand McNally & Company, pp. 142–93.

Streeck, W. (2008), 'Flexible markets, stable societies?', MPIfG Working Paper 8/6. Cologne: MPIfG.

Streeck, W. (2009a), *Re-Forming Capitalism: Institutional Change in the German Political Economy*. Oxford: Oxford University Press.

Streeck, W. (2009b), 'Flexible employment, flexible families, and the socialization of reproduction', MPIfG Working Paper 9/13. Cologne: MPIfG.

Swenson, P.A. (2002), *Capitalists against Markets: The Making of Labor Markets and Welfare States in the United States and Sweden*. Oxford: Oxford University Press.

Tåhlin, M. (2013a), 'Economic crisis and employment change: the great regression', in Gallie, D. (ed.) (2013), q.v., pp. 30–57.

Tåhlin, M. (2013b), 'Distribution in the downturn', in Gallie, D. (ed.) (2013), q.v., pp. 58–87.

Talani, L. and Cerviño, E. (2003), 'Mediterranean labour and the impact of economic and monetary union: mass unemployment or labour market flexibility?', in Overbeek, H. (ed.), *The Political Economy of European Employment*. London: Routledge, pp. 199–226.

Taylor-Gooby, P. (ed.) (2004), *New Risks, New Welfare: The Transformation of the European Welfare State*. Oxford: Oxford University Press.

Tóth, A., Neumann, L. and Hosszú, H. (2012), 'Hungary's full-blown malaise', in Lehndorff (ed.) (2012b), q.v., pp. 137–54.

Traxler, F. (2003), 'Bargaining, decentralization, macroeconomic performance and control over the employment relationship', *British Journal of Industrial Relations*, 41, 1: 1–27.

Traxler, F., Blaschke, S. and Kittel, B. (2001), *National Labour Relations in Internationalized Markets*. Oxford: Oxford University Press.

Traxler, F., Brandl, B. and Glassner, V. (2008a), 'Pattern bargaining: an investigation into its agency, context and evidence', *British Journal of Industrial Relations*, 46, 1: 33–58.

Traxler, F., Brandl, B., Glassner, V. and Ludvig, A. (2008b), 'Can cross-border bargaining coordination work? Analytical reflections and evidence from the metal industry in Germany and Austria', *European Journal of Industrial Relations*, 14, 2: 21737.

Tzanov, V. (2011), 'Inequality at work emerging in the current crisis in Bulgaria', in Vaughan-Whitehead (ed.) (2011), q.v., pp. 103–42.

UNCTAD (2013), *World Development Report*. New York: United Nations.

UNDP (2013), *Human Development Index*. New York: UNDP.

UNEP (2012), *United Nations Sustainability Index*. New York: United Nations.

Van den Berg, A. and De Gier, E. (2008), 'Research in transitional labour markets: implications for the European employment strategy', in Rogowski (ed.) (2008b), q.v., pp. 63–106.

Vandenbroucke, F., Hemerijck, A. and Palier, B. (2011), 'The EU needs a social investment pact', Opinion Paper, 5 May 2011. Brussels: Observatoire Social Européen.

Vaughan-Whitchcad, D. (ed.) (2011), *Work Inequalities in the Crisis: Evidence from Europe*. Cheltenham, UK and Northampton, MA: Edward Elgar.

Verhulp, E. (2008), 'The employment contract as a source of concern', in Knegt (ed.) (2008), q.v., pp. 47–73.

Visser, J. (2013), *The ICTWSS Database 4.0 2013*. Amsterdam: AIAS.

Wadensjö, E. (2009), 'Sweden', in De Beer and Schils (eds) (2009b), q.v., pp. 1–26.

Weber, M. (1919), *Wirtschaft und Gesellschaft*. Tübingen: Mohr.

Whiteside, N. (2014), 'Privatization and after: time, complexity and governance in the world of funded pensions', *Transfer*, 20, 1: 69–81.

Wilkinson, R.G. and Pickett, K. (2009), *The Spirit Level: Why More Equal Societies Almost Always Do Better*. London: Allen Lane.

Wilthagen, T. (2002), 'Managing social risks with transitional labour markets', in Mosley, H., O'Reilly, J. and Schömann, K. (eds) (2002), *Labour Markets, Gender and Institutional Change: Essays in Honour of Günther Schmid*. Cheltenham, UK and Northampton, MA: Edward Elgar, pp. 264–89.

Wilthagen, T. and Tros, F. (2004), 'The concept of "flexicurity": a new approach to regulating employment and labour markets', in 'Flexicurity: conceptual issues and political implementation in Europe', *Transfer*, 10, 2.

World Bank (2004–2009), *Doing Business*. Washington, DC: World Bank.

World Bank (2011a), *The Changing Wealth of Nations*. Washington, DC: World Bank.

World Bank (2011b), *Migration and Remittances Factbook 2011*, Second Edition. Washington, DC: World Bank.

World Bank (annual), *Carbon Dioxide Emissions*. Washington, DC: World Bank.

World Bank (website a), data http://www.data.worldbank.org/table/2.9, 3 September 2014.

World Bank (website b), data http://www.data.worldbank.org/table/2.15, 3 September 2014.

World Bank (website c), data http://www.data.worldbank.org/indicator/ SE.XPD.TOTL.GD.ZS, 3 September 2014.

World Trade Organization (annual), *World Trade Statistics*. Geneva: World Trade Organization.

Zeitlin, J. and Trubeck, D. (eds) (2003), *Governing Work and Welfare in a New Economy: European and American Experiments*. Oxford: Oxford University Press.

Index